Objections to Dualism

Essays in the Philosophy of Mind

Steven M. Duncan

An Amazon CreateSpace Book

DEDICATION

Dedicated to the Forgotten Man, who stands bemused and uncomprehending as the once unimaginable becomes the reality of our time. May he take hope and comfort from what I have written here.

CONTENTS

PREFACE

The Essays in this collection were written over a period of time and uploaded separately to the Philpapers website between 2009 and 2016. I have rearranged them to create a better narrative flow and rewritten them in spots to reflect later developments in my views. However, they remain largely as I wrote them and there is a significant amount of overlap between the papers that some readers may find repetitive and tedious. I apologize for this and hope to repair the defect in a projected companion volume to this book in which I draw some novel conclusions to which the studies of this volume are closely related.

Chapter One

How Is Neuroscience Possible?

By neuroscience, I refer to the scientific study of the brain *qua* material thing, a structured set of interrelated tissues and structures constituting one of the major functioning organs of the human body. This study, a branch of medicine and natural science, consists of two main divisions. The first is *neuroanatomy*, which explores and studies the various kinds of tissues and structures existing in the brain: the cerebrum, the cerebellum, the brain stem, and so on, down to the microscopic level of individual brain cells (such as neurons) and the structures to which these cells belong. The second division, *neurophysiology*, is the study of the living brain and the electrochemical processes occurring there. In part, we are concerned with mapping these processes for their own sake. By and large, however, we study these processes with a special emphasis on their relation to mental events and processes, such as conscious awareness, sense perception, memory, imagination, and so on, which we believe we have good reason to think are in some way related to the living brain and the electrochemical processes occurring there.

In pursuing this second project, neuroscience touches on questions that have traditionally been thought to fall in the province of philosophy, and has inspired philosophical research program under the banner of "cognitive science" or "neurophilosophy," intended to "naturalize" the mental and incorporate it without remainder into a broadly physicalist worldview.

Neuroscience, I think, inspires but does not require any such project in order to be viable as a science. However, many people, some of them neuroscientists themselves, have jumped on the "cognitive science" bandwagon, apparently convinced that anyone with even a passing acquaintance with the results of neuroscientific research must concede that conscious awareness and mind are wholly explicable in naturalistic, physical terms. Those like myself who resist what seems to many to be the obvious implication of modern science, are often dismissed as at best uninformed and at worst in the grips of a pre-scientific view of the world (sometimes called "folk psychology") and thus little better than superstitious cranks.

Since neuroscience is an actual, going concern within that project of theoretical inquiry known as natural science, we must therefore conclude that it is possible. Those who take the positive results of neuroscientific research as a platform for the grand, speculative constructions spun out by the "cognitive scientists" take their stand on an apparently solid foundation. If, however, we raise the question that serves as the title to this essay, I think we will find that the general thrust of these grand, speculative constructions not only does not follow from the results of neuroscientific research but would, if true, make neuroscience (and indeed, all natural science) impossible. If the argument of this collection is correct, the philosophical materialist assumptions that inspire and undergird so-called "cognitive science" and "neurophilosophy" create severe epistemological and conceptual difficulties both for the pursuit of theoretical inquiry in general, and for neuroscience in particular.

The argument of this essay enforces the following conclusion: if the basic claims of "cognitive science" are true, then we can have no reason to believe the claims of neuroscience that inspire them in the philosophy of mind. Therefore, we must choose either neuroscience or "neurophilosophy" – we cannot have both. The very conditions necessary for the possibility of natural science as a going concern in the world (hence of neuroscience as well) prove to be incompatible with the substantive truth of the presuppositions of "cognitive science." It does not follow by itself that these substantive claims are false, but we will be hard pressed to make any sense out of theoretical inquiry of any kind, including natural science and philosophy, on the assumption that they are true. Therefore, since it turns out that we could never have any reason for supposing that these claims are actually true, even in principle, it is eminently rational for us to decline belief in these claims, even if (as it happens) they are true.

I am sure that many will be inclined to dismiss the foregoing claims out of hand, and many more will be extremely resistant to accepting them, no matter what sort of argument is offered on their behalf. For one to read an essay with the "refute" button on is common enough among philosophers, especially when the reader has a strong, pre-philosophical commitment to a cherished view. As such, one might expect that I will be presenting some elaborate, convoluted argument for the conclusion I am trying to enforce. Not at all. My argument will be relatively brief and to the point, and is really the conjunction of three briefer arguments. Before presenting it, however, I need to make some banal points about the nature of theoretical inquiry as practiced by everyone who engages in it, philosopher and natural scientist alike.

The Nature of Theoretical Inquiry There is no space here for me to construct a complete philosophy of science. What follows here is simple a casual reflection on the process of theoretical inquiry as engaged in by researchers, regardless of their field of inquiry – a "folk psychology" of theoretical inquiry, if you will. I begin from the observation that theoretical inquirers generally adopt a realist stance with regard to their chosen form of inquiry, whatever it happens to be. We assume from the beginning that the object of inquiry is something existing and constituted independently of our thoughts, opinions, and even our awareness of that object. This means that, e.g., in studying the brain we are studying something that really exists and inherently possesses whatever features, structures, and functions belonging to it independently of anyone's opinions about this, or even awareness that the brain exists. The brain is not invented by us, nor is it a theoretical posit or the product of theoretical inquiry – it exists as something in its own right whether we believe this or not.

We also assume that the object of inquiry is such that something significant that can be said about it, which it is the goal of theoretical inquiry into the brain is to arrive at – the *truth* about that object. Theoretical inquiry into the brain has as its product the objective truth about the features, structures, and functions of the brain understood as a bodily organ. At the same time, this in turn presumes that despite its objectivity, the objective truth abut the brain, the object of theoretical inquiry in this case, is capable of being known by us, at least in principle. That the brain should exist, that there should be some truth about the brain, and that this truth is somehow accessible to us and capable of being known by us – all of these are necessary if theoretical inquiry about the brain, and thus neuroscience, are to be possible, both in principle and as a going concern in the world.

If any of these prior conditions failed to be case, inquiry into the brain, or inquiry of any sort, would be largely pointless. More than this, we take it for granted that the results of this inquiry are capable of being publicly expressed and understood by anyone properly situated to receive it. The knowledge we seek through theoretical inquiry, then, is *propositional* knowledge, capable of being articulated in and expressed through language.

Theoretical inquiry, then – whether about the brain or anything else - is a *goal-directed* endeavor. It has an end or purpose, which is to acquire knowledge of the truth about reality for its own sake and express that knowledge in the form of propositional truths about the brain. This process also has a *norm*, i.e. reality itself, existing as such, taken to be touchstone for any claims made about the brain and to which our inquiry needs to be subordinated. Knowledge of the natural world, including the brain, is of contingent entities and states of affairs; as such, it cannot be acquired simply through *a priori*, armchair reflection. Neither does it lie ready to hand and available to causal sensory observation. To the contrary, we can acquire this objective knowledge of the brain only through concerted empirical investigation. In this process, our rational powers of observation, interpretation of data, memory, and rational inference (both deductive and inductive) must play a vital role in both the formation and the justification of our beliefs about the brain expressed in language as substantive, true propositions about the world. It is likewise the case that theoretical inquiry must be *methodical* and guided by *discursive* reason if it is to have any hope of reaching knowledge of the truth about the object of inquiry. Mere causal observation and unchecked speculation will not do.

In natural science, for example, the process of inquiry takes the form of the stereotypical *scientific method*. Beginning from some striking phenomenon that evokes wonder and curiosity, we proceed to observe carefully the phenomenon using the five senses, in order to acquire further data upon which to ground a possible explanation. The possible explanation, itself the product of imagination, is then formulated as an *hypothesis* capable of being tested in experience. Certain observable consequences are inferred from that hypothesis, and further observations, acquired either through direct sense-perception or through such perception mediated by artificial conditions of our own devising (such as a controlled experiment or a computer simulation), are sought. These consequences, if in fact observed, are said to confirm the hypothesis, and to disconfirm it if competent researchers fail to observe or reproduce them.

We take a sufficient number of repeated confirmations of the hypothesis to have justified it sufficiently to raise that hypothesis to the level of a theory and to incorporate it into the standing body of scientific knowledge. That standing body of well-confirmed results continues to grow through time and becomes a permanent human achievement capable of being passed down to subsequent generations, added to, and brought to ultimate completion. This account of the scientific method is no doubt over-simple and has been challenged by many contemporary philosophers and historians of science. Whether right or wrong, however, I take it that this is a correct, if superficial, description of what theoretical inquirers such as neuroscientists take themselves to be doing in the course of their research. To simplify this even more, I want to focus on just one aspect of this process: the role played by data and evidence in the formation of rational beliefs about the objects of theoretical inquiry.

Within the context of theoretical inquiry, we suppose that the presence (or absence) of good reasons for belief, in the form of relevant observations, evidence, and sound arguments, both deductive and inductive, is highly relevant to the question of what we ought to believe about the nature of things. In general, or at least ideally, a rational belief is one that is occurrently held on the basis of good reasons (plausibly truth-connected grounds derived from sensory observation or sound argumentation) that one correctly recognizes to be such. A belief is dismissed as irrational if it is willfully held on inadequate grounds or arguments, held in abeyance of such grounds, or especially if it is held contrary to the weight of evidence or argument judged by competent inquirers to be relevant to the acceptance of that belief. The primary goal of theoretical inquiry is to provide these grounds and arguments in order that we may form our beliefs in accordance with them and thereby arrive at the best approximation to the truth our circumstances will allow. These beliefs will be justified by those good reasons, recognized by us to be such, and occurrently embraced by us on those grounds and arguments. Those reasons, then, *just as such*, will play a significant and, to the extent that we are rational, leading role in both the justification of those beliefs and the explanation of why we hold them and persist in holding them as well.

For this reason-seeking and reason-giving activity to have any point, however, it has to be the case that these good reasons, whatever they are, are in fact capable of influencing our occurrent beliefs. In other words, it must be possible for reasons *as such* to affect our judgments and the beliefs we arrive at as the result of theoretical inquiry, since only these are directly relevant to the question of the objective truth about reality of those beliefs. Further, theoretical inquiry itself must be structured explicitly and consciously carried on in accordance with the canons of method and laws of logic supported by intellectual virtues such as love of truth, commitments to rationality and objectivity, and an attitude that is critical rather than rigidly dogmatic or carelessly skeptical. All of this implies that theoretical inquiry requires that the researcher have considerable rational autonomy, which includes both the capacity to be affected by evidence and argument *just as such*, as well as the power to conform one's beliefs to the evidence and the results acquired through properly applied method. The mind of the researcher must be penetrable by such reasons considered as such, and his or her belief-structure capable of reflecting that influence through conscious, willful adherence to propositions received as true precisely and ideally *solely* on the basis of reasons and evidence. Otherwise, theoretical inquiry will be nothing but a sham and an illusion – something other than what it has to be in order to be what we take it to be.

The same will hold of any special branch of theoretical inquiry, such as neuroscience. If neuroscience is to be possible as a going concern within natural science, then its object, the organic brain, must be capable of empirically investigation by researchers using the senses to observe the brain and identify its various component tissues and structures through anatomical observation. Further, the various processes going on in the living brain must be capable of being measured, monitored, and recorded in order that we may arrive at plausible hypotheses about the functions of the various structures and parts of the brain that compose that organ. These hypotheses need to be capable of confirmation or disconfirmation by various observational and experimental means, and the resulting data and interpretations capable of being reported to and repeated by others. In turn, all of this has to have some effect on what we believe, i.e. take to be the objective truth about the brain. Neuroscientists take it to be the case that, to the extent that we are rational, we will accept the outcome of their researches as true on the basis of their authority due to the fact that these results are justified by the evidence presented for them, regardless of our "druthers." They thereby presuppose that it lies within our power to do so.

However, if we accept the leading ideas informing "cognitive science" and "neurophilosophy" none of these claims can be true. The project of "naturalizing" consciousness and the mind has three main pillars: physicalism about the external world, materialism about mind, and neurophysiological determinism. Each of these, I contend, produces insuperable epistemological problems for neuroscience considered as a branch of theoretical inquiry, as it does for all science and philosophy. I will now proceed to say why I think this is the case.

Physicalism and Knowledge of the Brain By "physicalism," I mean what I have elsewhere called *Galilean Physicalism*, i.e. physicalism about the external world.[1] Galilean physicalism is an ontological claim about what really exists "outside the mind" and has been the common assumption of philosophers and scientists since Galileo first drew the primary/secondary quality distinction in the dedicatory letter prefaced to his treatise on comets, *Il Saggiatore*.[2] According to this view, the only things that really, ultimately, or fundamentally exist are the entities and properties that are posited or "quantified over" by physicists in the process of constructing mathematical models of the external world. The substantive picture, still affirmed by most of us today, is that nothing at all ultimately exists "out there" except matter swirling in the void and taking the form of various sorts of particles possessing a few simple properties and interacting in accordance with

---

[1] See, especially, my books *Physicalism and Scientific Realism* and *Reason and Illusion*, both published by Amazon CreateSpace, 2022.
[2] See Michael R. Matthews, ed., *The Scientific Background to Modern Philosophy*, Indianapolis, IN, Hackett, 1989, 56-61.

simple, non-purposive mechanical laws. Since the nineteenth century, forces have also been seen to be an irreducible part of the physical world, and the twentieth century has added space-time and "energy" to the mix. Everything "else" is merely a construction out of these particles, forces and so on, hence reducible to them without reminder. Few have been willing to openly affirm that such things as tables, chairs, trees, the bodies of persons, etc. are non-existent or merely fictional, even though this would seem to be an obvious implication of commitment to physicalism.[3] It is far more common for philosophers and scientists to assert both the truth of physicalism and yet affirm just as dogmatically that chairs, tables, and so on do obviously exist even as they insist that such entities are "nothing in addition" to the physical posits out of which they are made – a claim that borders on the self-contradictory.

The classic problem here, of course, is that of Eddington's two tables.[4] First, there is the table as a material thing, perceived by the senses as a solid, singular, medium-sized material thing composed of wood and having a specific color, weight, and various proper and constitutive parts. Second, there is the table *qua* physical object, which is simply a cloud of interacting atomic and subatomic particles externally related to one another by various forces. This physical object possesses none of the perceptible qualities we sense the table to possess – indeed, it is quite invisible – and consists largely of empty space. Rather than existing as a unit and being sharply delineated from other objects around it, it has only hazy boundaries and cannot be altogether distinguished from other clouds of atoms around it. There is simply one, uniform sort of matter differing in particle concentration throughout space-time. Despite the fact that the senses tell us that the first is the real table, if we take science seriously, the palm must go to the second. Although Eddington's philosophically unsophisticated handling of some of these ideas exposed him to some well-deserved philosophical ridicule,[5] it does not follow from this that his problem can

---

[3] See, for example, Peter Van Inwagen, *Material Things*, Ithaca, NY, Cornell University Press, 1990, and Trenton Merricks, *Object and Person*, Oxford at the Clarendon Press, 2003, both of whom deny the existence of composite material things. James Ladyman et al, *Every Thing Must GO!* New York, Oxford, 2007 go even further and deny the existence of simple material substances in favor of a "structural realism" that dispenses with substances altogether and that they claim is the only ontology compatible with the latest physics.
[4] See Sir Arthur Eddington, *The Nature of the Physical World*, London, MacMillan, 1929, ix-xvii.

simply be dismissed without further discussion. Despite the criticisms, most philosophers and scientists continue to endorse the physicalist perspective on this issue and take it for granted that the physical table is the real one.

However, if the foregoing is true, then certain serious epistemological problems seem to be unavoidable, at least within a scientific realist perspective. Ever since Galileo initiated the New Science, the appearance/reality distinction has loomed large in Western epistemology, along with all the skeptical worries to which this distinction gives rise. If the table *qua* physical object is the real (and the only real) table, then what is the status of the table as it appears to the senses? On the physicalist ontology, there appears to be no place for it in the external world, where invisible, imperceptible matter swirls, indifferent to our desire to know. It has been the common habit since Galileo and Descartes to evacuate the visible, perceptible table to the mind, where it exists as a subjective, mind-dependent mental image that at best represents without resembling the physical object that in some manner causes that image to appear in the mind. On this point of view the merely apparent, mental table can be called the *phenomenal* table, whereas the table *qua* physical object can rightly be called the *noumenal* one.

The difficulties for this view are too well-known to require extensive restating here. How does the phenomenal table portend, even as a fiction, the noumenal table? How does the phenomenal table represent the noumenal table in the first place? How do we even know that there is such a thing as the noumenal table? Even if there were, given that the table is noumenal and lies in principle beyond our sensible apprehension, how can we even conceive of such objects, let alone know, that the claims we are making about them are true? How then is natural science, even physics itself, possible for us as a mode of theoretical inquiry into the nature of reality? Despite much effort on the part of many clever thinkers, I doubt whether anyone has satisfactorily solved these problems or shown how they can be evaded without abandoning scientific realism. It is far more common for philosophers and scientists to simply dismiss these problems as trifling, philosophical ones and assert dogmatically that if science says something, then it must be true and then, as Dr. Johnson would say,

---

[5] See L. Susan Stebbing, *Philosophy and the Physicists*, London, Routledge, 1937, 45-61 for a hilarious discussion of Eddington's ideas, many of which are on the mark.

"there's an end on it." When they do this, of course, they are simply refusing to countenance the problems here. This does not make them go away.

To show up this point more clearly, let's apply the foregoing to neuroscience as described above. Both neuroanatomy and neurophysiology focus on the empirical investigation of the brain, which we apprehend by means of sense perception as a material thing, in particular, a bodily organ performing various functions within the overall economy of the body's operation as a living thing. However, on the assumption that Galilean physicalism is true, the ontological status of the brain *qua* material thing is no less problematic than that of any other material thing. If we are to study the brain at all, then the brain must be apprehensible through the senses and so must be, in that sense, phenomenal or empirical – present to conscious awareness by means of the senses. However, being invisible and imperceptible, the noumenal brain (i.e. the brain *qua* physical object) cannot be present, *as such*, to conscious awareness by means of the senses. The phenomenal brain, then, cannot be (in any ontologically useful sense) the same thing as the physical brain apprehended by the senses and present to conscious awareness. We thus have two brains, a phenomenal and a noumenal one, corresponding to Eddington's two tables.

Neuroscientists take it for granted that the brain that they study, a bodily organ consisting of various tissues and structures accomplishing various kinds of tasks and functions within the overall economy of functioning in the body, is the real brain – a material thing existing in the external world. Physicalism, however, tells us otherwise and leaves the status of the phenomenal brain accessible to scientific study in the air. If we follow the standard resolution of the two tables problem familiar from the tradition, the phenomenal brain is simply a collection of sense-data existing in the mind due to the causal influence of the noumenal brain on the mind. The phenomenal brain, then, is something that exists only in the mind as a mental image, or series of such images and thus is not an external object at all. (As one French neurologist put it, "What we call the brain is really just a process going on in the brain" – a claim that the slightest reflection shows to be utterly incoherent.) If physicalism is true, then it appears that neuroscientists are simply mistaken if they think they are studying the real, physical brain when they investigate the phenomenal brain.

It is natural at this point to expect an appeal to materialism about mind in aid of a solution to this difficulty. According to materialism, the mind *is* the brain, and more than this, *nothing but* the noumenal brain.[6] Consciousness, then, is nothing but a purely physical process occurring in the noumenal (i.e. purely physical) brain. Our awareness of the phenomenal brain, then, is identical with some part of that purely physical process occurring in the noumenal brain, each component of which is identical with some physical brain-state. Therefore, since mind and brain are identical, awareness of the phenomenal brain, occurring in conscious awareness, *must be* identical with awareness of the noumenal brain as well, so that awareness of the noumenal brain is itself part of a process occurring in the noumenal brain.

However, identity in this sense cuts no epistemological ice. When Medea meets Orestes in disguise, she sees a man, and in seeing a man apprehends a man, and in apprehending a man is aware of a man. Since that man is her brother Orestes, there is a sense in which she is therefore aware of Orestes in being aware of the man who is identical to him. However, it does not follow from this she *knows* that she is apprehending Orestes or even *could* do so given her current apprehension of the man she putatively sees. In the same way, if I am struck in the back of the head with a baseball bat, I am aware of being struck, and of being struck by something. Since the something that struck me in this case is a baseball bat, in being aware of being struck by something I am therefore also aware of the baseball bat with which I was struck. Even so, it does not follow that I know even so much as that I was struck by a baseball bat or even that I *could* know this based on my apprehension of the bat in the process of striking me. If I were to awaken from my concussion and spy a bloodied club next to my head, I would automatically assume that it was this and not the baseball bat that struck me. However, I may simply have been the victim of a serial clubber who always leaves the weapon used in his previous attack at the

---

[6] As Jerome Shaffer pointed out many years ago, mere identity in this context is not enough to constitute the materialist position; an idealist also claims that the mind and the brain are identical, differing from the materialist in asserting that the brain is nothing but a sequence of sense-impressions occurring in the immaterial mind. A materialist about mind has to defend the thesis that the mind is nothing but the brain, i.e., consists of nothing but physical posits and relations between them, a claim that borders on the unintelligible. See his Jerome A. Shaffer, "Mental Events and the Brain," *Journal of Philosophy*, Vol. 60, March 1963, 106-120.

next one in order to taunt the police.

Of course, if Medea had lifted the man's hood or if a video surveillance camera contained footage of my attack, then additional information could have made this knowledge possible in principle for her and for me in these cases. However, the cases we have just been discussing are not parallel with that of the phenomenal and the noumenal brain. It is not possible for me to acquire any facts about the noumenal brain, including the (contingent) identity of the phenomenal with the noumenal brain, by some further empirical investigation, even if they are *in fact* identical. Our apprehension of the phenomenal brain by means of the senses is our only possible source of information about the noumenal brain and, as we have seen, even if in apprehending the phenomenal brain we in some sense apprehend the noumenal brain as well, we do not do so in such a way as to yield us any knowledge about it. As such, Materialism neither addresses nor removes the difficulty about acquiring knowledge of the noumenal/physical brain from the apprehension of the phenomenal brain. Nor is this altogether surprising, since it is simply an application of the problem of the external world, itself the product of modern philosophy's commitment to Galilean physicalism to a particular context, i.e. neuroscience.

Materialism and Neuroscience Materialism not only does not help the cause of neuroscience, it positively undermines its possibility as a branch of theoretical inquiry by undermining the very possibility of theoretical inquiry itself, at least as described above. Just as materialism asserts that the mind is nothing but the noumenal brain, it also contends that our perceptual experiences, thoughts, judgments, inferences, and beliefs are nothing but physical states of that brain, exhaustively describable in physical terms. More than this, their existence, order, and succession is fully explicable in terms of the operation of purely physical causal antecedents governed only by the physical laws of motion. These causes, in turn, provide all of the necessary and sufficient conditions for the occurrence of each of these physical events in precisely the order in which they occur. This means that each of my thoughts occurs in precisely the order in which they occur due solely to the operation of physical causes over which I have no control and to which my thought-processes as engaged in and lived by me make no causal contribution. As such, the actual contents of my mental processes, just as such, play no role whatsoever in explaining what I perceive, think, judge, infer, or believe. Indeed, if materialism about mind is true, mental contents, considered as such, possess no causal powers of their own; they are either mere epiphenomena or their causal powers are reducible to, identical with, or nothing in addition to those exercised by the brain states with which they are identical.[7]

On this view, then, theoretical inquiry of the sort represented by philosophy and natural science, including neuroscience, is an *illusion*. The neuroscientist may believe that based on his or her perceptual observations he or she is acquiring data about the structure and functioning of the brain, that reflection on these observations leads him or her to make certain judgments about what those structures and functions are, and that assent to those judgments taking the form of beliefs are justified by good reasons and sound arguments. In fact, however, his or her phenomenological description of the process of theoretical inquiry as he or she actually experiences his or her own participation in it turns out to be a mere exercise in "folk psychology." However things may *seem* to him or her while engaged in actual neuroscientific research, the neuroscientific story about what happens when we do neuroscience is much different.

According to that story, all that is *really* going on is that certain electrochemical events are occurring in the noumenal brain, events that we do not even so much as apprehend in any way that is useful to us for the acquisition of knowledge, let alone control or guide through any sort of reflective, intellectual process of discovery. To the contrary, if the materialist account of what goes on when we do neuroscience is correct, neither our observations, reflections, judgments, inferences or beliefs *as we undertake these operations in lived experience as self-conscious rational beings* play *any* substantive role whatsoever, let alone an essential one, in determining either the course or the outcome of neuroscientific research. They are preempted from making any such contribution by the fact that causation on the purely physical level occurring in the noumenal brain has already determined these

---

[7] This appears to be the view of Jaegwon Kim; see his *Physicalism – or Something Near Enough*, Princeton, NJ, Princeton University Press, 2005. Although he reluctantly admitted both the existence and the irreducibility of *qualia* to physical states of the brain, Kim continued to argue that there is no such thing as mental causation *per se*; all mental causation is ultimately and exhaustively reducible to physical causation occurring in the brain.

matters down to the last detail. As such, if my theoretical inquiry has succeeded in reaching the substantive truth about the brain this is something that from the point of view of its physical causes – and that is the only point of view that counts if materialism is true – can only be regarded as fortuitous and accidental.

One might think that this need not make any real difference to theoretical inquiry, regarded as the search for truth. After all, the possibility that this purely physical process might instantiate or realize a truth-tracking instance of theoretical inquiry cannot be ruled out in advance. Further, does it not lie within our power to *review* our results and thereby convince ourselves that our observations are in fact correct, our judgments sound, and our beliefs about the brain based on experiment and argument sufficient to justify those results? The answer to this, unfortunately, is a resounding "No!" if materialism is true. Our attempts to review our results by reexamining the data, the experimental outcomes and the arguments upon which our beliefs are based must, if materialism is true, themselves are at best the *epiphenomena* of some process going on in our brain, the occurrence of which is the consequence of purely physical causes over which we had no control and to which we make no contribution. In turn, each of the components of this process will be a physical brain-state wholly determined by the operation of purely physical causes operating in accordance with the truth-indifferent laws of motion. As such, it is no more intrinsically truth-connected than any other brain process, and so it can offer us only cold comfort that our efforts at review seem to confirm our original results. As such, the mere logical possibility that such a process could accidentally instantiate an instance of theoretical inquiry, let alone successful theoretical inquiry, through some chance process does not give us any reason to suppose that something like this would ever actually happen. To suppose that it could happen over and over again seems incomprehensibly unlikely.

Neurophysiological Determinism and Neuroscience A final, fatal difficulty for the materialist's attempt to "naturalize" neuroscientific research resides in the thesis I call neurophysiological determinism.[8] If materialism about mind is true, then all of our mental processes and their

---

[8]This is a *precis* of the argument of Chapter 2 below, "The Consequences of Neurophysiological Determinism" applied to the present context.

products are fully and completely explicable of the operation of purely physical causes operating in the brain of which we have no epistemically significant apprehension. These causes, in turn, fully determine the course of the neuroscientist's theoretical inquiry, from beginning to end, prior to him or her even beginning to undertake the research constitutive of that inquiry. If that is so, then the neuroscientist has no effective control over the course of his or her research – that has already been determined by forces outside of his or her control. All of his or her observations, thoughts, judgments, inferences, and beliefs are already in the cards before the scientist even begins to collect the data. Although it may appear to the neuroscientist that he or she is being open, objective, and sensitive to data, experimental results, and the logical force of reason and argument, once again this is only the way it *seems* to him or her from the first person point of view. From the objective, third-person point of view, this facile self-awareness is superseded by a genuinely scientific account according to which theoretical inquiry is no genuine activity at all, let alone an intellectual pursuit of truth, on the part of scientists. Instead, it is simply something that *happens* to them, something individual scientists undergo as the result of the operation of causes over which they have no control and are powerless to evade, alter, or correct.

More than this, we find further reinforcement for a point we made in the last section. Neuroscientists suppose that their beliefs are based on observation, reflective thought, judgment, empirical evidence, and rational argument. They furthermore suppose that it is precisely the epistemically significant aspects of observation, judgment, empirical evidence, and rational argument that exercise the greatest influence in forming their substantive beliefs about the brain. Indeed, if this is not so, then it would seem that theoretical inquiry in general and neuroscience in particular would have no guarantee of being truth-connected, no matter how thoughtfully and carefully its researches were undertaken. Yet, as we have seen, if materialism about mind is true then we have no reason at all to believe this. The operation of purely physical causes in the noumenal brain leave no room for observation, reflective thought, judgment, reasoning, deliberation, discussion, and so on to rationally influence our substantive beliefs.

The epistemically significant aspects of our mental states are thereby excluded from playing any role at all, let alone the leading role, in theoretical inquiry. These can have influence only to the extent that they are caused to have it in virtue of the causal powers residing the non-rational, purely physical states of the noumenal brain with which they are identical operating in accordance with the laws of motion. Despite appearances, then, no one has ever held a belief based on observation, judgment, empirical evidence, or rational argument, except insofar as they were caused to do so by brain processes that they neither control nor direct and which reach predestined results causally determined from the beginning of time. In that case, neuroscience is itself impossible as an exercise in theoretical inquiry as traditionally understood.

Why Externalism won't Help The proponent of materialism may well wish to question a hitherto unstated presupposition of the foregoing arguments. According to the standard account of the theoretical inquiry as I have presented it, it is not enough that I actually possess adequate grounds for my beliefs; it is further required that those grounds be accessible to me and be the actual grounds for my belief. This is a version of the epistemic theory known as *internalism*, one that requires access to the justificatory grounds for one's beliefs as a condition for the rationality of one's beliefs. Perhaps, however, one could craft an *externalist* account of rationality, according to which it is not necessary that one be able to access the rational grounds for one's beliefs in order for those beliefs to be rational. Rather, it will be *sufficient* for a belief's being rational that it be produced by a causal process (consisting wholly, e.g., of purely physical brain states) that (physically) realizes or instantiates a line of reasoning that, if it *were* available to the subject thinking it, *would* justify that believer's belief. This sort of thing is much more amenable to the materialist point of view than the standard view outlined above, which no doubt accounts for some of its current popularity. However, it is not without its difficulties.

Externalism is most plausible in those cases in which the focus is what some philosophers have called *basic beliefs*, i.e. judgments arising spontaneously from direct experience, and which are thus elicited by non-propositional grounds.[9] Externalism is much less plausible where our focus

---

[9] See Alvin Plantinga, *Warranted Christian Belief*, New York, Oxford, 2004 175-117; so far as I know, Plantinga no longer distinguishes "basic" from "properly basic" beliefs, apparently taking it that every basic belief is properly basic unless we have good reason to suppose otherwise – basic beliefs are thus innocent until proven guilty.

is theoretical inquiry as the search for substantive truths about the nature of things that do not lie ready to hand in the way that perceptual knowledge at least appears to do. After all, theoretical knowledge appears to be explicitly based on and thus a product of, conscious discursive reasoning rather than any merely mechanical causal process. However, some philosophers have suggested that perhaps a generalized version of externalism could be enlisted to secure the reliability or proper functioning of our cognitive faculties, such that rational beliefs are those produced by cognitive processes causally hooked up to the world in such a way as to track truth. Even in the simple case, however, this is problematic.

Suppose I am "appeared to treely" at the current moment and wonder whether I am actually seeing a tree. The externalist can apparently do no more than tell me that, if my "being appeared to treely" has been caused by a reliable (i.e. truth-tracking) cognitive faculty of perception, then it is rational for me to be believe that I am seeing a tree and if not, then I am not rational in so believing. This is not very helpful; in a certain sense I already knew this, so to have it reiterated is not responsive to the question asked. Again, imagine Seyton telling Macbeth, "My Lord, if the dagger thou seest before ye be caused by a reliable, truth-tracking cognitive faculty, then certes, m'lud, there be a dagger before ye, yet if not, then it be none but an hallucination." What should Macbeth decide about his dagger? Perhaps Macbeth and I can investigate the question of whether we possess reliable cognitive faculties. However, not only is this against the spirit of the externalist enterprise, since it is once again the search for internal justification for my belief about the reliability of my cognitive faculties, it appears that it couldn't possibly succeed. We have no cognitive faculties to use other than those we already possess in order to resolve the question, yet it is precisely these faculties that are being called into question in asking it. As such, no progress will have been made regardless of what conclusion we arrive at. If my cognitive faculties certify themselves, then my reasoning will have been circular and so useless. If my cognitive faculties undermine themselves, then we can have no confidence that they have reached a sound result in this case, either. In either case, the question remains unanswered and indeed, appears to be unanswerable from the externalist point of view.

In the next place, let us ask the externalist why we should think that externalism is true. I suppose that a consistent externalist would have to decline to answer that question and respond that if a reliable, truth-tracking cognitive faculty has produced one's belief in externalism, then it is rational to believe externalism, and if not, not.[10] But of course this is not how externalists respond to this question. Quite the contrary, externalists are well prepared to argue for their view using philosophical arguments intended to persuade us of the truth of their conclusions on the basis of the evidence provided by the premises. Most commonly, they argue for externalism *indirectly* by presenting arguments against internalism: we are told, for example, that internalists cannot evade the problem of the criterion. However, this is still to argue as an internalist would argue, a strategy that cannot succeed, since the success of any such argument would epistemically undermine itself and leave us with no way to either affirm or deny its conclusion. More than this, for such a strategy to succeed, it would have to be case that it was possible for me to affirm the conclusion on the basis of the premises in the first place, something which we have surely seen by now is not possible if materialism is true. So, externalism has not helped us to evade that difficulty after all.

We must conclude, then, that there can be neither externalist nor internalist grounds for affirming the truth of externalism. Even if there were, they could not help the cause of materialism. Externalism appears to be the sort of view that can only be attractive to someone like Aristotle (arguably the first externalist) who already believes that, since the world was eternal and human beings had always existed, that we already possess all substantive truth and is therefore inclined to regard any skeptical doubts as frivolous.[11] Given the foregoing, however, one may well question whether this attitude is warranted for us.

Why Evolutionism won't Help One might be tempted to supplement the externalist account with an appeal to evolution. Ever since Quine's famous article, evolutionary epistemologists have attempted to argue that we could

---

[10] I remember hearing Daniel Dennett many years ago, who reported that, in a debate with a behaviorist, he had gotten his opponent (I think his first name was Ed) to admit that all of our beliefs were the result of positive reinforcement, *including that one.* Dennett saw this as sufficient to dismiss his opponent's view as absurd; however, I believe that a parallel argument applies equally well to his own position, and to any position like it as well.

[11] As opposed to Plato, who gives the classic internalist definition of knowledge as justified true belief, Aristotle defines knowledge as the conformity of the intellect to its object, something that he thinks is automatically produced by the causal influence of external material things on the senses.

explain knowledge as the product of some sort of evolutionary process occurring in natural history.[12] The feeling seems to be that all knowledge is potentially valuable for survival and cognitive error likely to involve fatal maladaptation to one's environment. Each organism, it is said, is a kind of "theory" about the way the world is, a theory to be either confirmed or refuted by how well adapted it is to its environment. As such, there would be selective pressure in favor of this sort of adaption, and thus a reproductive advantage, expressed as differential reproduction, to those organisms whose "theories" are greater in their conformity to reality, and thus to the truth about things.

Given the prior commitment to externalism, such an appeal will simply be to the *possibility* of such an account as a potential explanation for the existence of truth-tracking cognitive faculties. We cannot, in this context, argue that such an account is substantively true, since to argue for it on the basis of scientific evidence would not only be to abandon externalism for internalism but also to beg the question, since we can only judge the evidence for evolution using the very cognitive faculties that have been called into question. I can only know that evolution is true if my cognitive faculties are sound, so I cannot argue that this is the case by appeal to the truth of an evolutionary account of their development. To do so would be to fall into the Darwinian equivalent of the Cartesian circle. Even so, it may be urged that such an evolutionary account could *explain* how truth-tracking cognitive faculties are possible and thus, how externalism could be true.

It might, if in fact there were any reason to believe that this proposal were at all likely. However, as some notable philosophers have pointed out, there is no realistic prospect for the suggestion that evolution would have endowed us with reliable, truth-tracking *cognitive* faculties. Evolution, so we are told, is driven solely by chance and necessity, and "rewards" only behavior that aids an organism's survival and differential reproduction. Evolution operates, not by endowing organisms with cognitive powers or states, but instead by forging adaptive links between behaviors and survival of the fittest understood in terms of differential reproduction.[13] As such, we can expect evolution to lead organisms to true

---

[12] See W. V. Quine. "Epistemology Naturalized," in *Ontological Relativism and Other Essays*, New York, Columbia University Press, 1969, .

"beliefs" only in those areas (such as basic sense perception) and those subjects (e.g., food, predators, and potential mates) that directly bear on survival and differential reproduction. Even in those cases, that an organism arrives at a true belief (or something like it) is purely fortuitous and accidental, having nothing to do with the fact that what is "believed" is true *as such*. Truth-tracking as such, then, cannot be an evolutionary "goal" for any organism and thus we cannot plausibly explain how reliable, truth-tracking faculties might have come about. For this reason, the standard evolutionary account of these matters, going back to Darwin's time, suggests that our cognitive faculties originally developed for some other function related to survival and differential reproduction, which having overcome their initial challenge, left these faculties idling and capable of being employed for other tasks. On that account, however, we have no reason to believe that these faculties are the least bit adequate to the task of tracking truth nor any way to explain why or how they became contracted to the pursuit of theoretical truth in some manner that connects this to differential reproduction. It is thus hard to avoid agreeing with Plantinga's judgment that the likelihood that we have such faculties, given naturalistic evolutionism is "low to inscrutable."[14]

More than this, given our concern here is with theoretical knowledge for its own sake and with the faculties that might have made this possible, we need to note that beliefs of this sort have very little direct impact either on survival or differential reproduction. There have been many religions, cosmologies, political ideologies, and scientific paradigms commanding the assent of human beings throughout our history. In all but very few cases, these allegiances make no significant impact on differential reproduction, not even belief in evolution itself. While it is true that modern science has contributed greatly to both human survival and human flourishing through the application of theoretical knowledge to the problems of life, the notion that evolution may have somehow provisioned us with reliable, truth-tracking cognitive faculties in order to make this remote end possible for us seems teleological in the extreme. However, as the proponents of evolutionism never tire of telling us, evolution is a "blind" process, incapable of any remote provisioning. This in turn suggests

---

[13] Sharon Street explains this nicely in her "A Darwinian Dilemma for Realist Theories of Value," *Philosophical Studies*, Vol. 127, No. 1, 2006, 109-166.

[14] See Alvin Plantinga, *Warrant and Proper Function*, New York, Oxford, 1994, 216-37.

that the odds against any such faculties surviving long enough in a population to emerge as useful in this way is highly improbable.

It is sometimes argued that the fact that we can build bridges that don't collapse and so on is proof that we have reliable, truth-tracking cognitive faculties. The suggestion is that, since our cognitive faculties must have evolved, that despite the long odds, evolution must have somehow accidentally produced them. To the contrary, on the standard, adaptive-link account of how evolution operates, it remains highly unlikely that evolution could have given rise to reliable, truth-tracking cognitive faculties. Any evidence that we do, in fact, possess such faculties supports, not the evolutionary "long shot" view but rather presents an obvious anomaly for the usual, adaptive link account of evolution, at least in this context. In that case, the very fact that we can formulate the theory of evolution and confirm it as a fact of natural history is evidence against the usual, adaptive-link account of evolution as applied to cognition. Externalism, then, borrows little support from such an implausible view.

So, then, how *is* neuroscience possible? I do not propose to give a complete answer to that question.[15] However, the thesis of this book is that neuroscience is possible for us as a branch of theoretical inquiry only if the mind is not the brain and the scientist who inquires is a self-conscious rational subject. For more of my reasons for thinking this, read on..

---

[15] See my Chapter 3 below for as much of answer as I can muster.

Chapter Two

The Consequences of Neurophysiological Materialism

Most of us believe that our mental contents play a central role in explaining what we believe about those contents and justifying our beliefs about them. For the most part, we take it for granted that we can know what those contents are simply by apprehending them reflectively in conscious awareness by introspection. Thus, I can know that I am presently aware of a red sense-datum (for example) simply through the fact that a red sense-datum is directly and immediately present in and to my conscious awareness as a content of my intentional field of conscious awareness, a fact that I am capable of making explicit to myself in reflection through directing my attention to that mental content. I thereby *apprehend* it, so that I am not merely aware of that red sense-datum but also aware of the fact that I am aware of it – something that is essential to and definitive of my being a self-conscious rational subject.

On this traditional, everyday account of the matter, the presence in and to conscious awareness of a particular mental content, in this case the red sense-datum, is essential to my claim to know this fact and thus the truth of the proposition expressing that fact. Further, this is so in two ways. First, the presence of that sense-datum in and to conscious awareness is explanatorily essential to my *apprehension* of it as a fact of my mental life, by providing both the *content* and the *object* of that reflective mental act. Secondly, that apprehension provides the *epistemic ground* for the truth of my beliefs concerning that mental content, such as that I am presently aware of a red sense-datum, that I apprehend that mental content, that I know these facts obtain, and thereby know the truth of the statements that express that knowledge. These beliefs, in turn, will be *rational* to the extent that they are explicitly based on grounds or reasons that *justify* those beliefs, or at least capable of being so based by and for those who hold them. These reasons, in turn, derive from our direct apprehension of our individual mental contents, *a priori* insights, deductive and inductive inferences, observation and experiment, etc. The systematic study of substantive questions using the procedures of discursive reason, which we may call *theoretical inquiry* and of which philosophy and natural science are examples, pursues truth and knowledge in a sustained, methodical way, hoping to arrive a general picture of the nature of things. At any rate, so it seems to common sense and has been affirmed by traditional philosophers as well.[16]

In this essay, I argue that if neurophysiological materialism is true, this ordinary picture of the role and significance of mental contents cannot be sustained. By *neurophysiological materialism,* I mean the thesis that each and every mental content present in conscious awareness, regardless of its attributes, is the product of the operation of non-mental, purely physical causes existing in the brain, causes whose operation cannot be apprehended *as such* even in principle but must be posited as extramental, theoretical entities. If this claim is true, we can always provide a *full* and *complete* explanation of the presence of any mental content in conscious awareness by reference to such causes. In that case, I argue, the presence in conscious awareness of those contents plays no essential role in any of the judgments we make or beliefs that we arrive at concerning those contents or their justification. This, in turn, generates insuperable epistemological problems for the neurophysiological materialist. I conclude that, since it is impossible for us to entertain the idea that our mental contents are irrelevant to judgment and belief, we ought to reject neurophysiological materialism, even if it cannot be disproven on scientific grounds alone.

---

[16] It is to be noted here that our concern in this context is solely with the contents of our own minds, not with the objects they putatively represent to us. The question, then, concerns our knowledge of our own thoughts and other mental states.

Suppose I believe, *allegedly* on the basis of my immediate experience, that I am currently perceiving a red sense-datum. If neurophysiological materialism is true, then there is a complete explanation of my believing this, one to be given in terms of the activity of non-mental, purely physical causes existing in my brain. This explanation will make no essential reference to my immediate experience or its contents at all. As such, my belief that I presently *perceive* a red sense-datum owes nothing to the presence in my mind of the *putative* red sense-datum I claim to perceive, even if it is there. In that case, that red sense-datum itself (even if present) is in no way the cause or ground of my belief that it is present to me. This is important, because as I have explained, I would ordinarily claim to *know* that my belief that I am now perceiving a red sense-datum is true on the basis of my direct and immediate apprehension of the red sense-datum itself as my current mental content.

If neurophysiological materialism is true, however, the red sense datum and my putative awareness of it played either no role whatsoever or some completely dispensable role in the acquisition of that belief. That is because if neurophysiological materialism is true, every mental state is the product of the operation of non-mental, purely physical causes existing in my brain and this includes all my beliefs, including my beliefs about my putative sensory apprehensions. Thus, for example, the fact that I believe that I am apprehending a red sense-datum will likewise be the product of the operation of non-mental, purely physical causes existing in my brain, which will completely explain why I am in that belief-state. Once again, then, my belief that I am presently apprehending that red sense-datum owes nothing to that apprehension itself, even if I am actually apprehending a red sense-datum at the present moment. Thus, if neuropsychological materialism is true, I have that belief solely due to the operation of non-mental causes existing in my brain, causes that have produced that belief in me in a manner indifferent to the presence or absence of the apprehension that is the object of that belief.

It follows, then, that my belief to the effect that my belief that I currently perceive a red sense-datum is based on my immediate experience of a red sense-datum is, after all, *false*. If neurophysiological materialism is true, the actual causes of my believing this are quite other than the one I take it to be, and this will hold regardless of whether that sense-datum is present to conscious awareness or even that I do in fact apprehend it. My conviction that my belief that I am experiencing a red sense-datum is based on my apprehension of that sense-datum has to be dismissed as an illusion, or at best, an example of the false, pre-scientific "folk psychology" that modern science supposedly supersedes.

II

This is a highly counterintuitive result, to say the least, but is it epistemically fatal? Couldn't my apprehension of the red sense-datum still serve as the *epistemic* or *justificatory* ground of the beliefs associated with it? After all, if I actually have it, why not?

Here is the reason why not. The foregoing argument will also hold for my belief that I am epistemically justified in believing that I presently perceive a red sense-datum in the same way as it did in the other cases. If neurophysiological materialism is true, this belief too will be the product of the operation of non-mental, purely physical causes existing in my brain in which my apprehension of that sense-datum, even if actual, will play no role, or only a purely dispensable one, in its acquisition. The same will hold, in turn, for my belief that I *actually* apprehend a red sense-datum at the present moment. If neurophysiological materialism is true, I hold that belief as well due to the operation of non-mental, purely physical causes existing in my brain.

For still the same reason, the same will hold for the *conjunction* of these two claims, i.e., that I am epistemically justified in believing that I perceive a red sense-datum at the present moment *because* I actually apprehend a red sense-datum at the present moment. This belief too will be the product of the operation of non-mental, purely physical causes existing in my brain in which that apprehension, even if actual, plays no significant (non-dispensable) causal or explanatory role. At no point in any of this, then, does my putative apprehension, even if actual, play any role that will permit it to serve as the causal or justificatory ground of my beliefs, even if they are true and even if that apprehension could in principle provide such grounds for that belief. At every point, the operation of non-mental, purely physical causes existing in my brain blocks me from asserting any claim that makes indispensible reference to that mental content itself in such a way that it makes an explanatory contribution to my actually holding that belief. In so doing, it also prevents my apprehension of that mental content from serving as the epistemic ground of that belief, constituting it as epistemically justified for me. This will hold even about such facts as those concerning the immediate contents of conscious awareness, even supposing that I do in fact apprehend them.

III

Surely, one will say, if I really do apprehend a red sense-datum, even if that apprehension is the product of non-mental, purely physical causes existing in my brain, I can be certain that I do apprehend it and so appeal to that apprehension to justify epistemically the foregoing beliefs. However, if neurophysiological materialism is true, it is perfectly possible that this claim is false. There is no reason to suppose that non-mental, purely physical causes existing in my brain might not produce *unshakeable conviction* that I am apprehending a red sense-datum when in fact, I am doing no such thing and there is no red sense-datum present to my consciousness *at all*.

More than this, it is arguably an empirical fact that this sometimes happens. Oliver Sacks, for example, has documented cases of people who sincerely believe, and claim with the sort of complete conviction that accompanies incorrigible belief, that they can see and have visual experiences even though they are blind and to have such experiences is physically impossible for them.[17] If my putative apprehension of a red sense-datum is the product of non-mental, purely physical causes existing in my brain, my mere testimony that this sense-datum is present to my consciousness is on a par with, hence no better than, that of the people described by Sacks. The presence or absence of that sense-datum, then, may well make absolutely no difference to the fact that I hold the belief that I do, and given the same causal antecedents, I would have believed it regardless of what (if anything) was going on in my conscious awareness.

---

[17] See the case study "The Last Hippie," in Oliver Sacks, *An Anthropologist on Mars*, New York, Vintage, 1996, 42-76.

On this view, such a circumstance could obtain for all of us at all times so that we would believe with perfect conviction that we have visual, auditory, gustatory, olfactory, and tactile sensations even though no such sensations actually existed as mental contents of any kind.

More than this, since my being in a particular belief-state is nothing more than for a certain physical brain-state to be realized in my physical brain, I would hold that belief – whatever this could possibly amount to on the view we are considering here – even if I was not, in fact, apprehending a red sense-datum at the present moment or even if I was apprehending nothing at all and my belief to that effect had no propositional content at all. In that case, my apparent apprehension of that red sense-datum would have to be an illusion and my belief to that effect would have to be false, since neither of these events would actually be occurring after all. Worst of all, my believing this would not, after all, even be so much as occurring as a mental content available in, to, and for occurrent conscious awareness. In that case, I could not possess occurrent conscious awareness of anything at all. My beliefs to that effect could be rescued from falsity only through being dismissed as unreal – not really occurring as part of what is going on in the world.

Indeed, if the view adopted, either directly or by implication by some hard-bitten materialists called Eliminitivism about mind is true, there is no such thing as lived experience, no mental contents or events, and no contentful mental states such as beliefs, etc. In that case, all of our claims to know, e.g., that I am currently seeing a red sense-datum, or anything at all on the basis of "lived experience" are in fact false, with the result that my status as a self-conscious rational subject is eliminated as well. Of course, if this is the case, so too is neuroscience as a going concern in the world of the sort we take it to be as a branch of theoretical inquiry, along with theoretical inquiry generally, rational thought, and rational discourse as well.

Now one may want to insist that, however it may be with people like those described by Sacks, *I* am actually aware of what I sincerely avow to be the case when I assert that I currently perceive a red sense-datum, and that this makes all the difference in the world between my case and theirs. However, on this supposition, the difference between my case and theirs crucially turns on the factual question of whether the red sense-datum is *actually present* in and to my conscious awareness while it is absent in theirs, despite their unshakeable belief to the contrary. How could I resolve this factual question? Of course, if Eliminitivism is true, I clearly cannot even so much as raise this question, let alone undertake a project of theoretical inquiry into the matter. In that case, the question answers itself due to the fact that it cannot be raised precisely because there are no self-conscious rational subjects capable of asking it in the first place.

If we turn back from the abyss and consider this question seriously, (something we could not do if eliminativism is true) it seems that I could easily answer it if I possessed a power of intellectual, introspective apprehension that made it possible for me to grasp, directly and immediately, my mental contents and their attributes *as such* and thus ground my beliefs and their justification on that apprehension. However, if neurophysiological materialism is true, *all* of my mental states, even my putative apprehensions of my own mental contents, are the product of the operation of non-mental, purely physical causes existing in my brain. As such, I never have direct, unmediated access to any of my mental contents sufficient to confirm either their presence or their qualitative properties: the operation of non-mental, purely physical causes existing in my brain always dispose of the matter independently of those contents and their attributes, whatever they might be and regardless of whether they are there or not.. I thus have no way to confirm that matter-of-fact, and thereby resolve that empirical question, in this or any other case. The truth of neurophysiological materialism preempts and excludes mental contents from having any influence over our beliefs about our mental contents, rendering them useless as an epistemic ground for any belief whatsoever, including the belief that I am actually aware of a red sense-datum at the present moment, *even if I am*! The same, of course, will hold of my belief that it *seems* to me that I perceive a red sense-datum at the present moment, and so on.

IV

One might want to protest that, given the fact that mental contents are nomically dependent on their corresponding neural correlates, that it was not causally possible for those antecedents to have obtained without the presence of the appropriate sense-datum in conscious awareness. On this view, part of what it *means* to be in a particular neural state *is* for the person in that state to be aware of a particular mental content, existing as the mental correlate of that particular neural state. Thus, one might argue that the people described by Sacks will have acquired their delusive belief in another way, one neurologically distinguishable from our own, and that given this their case may safely be put aside.

One can say such things, of course, but this claim can hardly be a *conceptual truth* about these states or knowable *a priori* in some way independently of the operation of non-mental, purely physical causes existing in my brain, at least if neurophysiological materialism is true. Nor, in any case, do mental states and their neural correlates appear to be internally related so that (like left and right) we can apprehend the one only if we at the same time apprehend the other. To the contrary, I can (apparently at least) have detailed knowledge of my own mental states through direct and immediate apprehension of their contents and properties without even knowing that I have a brain or believing that the brain has anything to do with cognition. The supposed correlations, then, are clearly logically contingent. Since apprehension of my mental contents as such does not carry with it the same – or indeed any – sort of apprehension of the supposed neural correlates upon which they somehow depend, that there is such a correlation here needs to be justified somehow. So how could we confirm that these correlations actually exist?

Apparently, this will only be possible if we can somehow empirically *confirm* these nomic connections between mental contents and their neural correlates. Leaving aside the problem of how we would establish the *nomic* (hence modal) aspect of this claim, the very project of establishing such a correlation using empirical methods is surely conceptually impossible if neurophysiological materialism is true. Such correlations cannot be established by neurophysiology alone, because such correlations make inevitable reference to mental contents and their qualitative attribute that cannot be empirically detected *except* through the presence of their neural correlates. So no such correlation can be established in this way without presuming what is not in evidence and begging the question.

Presumably, we could establish such correlations only by matching people's reports about their subjective mental contents and the properties of those contents with publicly observable brain-states.[18] This, however, presupposes that the experimental subjects do actually possess mental contents and can accurately describe the qualitative attributes of those states. Such correlations could be established only if those subjects had some sort of direct, unmediated access to their own mental states and their qualitative attributes by means of a faculty that apprehends them directly and immediately, hence independently of the influence of non-mental, purely physical causes existing in our brains. However, if neurophysiological materialism is true, we have no such access, and any such project is stillborn.

Indeed, for reasons we have seen, if neurophysiological materialism is true, we are in no position to affirm with any confidence that any such mental states or properties even so much as exist, let alone that any form of theoretical inquiry that supposed this was even so much as possible. Thus, if neurological materialism is true, such correlations, then, cannot be even so much as established in the first place, let alone used to prove that such contents are nomically connected to their supposed neural correlates. As such, we are blocked from establishing either the dependence or the identity of mental events with their supposed neural correlates through knowledge of any such correlations, even in principle.

Worse even than this, we have to note that, in order to make these correlations, even on the side of neurophysiology, it has to be possible for us to observe the brain, its states, the outcomes of scientific experiments, and so on, since only in this way could we acquire the empirical evidence required to establish that such correlations exist. However, any such observations, depending as they do on sense-experience, would have to be mediated to us by our own conscious states and their contents, which

---

[18] As I shall insist immediately below, however, all publicly observable things, events, and states-of-affairs are mediated by subjective mental states that are directly apprehended by individual observers, so that there is no prospect of supplying such correlations in any event.

putatively inform us of the relevant empirical facts. However, as I have just argued at length, if neurophysiological materialism is true, our conscious states have no role whatsoever to play in the formation of our beliefs about the external world. All such contents are preempted in this role by the operation of non-mental, purely physical causes existing in our brains, which given the foregoing we can never apprehend, even in principle. Thus, if a scientist believes that he or she can arrive at such correlations based on the empirical evidence derived from observation and experiment, and neurophysiological materialism is true, he or she must surely be mistaken about this, even if everything that he or she is inclined to believe due to the operation of the non-mental, purely physical causes existing in his or her brain is in fact true about the world.

In that case, scientific judgments and beliefs supposedly based on observation and experiment owe nothing at all to these correlations considered *as such*. Instead, those judgments and beliefs are simply the product of the operation of non-mental, purely physical causes that operate indifferently to the presence of any such contents, and can (for all we can possible know if neurophysiological materialism is true) in principle realize their effects without them. In that case, no such correlations are possible for us as the outcome of theoretical inquiry undertaken by the neurophysiologist. More than this, it is not clear that any form of theoretical enquiry, not even neurophysiology itself, is possible even in principle.

Science will not be possible unless it is possible for us to apprehend the external world in some fashion, to make observations and measurements, form hypotheses, construct and observe the outcomes of experiments, and to reason from (observable) effects to (usually hidden) causes. In turn, the very possibility of all these operations requires that our beliefs be based on the input of the senses and the judgments they evoke, and which are subsequently accepted as beliefs on the basis of that evidence. However, by preempting their influence, non-mental, purely physical causes existing in the brain exclude anything like this from being a correct depiction of what is happening when a scientist does his or her work. At best, the account of scientific reasoning sketched above constitutes a kind of "folk psychology" of scientific inquiry, one that a truly scientific description of the matter would show to be a mere, pre-scientific illusion. However, it is not immediately clear what such a view could even amount to, let alone formulated and verified in a way consistent with its own claims and within its own strictures. I leave it to others to ponder that speculative question.

For my part, I think that the standard account of intellectual inquiry, far from being a folk-psychological myth, cannot be denied without destroying not only the possibility of theoretical inquiry, but of human rationality itself. Any successful scientific inquiry would provide a *pro ambulo* refutation of the claims of neurophysiological materialism. In that case, our very success in establishing correlations between mental events and their supposed neural correlates, must be taken as evidence *against* neurophysiological materialism rather than support for it (as it is universally taken to be). To the contrary, it ought to be taken to be evidence that we have a capacity to apprehend, directly and immediately, our own mental contents without the mediation of non-mental, purely physical causes existing in the brain.

V

This sort of argument can be extended to every other sort of knowledge claim: mathematical and logical truths, *a priori* truths, claims based on deductive and inductive inference, empirical claims based on observation and experiment, and so on. If we know anything at all, including the truths of modern science, we know that neurophysiological materialism *must* be false.[19] Having illustrated how this argument works for what it is presumably the most difficult case, I leave further extensions of this argument to these other cases as an exercise for the interested reader. Let's cut to the chase.

The upshot is this: only if I am able to both apprehend my mental contents and to make some reflective judgments independently of the operation of non-mental, purely physical causes existing in my brain is it possible for me to have any knowledge at all, even of the facts that I would

---

[19] Of course, it doesn't follow from the foregoing that we do know anything, or that neurophysiological materialism is false. However, for reasons that will emerge below, we need never worry that someone might actually prove that this is the case.

claim to know with the greatest certainty. This prospect of neurophysiological materialism does the Evil Genius argument one better but, like the argument from the possibility that I am insane, it destroys itself as a ground for skepticism, by destroying rationality altogether. If I cannot have the kind of direct access to my mental contents that is required in order for them to play some role in the production of the thoughts by means of which I reflect on them, then rationality is an illusion and all reflective thought comes to an end. I may think that I am capable of reflective thought, and believe that I actually engage in it, but that is only because I have been caused think this by non-mental, purely physical causes existing in my brain.

Indeed, if Eliminitivism is true, not even this can true – it is false that I even so much as occurrently entertain any such belief. In the same way, should I try to reflect on that fact, it will obtrude that I have been caused to think that I have been caused so to think, and so on, by other causes of the same sort. The operation of non-mental, purely physical causes always serves to break the connection between reflection and its object, interposing itself between them so that the reflective act never attains its putative object or does so, if at all, only indirectly and merely accidentally. Our subjective experience testifying to the contrary must be rejected as false if neurophysiological materialism is true and as non-existent if Eliminativism is true. In that case, I can never genuinely think at all in the sense that thinking is related to rational belief as traditionally understood.

In that case, theoretical inquiry as we ordinarily take it to be will be impossible as well since the purpose of such inquiry is presumably to arrive at rational beliefs about substantive matters of fact. After all, I can think to some purpose in this regard only if my occurrent thoughts are responsive to my mental contents, logic, and governed by the rules of inquiry rather than merely being the product the operation of non-mental, purely physical efficient causes existing in my brain, as must be the case if neurophysiological materialism is true. Since philosophy and natural science are branches of theoretical inquiry, the truth of neurophysiological materialism will also exclude those activities as well, and for the same reason. At the same time, if I cannot do natural science, then I cannot provide scientific evidence for the truth of neurophysiological materialism –

presumably the only sort of evidence relevant to determining the truth or falsity of that theory.

Given the foregoing, we need never fear that science will prove that neurophysiological materialism is true, since any such proof would be at the same time proof that science, as a mode of theoretical inquiry, is impossible for human beings. Neurophysiological materialism, then, is epistemically self-refuting. It does not follow from this, of course, that neurophysiological materialism is false. A transcendental argument of the sort I have been constructing here cannot arrive at any such substantive result.

However, this is cold comfort for the proponent of neurophysiological materialism. If I am even to be able to seriously consider the question of whether neurological materialism is true, it has to be possible for me to arrive at a rational judgment concerning this substantive, factual question. If neurological materialism is true, however, then as we have there is no way for me even to begin to do this. Indeed, I cannot even so much as entertain the possibility that neurophysiological materialism might actually be true since its actual truth would exclude my being able to do so. Thus, regardless of whether neurological materialism is true, I can only proceed on the assumption that it is false if I am to consider the question of its truth *at all*, since the falsity of neurophysiological materialism is a necessary condition for this to be possible. Thus, if I can even consider this question, I can do so only from a perspective that presupposes that neurophysiological materialism is false. In that case, the question answers itself.

In that case, of course, further discussion of the question is clearly otiose. Surely, then, we are well within our rights as rational beings to reject any such theory, even if the foregoing argument does not (as it does not from the rational point of view) *prove* that this theory is false. It would never be reasonable to accept it, even on a provisional basis, since to do so would constitute intellectual suicide given the implications of that theory. To do this would not even be intelligible if there was no alternative, and this is clearly not the case.

Quite the contrary: I am much more certain that I directly and immediately apprehend my own mental contents than I am of the truth of any scientific theory, let alone a philosophical theory like neurophysiological materialism. Indeed, I would claim to know this fact with *incorrigible* certainty, a certainty that excludes all possibility of error or deception, despite the fact that I cannot prove this to anyone from the external, objective third-person point of view. Thus, to the extent that neurophysiological materialism is inconsistent with that incorrigible fact, I must reject it as obviously false. Further, this common sense assumption of traditional philosophy proves to be self-referentially consistent and intuitively satisfying as the basis for an account of apprehension, judgment, inference, and rational belief-formation, a fact that shines out in relation to the supposed neurophysiological "alternative." Therefore, given that neurophysiological materialism proves to be inconsistent with that sort of account and is itself of doubtful coherence, it appears to me I have every right as a rational being to reject neurophysiological determinism as false.

If the neurophysiological materialist thinks otherwise, then there are some questions he or she needs to consider and answer before undertaking a criticism of these arguments or further articulation of this view. First, what is it to think? How does the neurophysiological materialist accomplish this feat? More importantly, how does the neurological materialist know that he or she thinks or what he or she thinks? As it stands, it is difficult to see how the neurophysiological materialist could do or know any of these things, since if his or her view is true none of these notions make any sense at all in such a manner as to make a rational discussion of these questions possible, so that such a discussion could be possible only on the assumption that the very view being discussed is false. In the case, the point is moot and, if despite all I have said, neurophysiological materialism is true after all, if I can say anything at all, all I can say is, "Welcome to the Abyss."

Chapter Three

Dualism and Neuroscience

In the first chapter in this book, I argued that, rather than being extended, or even complemented by such research programs as "cognitive science" and "neurophilosophy," neuroscience – by which I mean the traditional studies of neuroanatomy and neurophysiology – understood as a branch of theoretical inquiry is in significant tension with these programs. That is because the very notion of theoretical inquiry as understood and practiced by philosophers and scientists inextricably belongs to and takes for granted what Sellars called "the manifest image" and is thus incapable of being incorporated into the "scientific image" without generating insuperable epistemological difficulties that threaten the very possibility of such inquiry. As such, the naturalistic (i.e., materialist and determinist) presuppositions of cognitive science and neurophilosophy systematically undermine all natural science, including the neuroscience that they hope to use as a basis for their speculative philosophical constructions. In so doing, they undermine their own views, and their own status as self-conscious rational subjects as well.

This is a surprising result for such a well-received view. At the same time, it seems to many to be a foregone conclusion that traditional Cartesian dualism is neither in the spirit of, nor even compatible with, the claims made on behalf of neuroscience. Here, however, we must divide cases. On the face of it, I see no reason to suppose that substance dualism is in any way incompatible either with the pursuit of neuroscientific research or with any of the substantive results that have actually emerged from that research. Certainly, there are ambitious claims made for the promise of neuroscience, mostly by philosophers and "cognitive scientists," concerning the nature of consciousness, mind, personhood, cognition, and much else. Most of those who promote such claims are decidedly hostile to substance dualism, but as I have argued elsewhere, we have little reason to believe these claims and, in fact, could not have such reasons, even in principle, as I explained elsewhere.[20]

In this paper, I propose to provide an answer to the question that served as the title for Chapter 1 of this book, i.e. "How is Neuroscience Possible?" I shall argue that, in order for it to be possible, we must first abandon the naturalistic presuppositions of neurophilosophy and "cognitive science:" Galilean physicalism, materialism, and determinism. Then, we must replace these naturalistic doctrines with their non-naturalistic antitheses: the ontology of material things, substance dualism, and freedom of the will. On this alternate picture (which admits of many different versions and much further development, so I claim no exclusivity or finality for the versions of these doctrines presented here), natural science, and theoretical inquiry as a whole, finds a natural home. Even if it must accept a somewhat chastened role in the exploration of the phenomenon of mind, the neuroscience actually done by neuroscientists will be at least possible and its discoveries genuine contributions to substantive scientific knowledge. That will have to do, just as it has largely done for actual working neuroscientists up to now, some notable practitioners of which were dualists.

Physicalism Must Go! When contemporary philosophers see the word "physicalism," they automatically think of physicalism about mind, the thesis that mind is nothing but a brain-process, ultimately reducible to or wholly dependent on, physical processes occurring in a wholly physical brain. That, however, is not the sort of physicalism I am attacking here – at least not directly.[21] Instead, I am attacking a view that has become so ingrained in our contemporary mindset that it goes for a foregone conclusion and is never even so much as formulated, let alone questioned.

---

[20] See, for example, "The Consequences of Neurophysiological Materialism," and "Can I know what I am Thinking?" – Chapters 1 and 4 in this book..

[21] I am attacking it indirectly only in the sense that physicalism about mind is often seen as the final, last detail needed to carry the Galilean physicalist program through to completion. If, as I have argued elsewhere, we abandon GP, then surely this particular motive for pursuing physicalism about mind ceases to apply.

This view I call *Galilean Physicalism* (GP) or *physicalism about the external world*. I am persuaded that it is this commitment to GP that generates the problem of the external world and the epistemological crisis that still bedevils Western philosophy. The basic problem is that GP cuts us off from the external world in such a way as to make knowledge claims about that world so problematic that neither common sense realism nor scientific realism can be sustained in the face of skeptical challenge. When pushed to the limit, GP is epistemologically self-undermining, and in so being, undermines science itself, understood as the branch of theoretical inquiry charged with discovering substantive truths about the extramental natural world.

In the case of neuroscience, for example, we find a familiar story played out. Neuroscientists depend on the senses to investigate the brain, which they perceive as a bodily organ consisting of various tissues and structures by means of which the brain is able to function in various ways that contribute to the overall economy of the living organism, specifically the body, of which it is a part. Everything that we know, and even can know, about the brain is derived, in the last analysis, from the findings of neuroanatomy and neurophysiology. Yet, according to GP, the real or *noumenal* brain, is nothing like the brain as it appears to us in conscious awareness *via* sense experience.

The real brain is simply a collection of atomic and subatomic particles externally related to each other by physical forces and interacting with each other in accordance with the laws of motion. Like Eddington's two tables, GP seems to present us with two brains, one a bodily organ, the other physical object with exclusively physical attributes. Given GP and the standard practice of preferring what Sellars called the Scientific to the Manifest image, we have to affirm the claim that, if either brain is the real brain, it is surely the latter.[22] In that case, however, the status of the brain as apprehended by the senses – call it the *phenomenal* brain – suddenly becomes problematic.

Neuroscientists take themselves to be studying the real brain. Yet given the notion that the real brain is a physical object and thus beyond being apprehended *as such* by the senses, the phenomenal brain we apprehend by means of the senses can at best be a subjective, mind-

---

[22] See Wilfrid Sellars, *Science, Perception, and Reality*, New York, Humanities Press, 1963, 1-40.

dependent set of sense-data existing (at best) only in conscious awareness, a sort of mental image of the noumenal brain. In that case, we face all of the familiar epistemological problems associated with the realism of Descartes and Locke. Since we have no access to the noumenal brain except through the phenomenal brain, how do we prove that the noumenal brain even exists, let alone that the very different phenomenal brain accurately represents it? Since there is no way for us to access the noumenal brain as such and so compare it to the phenomenal brain to which we do have access through sense perception, it would appear that these questions are unanswerable, even in principle. If one were to adopt a skeptical, or instrumentalist, interpretation of neuroscience, I think it would be very difficult to show that this view was untenable. It would be even more difficult to establish that neuroscientific realism is a tenable view.

Galilean Physicalism is a philosophical, indeed an ontological rather than a scientific, thesis. Many people, including Galileo himself, seem to have thought that GP is the only, or at any rate the most natural ontology for natural science. However, as I have argued that Descartes was at least inchoately aware, quite the opposite is the case – something that has become increasingly obvious to contemporary metaphysicians.[23] In that case, the epistemological difficulties that so many people tend to dismiss as at worst just skeptical sophisms and at best merely philosophical problems that, like all philosophical problems, can be deferred indefinitely instead indicate that there is a significant logical tension between the practice of natural science and the GP ontology. If I have said enough to persuade the reader to take this worry seriously, this may be an appropriate time to suggest an alternative.

The Ontology of Material Things Fortunately, a number of contemporary metaphysicians have been exploring the idea of rehabilitating an ontology of material things, largely upon neo-Aristotelian lines.[24]

---

[23] See my *The Proof of the External World*, Eugene, OR, Wipf and Stock, 2007, Chapter 1. Peter Van Inwagen and Trenton Merricks have argued (both assuming that GP is true) that physical objects cannot have proper parts and that therefore material substances (a class of entities that would include what we usually take to be the brain) do not exist. James Ladyman and his associates have argued that, if we are genuinely interested in basing our ontology on natural science that not even physical objects exist in the last analysis. See Van Inwagen (1990), Merricks (2001), and Ladyman *et al*, (2007), all *op cit*. The full references for these works are given in Chapter 1 above.

[24] Among these philosophers, I might mention E. J. Lowe, David S. Oderberg, Lynn Rudder

According to this view, material things are not only real but also ontologically fundamental. Material things, the intentional objects of the mental events and acts dependent on, on sense perception, are composite substances, consisting of significant form or *structure* and matter. The epistemological significance of this view is as follows. Material things are present *in* and *to* conscious awareness by virtue of their substantial forms, which forms are present in things as their natures and in a different way in the mind, so that the form as known is numerically identical with that form as it exists in things. Thus, in apprehending/knowing the content of my own mental act of sense perception, I at the same time apprehend/know that material thing of which I am thereby aware *formally* and *intentionally*.

To the extent that *matter* (Aristotle's material cause) is also perceptible, it too is material substance and a composite of form and matter. However, matter as understood by modern physics is not apprehensible and is conceivable only as a Lockean *substans* or *substratum*. What I call physical *objects* are theoretical entities, and as such are explanatory posits that represent our best attempts to model the noumenal world consisting of the "hidden natures" of material things using the imagination, scientific method, and the clues provided for us by sense-experience. The descriptions we offer of these noumenal entities neither are pure fictions nor literally true descriptions of things-in-themselves, but instead schematic, analogical *models* of those hidden natures.[25] These models, whether based on analogies derived from the senses or purely mathematical in nature, aim to be structurally isomorphic to what they describe and in so doing capable of both explanation and prediction within the realm of sense experience. To reach explanatory bedrock, such models

---

Baker, Amie Thomasson, Kathrin Koslicki, and Crawford Elder. I in no way want to suggest that these (and allied figures) constitute a school or movement, or that they would altogether agree with each other even on their basic outlook. Especially, I in no way wish to suggest that any of these figures would endorse any of the things that, after the next sentence in the text, I will offer by way of a suggestion for implementing this program. These ideas are entirely my own and cannot in any way be blamed on the aforementioned – or anyone else, for that matter. Neither do I agree with everything these figures have written. Although I resonate strongly with neo-Aristotelianism in metaphysics, I am still a Cartesian dualist and thus more inclined to side with Plato than with Aristotle on some key issues. The main attraction of these views is their role as providing a plausible alternative to Galilean Physicalism in ontology.

[25] See, on this point, Mary Hesse, *Models and Analogies in Science*, Notre Dame, IN. University of Notre Dame Press, 1965 and Ian Barbour, *Issues in Science and Religion*, Englewood Cliffs, NJ, Prentice-Hall, 1974.

must *posit* some sort of ultimate level of entities existing as *simple* substances, possessing simple attributes, relations, and subject to the smallest possible set of simple laws.

Whatever can be apprehended and in that sense known by us through sense perception is the consequence of the presence of substantial form in and to conscious awareness. What modern science calls matter (ideally, a set of uniform simple substances possessing only quantitative properties, related to each other by simple forces, and interacting in accordance with mechanical laws of motion) is not perceptible as such, and thus not capable of being directly apprehended or known by us. However, unlike Descartes and Locke, we must not assume that nothing can be known except what can be directly apprehended.[26] The great success of the scientific method in modeling external, noumenal reality in an illuminating way shows that this is false. While nothing can be comprehended by us without first being apprehended by means of the senses, it does not follow that only what is apprehended can be plausibly said to be known – or knowable.

Applying the foregoing to the brain, the following picture begins to emerge. The brain *qua* bodily organ is a material thing and constitutes the real brain. In sense perception, the brain's substantial form, which exists in it as the brain's structural principle or nature, comes to exist in conscious awareness in a different way, as the unifying, structural principle of the sense content of the mind's perceptual act when the brain is observed and studied. In so doing, it exists in conscious awareness in a manner isomorphic to the way it exists in the thing itself – the noumenal brain. In this way, the brain *qua* material thing is formally and intentionally present in and to conscious awareness and thus apprehended/known by the perceiving subject. In the same way, the *matter* of the brain, i.e. the tissues and structures studied by neuroanatomy, as well as the functions and processes studied by neurophysiology, are also apprehended by the senses. In this way, they are known by neuroscientists through the senses, and thereby made capable of being theoretically comprehended by them as well. Although neuroscience needs no more than this to be possible as a *bona fide* science, using the general categories of physics as adapted to the particular

---

[26] See Locke's *Essay*, Part IV, where he expresses both pessimism and skepticism about our ability to penetrate the secrets of nature, even by means of natural science.

context of the brain *qua* material thing, it is also possible to reconstruct the brain as a physical object and its structures and processes as physical processes as well. In so doing, neuroscientists are attempting to provide a *model* for the noumenal brain, at least insofar as the part of the brain that is hidden from sense-experience can be plausibly conjectured and reconstructed from what we do experience through the senses. Since this reconstruction is limited, partial, and analogical rather than fully literal, this will not do as a "reduction" of the brain to a physical object, which somehow supersedes or makes the brain *qua* material thing ontologically superfluous. There is no bar, however, to our accepting the well-confirmed results of such an inquiry as an indirect, if partial, apprehension of the brain *qua* physical object by means of a theoretical construct allowing us to intellectually *comprehend* the brain as a noumenal thing-in-itself.

There are not, on this view, two brains, one phenomenal and the other noumenal. There is only one brain, a composite substance consisting of form and matter, and two ways of knowing it: perceptually, as a material thing, and theoretically, as a physical object. The "phenomenal" brain is simply the brain as apprehended by the senses, and the "noumenal" brain the brain as comprehended according to the categories of physics. These are simply two different ways of looking at the same thing, one literal and epistemically fundamental, the other analogical but still our best account of the brain's *ultimate* but hidden constitution. The two pictures thus complement, rather than compete with one another, and there is ample room for everyone to engage in his or her preferred mode of theoretical inquiry without stepping on anyone else's toes. At the same time, no one gets the privilege of proclaiming that his or her perspective supersedes all others or makes the other's research superfluous.

Materialism and Neuroscience The second great epistemological bugbear threatening the possibility of neuroscience is materialism about mind, according to which conscious awareness and all its states and contents are either nothing but – or are wholly dependent upon – purely physical states of the brain externally related to one another merely by mechanical efficient causes. The essential difficulty is a version of the problem of mental causation applied to our own thoughts. If any science, including neuroscience, is to be possible, it has to be the case that we can engage in theoretical inquiry. This, in turn, presupposes that we can arrive at well-confirmed beliefs on the basis of observation, experiment, and sound logical reasoning. The difficulty arises from the fact that, if materialism is true, we can always provide a complete causal explanation for any mental state in terms of purely physical, non-rational causes occurring in the noumenal brain. Data, reasoning, and evidence are thus disbarred from contributing *as such* to the formation of our judgments and beliefs. Instead, they will be capable of so doing only insofar as judgment and belief were produced by the brain state with which these reasons are to be reduced or upon which they supervene. In either case, this will simply be accidental and fortuitous from the physical point of view. Given this, neither evidence, reasoning, nor argument, considered in themselves or as such, contribute in any way to what I end up believing.

For the same reason, neither is data, reasoning, argument, etc., capable of epistemically justifying my judgments or beliefs in order that they might be rational. My judgment that a particular argument is valid and sound and thus justifies its conclusion, being itself either nothing but, or wholly supervenient upon, a purely physical state of the noumenal brain, will be itself the product of wholly physical causes existing in that brain, just like every other mental state. Once again, my putative apprehension of the argument and its logical properties either played no role at all in my arriving at my judgment, or did so solely in virtue of its association with a purely physical brain state, hence only accidentally and fortuitously as the byproduct of a purely physical process occurring in the noumenal brain. In no way, then, is that judgment the product of any sort of rational process considered as such, in the manner we usually conceive of it.

If science is to be possible, theoretical inquiry, the pursuit of truth for its own sake, must be possible. In turn, theoretical inquiry will be possible only if rational belief is possible as well. For rational belief to be possible, it has to be the case that data, evidence, reasoning, and argument play the leading, indeed, to greatest extent possible the *exclusive* part in determining what we come to believe. It has to be possible for me to assent to the truth of a proposition solely on rational grounds, without the interference of any non-rational, merely efficient causal conditions. In this sense, the operation must be *autonomous*, just as we normally take it to be when we engage in philosophy, natural science, or any other form of intellectual inquiry.

The neuroscientist, for example, supposes that, in engaging in scientific research he or she is discovering the substantive, empirical truth about the how the brain works and what it does. What a surprise, then, to discover that this view must be mistaken if materialism is true. The neuroscientist's careful observations, elegant experiments, well-confirmed findings, and rationally compelling arguments are all, if materialism is true, no factor at all in determining what he or she believes, except insofar as purely physical processes going on in the noumenal brain with which they are associated have played a purely mechanical, efficient causal role in producing those beliefs. From the physical point of view, the presence or absence of those mental contents makes no difference to the causal processes that produce those beliefs. The neuroscientist, then, utterly lacks rational autonomy even as he or she pursues the substantive truth about the brain. The noumenal brain, by sundering any connection between beliefs and the reasons that justify them, simply will not allow it. A neuroscientist who is also a materialist must come to the conclusion that reason, as such, is an illusion, and in the end, that the very science that he or she practices, conceived of as being a product of reason, is an illusion too.

I have discussed various attempts to evade this conclusion at length elsewhere.[27] For now, I can do no more than hope that, given what I have said, the reader might be willing to entertain an alternative, at least hypothetically. Although this could possibly be false, I shall nevertheless proceed hopefully.

Dualism and Neuroscience If theoretical inquiry is to be possible, then rational belief must be possible as well. Rational belief will be possible only if reason is autonomous in its operation, so that it is possible for us to form our beliefs in accordance with evidence and argument rather than simply arrive at our beliefs solely due to the operation of non-rational, purely physical, efficient causal process occurring in the noumenal brain. By exploring the necessary conditions for the possibility of this sort of rational autonomy, we will also discover the necessary conditions for the possibility

---

[27] See the other chapters in this volume.. I have done so at still greater length in *Reason and Illusion*, Amazon CreateSpace, 2022. Many people will be resistant to this conclusion, I suppose that I will have to do so at even greater length on some future occasion if there is the opportunity. However, by now the intelligent reader can probably supply the appropriate critique for him- or herself without my help if only he or she has the will, leisure, and interest to do so.

of theoretical inquiry, natural science, and therefore, neuroscience as well.

In the first place, then, since reason is surely an illusion if materialism is true, the principal necessary condition for the possibility of rational belief is that materialism about cognition be false. This means that rational thought must be immaterial, in at least the minimal, negative sense that it is neither reducible to nor wholly dependent on physical processes occurring in the noumenal brain *qua* physical object. Instead, the exercise of our cognitive faculties needs to be in some way independent of the influence of such causes, so that we can arrive at our beliefs on the basis of data, empirical evidence, inductive and deductive argument, and so on. This also means that mind, and the self-conscious rational activity through which theoretical inquiry takes place and arrives at rational belief must be immaterial as well *so far forth*. This is a long way, of course, from showing that the mind is immaterial in the *positive* sense. However, it does at least suggest that this might be a metaphysical possibility. Here I can do little more than suggest the outline of a view that I have defended more fully elsewhere.

Let us begin with the idea of the soul as a simple, sempiternal, spiritual substance capable of only one simple, undifferentiated activity – *per se* causation in relation to the body.[28] Since the soul is not subject to space or time, this activity on its side or in relation to itself shrinks to a single, undifferentiated moment – the *now*, which taken in itself is simply a zero-dimensional moment of undifferentiated *duree*. In relation to the object upon which the soul exercises this power of *per se* causal influence, i.e. the body, it acts as *causa in esse*, serving as the metaphysical principle sustaining the body's operations across space and through time, becomes localized in space and extended through time. In its act in relation to the body it sustains, the soul is an *endurant* entity, wholly present in and to each temporal moment at which it acts due to its body being extended in space and time. The soul considered as such is a theoretical posit and knowable only through its effects.

The primary exercises of the soul's *per se* causality is in its role as the *principle of life* of the body. While the body *qua* material things has its

---

[28] I have discussed this at greater length in a new book, *How Free Will Works*, Eugene, OR., Wipf and Stock, 2011.

own substantial form (encoded in its DNA), the soul is the substantial form of the body *qua* living organism, i.e. the composite substance composed of and by both soul and body. Hence, the soul is the principle of substantial unity of the body and principle of its ongoing organic operations and does this through being the *per se* or sustaining cause of the body's organic operations in space and over time. The presence of the soul accounts for the organism's property of being "self-organizing," i.e. being able to maintain the same pattern while incorporating new parts, regarded since Aristotle as a primary difference between living and non-living things. This power it exercises independently of conscious awareness and its operation in this regard is not accessible to that awareness.

Consciousness (awareness-as-such) is the interface between the soul and the body by means of which the soul is able to monitor the body's state and condition, and by means of this to interact with the external world of material things. Conscious awareness arises due to the fact that the soul is present to the body, and capable of monitoring changes in it. Some of these changes are the consequence of changes in the body that hamper, retard, or interfere with the soul's ability to exert uniform *per se* causation with regard to its operations. Others are changes that are the result of interaction with other bodies, producing changes in the sense-organs and bodily-based appetites, emotions, passions, etc., that once again affect the soul's influence on the body.

Conscious awareness is constituted by and occurs in an intentional field of awareness that, while immaterial, arises at the interface of the soul and the body and thus participates in space and time inasmuch as the lived experience encountered in that intentional field of awareness is both perspectivally localized in space and reflects the passage of events as these succeed each other in the world. Conscious awareness is thus a third thing serving to unite body and soul into a single subject of experience, something for which both soul and body provide necessary conditions. The temporally and spatially ordered contents that appear in consciousness are largely the provision of the body that, being a material thing that is both localized in space and is itself subject to temporal passage and real change, occupies a volume of space and undergoes both immanent and extrinsic change in real time.. Conscious awareness is thus a third thing serving to unite body and soul into a single subject of experience, something for which both soul and body provide necessary conditions. It stands to the body in a manner analogous to the way in which the intentional field of a mirror and its contents stand to the reflective material thing we call a mirror. At the same time, the rational soul becomes a self-conscious rational subject by being conscious in and by means of that intentional field and realizing certain latent capacities and powers in relation to and by means of its presence to that intentional field. The soul thus becomes the subject of lived experience, interaction with the external world, capable of reflection on that experience, and *qua* rational capable of engaging in theoretical inquiry.

A soul that has become conscious we can call a *mind*. Mind is a *perdurant* entity, existing for the soul *qua* substance simply as a power realized and exercised in the intentional field of consciousness as both subject and agent. The soul possesses the power intrinsically, but the realization and exercise of this power depends on conditions outside the soul, and in particular, in the body. Nevertheless, anything that has a mind is conscious, and thus counts as a *res cogitans*. Yet not all souls that become minds are rational souls. Non-human animals are conscious but non-rational because they lack the power of *reflective awareness* of their own mental states. By contrast, a *rational* soul is one possessed of the power of reflective awareness, and thus capable not only of being conscious, but also of being aware of the fact of being conscious as well and of its own mental states, their properties, and contents as such.[29]

A rational soul that has become conscious and so a mind is thereby present in this intentional field as a self-conscious subject, a *person* or *self* and possesses additional conscious powers as a result. The human soul, at any rate, is not always conscious or capable of rationality in all circumstances. For this reason it is not always actively a self, hence does not possess realized or occurrent selfhood in all circumstances. Nevertheless, this power belongs to the rational, human soul by nature, hence is essential to it and thus present even when, due to external circumstances, it is incapable of being exercised. A rational soul lacking conscious awareness, rationality, and selfhood is thereby deprived of something that belongs to it by nature, like an eye that is blind. Nevertheless, since personhood belongs to a rational

---

[29] For more on this see Chapter 4 below.

soul by nature, on this view, a rational soul is a personal being even when it is not a self, due to some accident adhering in the body, such as having an undeveloped brain, being asleep, or even being in an irreversible coma. As such, a rational soul is still a person, even when it lacks active selfhood. In this way, we can thus concur with Boethius' definition of *person* as *an individual substance of a rational nature*. This definition does not limit personhood solely to those who are in active possession of consciousness, rationality, or self-awareness.

That we are capable of apprehending the contents of consciousness, and by means of them extramental things, is due to the fact that both the body and the things with which the body interacts are material things, composed of both form and matter. We cannot apprehend matter as understood by modern science by means of the senses. However, since substantial forms are capable of becoming *intentional species*, existing in various media, including the intellect, without becoming the natures of those things, it is therefore possible for us to apprehend material things through apprehending their substantial forms. More than this, since these substantial forms are immaterial, they are connatural to the conscious mind, and are thus capable of being the contents of conscious awareness. As Aristotle says, the intellect is potentially all things through the presence of their substantial forms in us.[30] Thus, viewed functionally, the purpose of the brain and its activities is to convey these substantial forms to conscious awareness, especially by means of the brain and its states and processes: it literally "in-forms" us through its activities.

On this view, the human body is a machine that has evolved to serve the needs of consciousness, and this is especially so in the way in which the brain has evolved. It is, I believe, much less likely that consciousness is some sort of accidental byproduct of the evolution of the organic brain than that the presence of consciousness itself is the primary factor in the brain's evolution. Human evolution, then, is not just about physical survival or differential reproduction considered as an end in itself. Indeed, very little of what human beings do, at least in ordinary circumstances, is plausibly explained by direct reference to these ends and few of the things that are so explicable would be worth continuing to do if

---

[30] *De Anima* 431b20-29.

an "evolutionary" account of these matters tying these activities to differential reproduction were to be accepted. After all, not even the most ardent evolutionist spends his time trying to have as many offspring as possible at the behest of his or her selfish genes! All enjoyment and everything that we can think of as worth having or doing is in some way related to and dependent on conscious awareness, and whatever promises to expand our capacity for conscious experience, whether in terms of intensity, range, or variety, naturally recommends itself to every sentient creature. In beings capable of self-consciousness, the pursuit of various kinds of intrinsic goods, capable of trumping the pursuit of sensuous pleasures and even overcoming the fear of death is widely recognized and prized by human beings.

From this point of view, the brain's role in cognition is to serve as an information processor, as the means through which substantial forms are made accessible to the rational soul, *qua* self-conscious subject, in conscious awareness. It does this by encoding the substantial forms of material things as the structural principle of perceptual brain states, and storing them the physical memory for further use. The brain does all this without being in any way aware of its doing so, for the brain is not conscious, nor is it even alive through its own act. Nevertheless, it plays an essential role in making conscious awareness possible, and is the source of all of our spontaneously arising mental contents, including our judgments. Only neuroscience, not philosophy, can tell us this part of the story, so I shall say no more about this here.

Thought is only possible if there is something to think about, and this is supplied by the brain through the introduction of substantial forms into conscious awareness. Both the forms themselves, and the thoughts about them, are immaterial. As such, we can learn no more about cognition by studying the brain than we can about Beethoven's Ninth Symphony by studying the various states and processes occurring in our stereo components when we are playing a recording of that work.[31] At best, brain

---

[31] I owe this image to Gavin Ardley, "The Nature of Perception," *Australasian Journal of Philosophy*, Vol. 36, no. 3, 1957, 189-200. It is especially apt, since even though the *performance* of Beethoven's Ninth that we hear when we play the recording is *utterly* supervenient on the non-musical processes that produce it, the study of those processes has absolutely no significance for or relevance to our understanding of that performance as either a piece of music or a work of art. The same holds, I contend, for the relation between the study of

activity and processes are necessary, not sufficient, for cognition. Further confirmation of this lies in the fact that the primary contribution of neuroscience to our understanding of cognition is in exploring how various kinds of brain diseases and illnesses affect our cognitive capacities by preventing the necessary conditions for normal, healthy cognition to occur. In this regard, the greatest interest and promise of neuroscience lies where it has traditionally been seen to lie – in the field of medicine as the basis for research intended to heal defects and traumas in the brain *qua* material thing so that, among other things, perception and cognition will be possible for those with mental deficiencies and injuries.

Much more than what I have said here is needed in order to make what I have said here even remotely plausible to most modern philosophers. This is not the place to say it and, at any rate, I have said this elsewhere. I only note that a dualist need not deny the necessity of the brain for conscious awareness, and especially for successful cognition. Nevertheless, the autonomy of reason needs to be preserved, on pain of undermining even the very possibility of neuroscience. To this topic we must finally turn.

Neurophysiological Materialism and Free Will As I have argued at length in the previous chapter, if the thesis known as neurophysiological materialism is true, then all of my thoughts are determined by non-rational, purely physical causes over which I have no control, exert no direction, and have no autonomous power to review. As such, whatever beliefs I arrive at, my arriving at them was something completely predictable from purely physical causes operating in my brain long before I even undertook my course of theoretical inquiry. Further, since those all-disposing, purely physical causes existing in my brain are at best only accidentally related to sound reasoning, I have no reason to believe the results of those inquiries once I know how they were produced. Neither am I in any position to confirm those results or verify them by further examination, since whether

---

cognition (or more simply, "thought") and the brain. If the stereo (or whatever) fails to function or to function as it was designed to do, then no proper performance will be heard; so too will thought be impossible if the brain cannot function or if its operation is defective. It does not follow that thought is nothing but a process occurring in the brain, or some process completely supervenient upon the functioning of the brain, or even usefully investigated by investigating the brain-processes that make thought possible for a finite mind.

I make such an examination, as well the results that I arrive at after doing so, were already determined by forces outside of my control. If I was determined to persist in my belief after reexamining it, or to change my mind, then I do so ineluctably, regardless of the facts of the matter. In that case, these results are no more trustworthy than those I originally arrived at, and no matter how many iterations of this process of examination I have been determined to engage in, the difficulty remains. The same, of course, will hold of specific forms of theoretical inquiry, such as neuroscience.

Although there are various ways in which defenders of determinism attempt to evade these implications of their view (when they actually engage them rather than simply dismissing them with scorn) I contend that none of them is successful.[32] If I am right, then the very possibility of rational belief and theoretical inquiry requires that belief in the substantive truth of a proposition must be a free act, made solely on the basis of reasons without interference from non-rational causes existing in my brain. Thus, rational belief and theoretical inquiry of all kinds, including neuroscience, are possible only if we have free will. However, since the brain is a machine and completely subject to the laws of nature, it follows that the brain is incapable of free choice. If we are to have free will, then, it must be the case that the soul as conscious and self-conscious mind exercises the power of free choice with regard to our beliefs in its guise as self-conscious rational subject. Thus, just as rationality presupposes free will, so also free will presupposes the existence of an immaterial soul that exercises that power of agency as conscious mind. In other words, if rational belief is to be possible in any field, including neuroscience, then either substance dualism, emergent naturalism, or idealism must be true.

It is sometimes argued that we do not, in fact, possess the power to believe or not believe at will. However, we need not interpret doxastic voluntarism as requiring this sort of Sartrean freedom. Instead, it is enough for our beliefs to be product of free, rational assent that it be possible for us to suspend judgment with regard to the truth of any proposition simply by withholding assent to that proposition. As Descartes and Hume show, this ability to suspend judgment in this way extends to any belief we possess about which we might even possibly be wrong, which includes nearly all of

---

[32] See Chapter 2 above and my *Reason and Illusion*, op. cit., 265-284.

our substantive beliefs. In most cases, we form our beliefs against the background of evidence that is less than logically compelling, and to which other rationally defensible alternatives exist. There can be no serious question in such cases that the judgments we make, viewed against the background of evidence and alternatives available to us, are free and the exercise of autonomous reason. If this were not so, then we could not be subject to doxastic obligation and willful irrationality – of which we strongly suspect philosophers who disagree with us – would be impossible.

I have elsewhere discussed the interaction problem for Cartesian dualism and offered my solution to it. Since the brain exists to process information and convey the forms of things to the mind in consciousness, its states and processes reflect those forms and their relations to one another. As such, these processes produce both spontaneous judgments and spontaneously arising lines of thought in conscious awareness tending to favor the various alternatives that (typically involuntarily) occur to us. The discipline of theoretical inquiry, constituted by the laws of logic and the canons of proper method, give us criteria for considering some alternatives and rejecting others, which neither need nor admit "correction" by neuroscientists, who depend on these same laws and canons to accomplish their own work. Such laws and canons, then, are clearly autonomous norms of thought presupposed by all theoretical inquiry of whatever kind, including neuroscience. In turn, these norms of thought sometimes conflict with our previous habits of thought. We manage our thoughts by selecting which to sustain or continue through the power of *per se* causation inherent in the soul. When we decide what to believe in accordance with logic, the canons of theoretical inquiry, and the preponderance of evidence, we are rational so far forth. When we either form beliefs independently of those canons or believe against the clear preponderance of evidence, we are willfully irrational, and since it was within our power to have done otherwise, we are rationally blameworthy for having done so. In many cases, however, the evidence is not dispositive for one side or the other; in such cases, more than one view may be rationally respectable those who hold different views equally entitled to their positions.

If neuroscience is to be a science, and therefore an exercise in theoretical inquiry, qualified researchers must undertake it with the end of arriving at the truth about the brain. These researchers, in turn, must be competent inquirers, and thus capable of applying the canons of theoretical inquiry to the pursuit of the study of the brain, its structures, and processes as well as forming their beliefs in accordance with those canons. This, in turn, requires that they possess rational autonomy and thus be capable of *freely* assenting to the truth of propositions on the basis of observation, evidence, and rational argument. This, in its turn, requires both that their beliefs not be the product of the operation of non-rational, purely physical causes existing in the brain and that we be capable of withholding assent, even from propositions to which we currently consent.

Thus, if neuroscience is a genuine science and neuroscientists capable of rational belief, then neuroscientists possess free will as well. In short, then: if neuroscience is to be possible, then natural science must be possible. Natural science, in turn, will be possible only if theoretical inquiry is possible. Theoretical inquiry, however, will only be possible if rational thought and discourse capable of arriving at rational belief is possible. This, finally, will only be possible if reason is *autonomous* in its operation. As we have seen, however, reason can be autonomous in the relevant sense only if physicalism, materialism about mind, and determinism are false and the brain has evolved to serve the needs of consciousness rather than merely producing consciousness as a kind of incidental effect or accidental byproduct. As such, neuroscience is possible only if so-called "cognitive science" and neurophilosophy are false. That is my final conclusion.

<h1 style="text-align:center">Chapter Four</h1>

<h2 style="text-align:center">Can I Know What I am Thinking?</h2>

An essay of many years ago asked the question "Am I Thinking?"[33] To most of us, this question answers itself. Indeed, as we would say, following Descartes, it is a necessary condition for even considering the question "Am I thinking?" that I be a *res cogitans* – a being that could *not* think could not even so much as consider such a question, or any question whatsoever. Nor, presumably, could such a being engage in discursive reasoning or in theoretical inquiry, such as philosophy or natural science. If we can even raise this question, then, its answer is *obvious*, since to raise this question is to engage in the very activity, thinking, about which it raises the question to begin with.

Most of us would also claim to *know* that we are thinking, and to know this fact with an incorrigible certainty that excludes all possibility of error. Augustine affirms that there are three items of knowledge – that he thinks, that he exists, and that he loves – of which "no Greek can

---

[33] See the essay "Am I Thinking?" in *The Practical Cogitator*, edited by Charles P. Curtis, Jr. and Ferris Greenslet, Boston, Houghton Mifflin, 1945, p. 1. According to novelist Nathanial Benchley, when his father (humorist Robert Benchley) died suddenly, a copy of this book, which the elder Benchley had just begun reading, was found on his person with the following marginal note written next to the title of this essay: "No! – and what if you were?" Neither the essay nor the comment was intended to be philosophical. Nevertheless, however unintentional, there is a sad commentary on contemporary philosophy of mind to be read in this brief exchange.

dispossess him." Descartes maintains that not even the Evil Genius could confuse or deceive him about this point. I stand with Augustine and Descartes on this point and presume that the reader does as well. However, reflection of this seemingly incorrigible fact has some surprising consequences for some of the more entrenched ideas dominating contemporary philosophy of mind. In this essay, I wish to call those ideas into question by reference to what I will call the standard model for self-knowledge of this sort, which I maintain is incompatible with those entrenched ideas. In particular, I shall claim that the standard materialist accounts of the nature of thinking makes our self-knowledge on this point extremely problematic and potentially illusory.

To begin, then, I will consider the standard account of our knowledge of our own thoughts and thus of the fact that we are thinking on those occasions that we advert to that fact. I will then present an argument – which I have developed in more detail elsewhere – for the conclusion that, on materialist models of mind of whatever sort, we can have no such knowledge. I shall conclude that, since we do in fact have such knowledge, that theories of this sort must be false and that I can know my own thoughts, and thus the fact that I am thinking, only if I have an immaterial mind and access to its contents independently of the operation of the brain. This result, though unpalatable to many, is nevertheless so straightforward and obvious that I cannot conceive of any response to my argument that does not wholly undermine the very activity of making it. In conclusion, I shall say why I think this is the case.

The Standard Account of My Knowledge of My Own Thoughts Let me now proceed to the standard account of how we know our own thoughts. To begin with, we have many mental contents, e.g. sensations, feelings, passions, that give rise to judgments prompting us to act in various ways. There is a broad (and in some contexts useful) sense, used by Descartes, in which every mental content counts as a thought and every sequence of related mental events counts as thinking. However, not all mental contents have to be conceived of as either potentially or actually known to those conscious subjects that possess them. On a standard, traditional view of the kind of conscious awareness enjoyed by non-human animals, for example, such creatures are capable of thought in Descartes' broad sense, but not in the more specialized sense in which we reserve that term for certain of our own mental contents. According to this traditional view, animals possess mental contents but neither a capacity for *reflective awareness* of those contents nor any *mental operations* over those contents. Rather, the mental contents animals possess and enjoy, being evolutionarily tied to non-conscious instincts and drives arising from adaptive links directed on survival and differential reproduction, simply exercise a direct causal influence over their behavior.

Not possessing any abstract concepts, the gazelle cannot say to itself "Heavens! That animal that has just come into view is a lion, a dangerous predator that may attack and eat me! Since I don't wish to be eaten, I had better run away." and then sprint away in an attempt to avoid that unhappy fate. Rather, the gazelle has evolved in such a way that whenever a dangerous predator comes into view, an instinctive reaction is triggered, adrenalin is released, the gazelle begins to sprint, and continues to sprint until the urge to sprint is relieved, after which it returns to grazing as though nothing had happened. Although a mental image, a feeling, and an overt behavior are all elicited by the presence of the lion, nothing like what we call "thought" in the human case comes into it. Even though we cannot agree with Descartes that animals lack consciousness or souls altogether, it is quite easy to agree with him that animal behavior is so largely mechanical that there is no reason to attribute anything like selfhood, cognition, or a capacity for inference to non-human animals. Despite the fact that in some cases we use anthropomorphic language to describe an animal's state of mind ("Fido believes that master is home," "Puff knows that if she waits long enough, the mouse will emerge from its hole" and so on), few if any of us want to *literally* attribute occurrent mental states with propositional contents to their subjects.

Indeed, modern evolutionary theory actually reinforces, rather than undermines, these traditional views, despite the fact that evolutionary biologists often help themselves to a question-begging use of the term "intelligence" intended to paper over the massive discontinuities between animal and human minds. The medievals, for example, attributed a quasi-cognitive "estimative power" to animals in order to explain how the lion judges when to pounce to capture its prey and the gazelle to run away when the lion gets too close.[34] We now suppose that lions and gazelles originally pounced and sprinted more or less at random in these circumstances and that those whose pounces and sprints were successful in either capturing prey or avoiding predators eventually outbred those whose pounces and sprints did not, thus allowing those characteristics to become widespread in their species. Although it may seem as though the lion and the gazelle are carefully weighing and judging when to act, that is merely an illusion. It is all mere chance and necessity after all.

What is missing in our literal depiction of animal behavior is the moment of *reflective awareness* of one's mental states and their contents. By contrast, reflective awareness is a standard feature of the sort of conscious awareness that human beings possess, even if this reflective awareness does not extend equally to all mental states and their contents at all times. It is not simply the case that human beings possess mental states with experiential contents; it is also very often the case that human beings are aware of those mental states and contents *as such*. It is only in this way that I can know that I am thinking in the full and complete sense that involves what we call cognition. In such case, I am reflectively aware of what I am thinking, and thus (at least inchoately and implicitly) of the activity of thinking itself. This in turn allows me to be aware of and thus to accurately report what my mental states and their contents are and thus to know how I feel, what I sense, what I am thinking, and what I believe. Without this capacity, no sort of sustained cognition would be possible, nor would the sort of discursive reasoning necessary for theoretical inquiry (e.g. philosophy and natural science) be either conceivable or possible as a going concern in the world.

All of the foregoing depends on my ability to *directly apprehend* my mental states and their contents by means of my *attention*. For the most part, our attention is directed outwards, toward the external world of intentional objects to which our conscious states mysteriously motivate us to concern ourselves. As with other animals, the original disposition of objects in our intentional field of awareness determining what is central and peripheral or constitutes foreground and background in that field is largely spontaneous and non-voluntary. Those objects that present themselves as central to and in the foreground of my intentional field of conscious awareness naturally

---

[34] See Robert Pasnau, *Theories of Cognition in the Later Middle Ages*, New York, Cambridge University Press, 1997, 53-4.

command the bulk of our attention and are thus that of which we are occurrently aware. In the human case, the lion comes into view and the human being *recognizes* that this is a lion, a dangerous wild animal, and immediately begins to *consider* how to get away from it. He or she is immediately and occurrently aware of him- or herself as potential prey, as being in a state of fear and terror, feels the adrenalin coursing through his or her veins, and as desperately desirous of attaining safety. Having made a happy escape, he or she rehearses the events in his or her mind, remembers how he or she felt, what he or she thought, and is grateful to be alive. He or she apprehends all of this in a reflective, self-conscious manner in real time as it happens or, if the speed of events overtakes reflectivity, in memory in a cool moment after the danger has passed. Other elements of the scene (such as the number of steps he or she took while running, or the size of the crushed rock in the asphalt path he or she travelled) may well fail to make an impression on the human being in this situation despite having passed through his or her perceptual field. Even so, there can be no doubt (at any rate, no coherent doubt) that occurrent reflective awareness is a standard part of the distinctive form of conscious awareness enjoyed by human beings. If we can even so much as entertain the question as to whether or not we possess such a capacity, the answer to that question has to be "Yes."

I can enjoy this sort of occurrent conscious awareness only because I directly apprehend my mental states and their contents by attending to them. Basic awareness of the sort we share with animals *plus* reflective attention *equals* direct apprehension of our mental states and their contents. More than this, it is only because I possess this power to directly apprehend my mental states and their contents that they are capable of becoming the *contents* and the *objects* of various sorts of mental acts, such as knowing and believing. Thus, due to the fact that I immediately apprehend my mental states and their contents that I am able to *know* what those states are and thus *that* I have them in the first place.

Through *voluntary control* of attention, I am able to alter foreground and background in my intentional field of awareness *at will*, concentrating on what would otherwise be peripheral elements, thus bringing them into centrality, while relegating normally central elements to the periphery, thus further solidifying my grasp on the full range of my mental contents.

Having focused on certain contents, e.g. propositional ones, I am then able to reason with and about them, deciding to assent to some, suspend judgment about others, and to positively dissent from still others, on the basis of reasons that seem to me sufficient to justify each of these propositional attitudes. In response to the promptings of curiosity or the challenge of new evidence, I may be driven to inquire into the truth of a particular matter, or seek the explanation for some surprising phenomenon, in which case I will initiate the search for theoretical truth for its own sake and do so by engaging in theoretical inquiry. When successful, discursive reason used in this way allows us to arrive at further, well-confirmed beliefs as the product of our own intellectual activity. All of this, of course, requires that it be possible for me to directly apprehend my mental states and their contents and thereby become reflectively aware of them. Without this, thinking in the sense we ordinarily take ourselves to be capable of would apparently not be possible.

Thus, I am able to *know* my mental states and their contents due to the fact that I *directly apprehend* them through the *reflective awareness* that naturally accompanies the distinctively human form of conscious awareness. This reflective awareness, in turn, can be directed voluntarily by me in such a way as to alter the constitution of my intentional field of awareness and increase my knowledge of, and appreciation for, its elements. More than this, I am able to *direct the course of my thoughts* in order to raise, investigate, and answer questions concerning the nature of things and thus arrive at substantive beliefs about reality by selecting, among the various lines of thought and inquiry that occur to me, which to pursue or ignore. This is what we attempt to do through science, philosophy, and other forms of theoretical inquiry.

More than this, such awareness is *necessary* if I am to have any knowledge of anything, whether subjective or objective. Even if it is possible for me to be *mediately* aware of certain objects by being aware of something else, it surely cannot be the case that I am aware of every object in this fashion. On this supposition, it would appear that in order for me to be aware of any object O would require that I am first aware of some prior object N, which would in turn that I first be aware of some prior object M, and so on *ad infinitum*. In that case, my conscious awareness of O would require an infinite, vicious regress of interposing objects, each of which was itself only indirectly apprehended through awareness of some further object. In that case, it seems that my awareness of O would not even be possible.

In order for me to be aware at all, then, awareness must *terminate* in something that I grasp directly and immediately in conscious awareness, *just as such*, as the *immediate object* of awareness. In the simplest such cases, the *intentional content* of my awareness and its *intentional object* will coincide in such a way as to preclude any distinction between appearance and reality. In that case, the intentional content of my act of awareness *is* the intentional object of which I am aware. In those cases, limited to mental states, their qualitative attributes, and their contents *just as such*, clear and distinct apprehension precludes all possibility of error and thus confers the *certainty* of incorrigibility on our judgments concerning those states, properties and contents. I can thus be said to *know*, e.g., my own thoughts, that I am thinking, and thus that I exist, in the strongest possible sense, one that exceeds that of any empirical, scientific claim, no matter how well-verified it may appear to be.

My direct and immediate, clear and distinct awareness or *apprehension* of my mental states, their properties, and their contents, is both necessary and sufficient for my *knowledge* of those states, properties, and contents, and thus to *justify* my claims concerning those states, properties, and contents with incorrigible, "demon-proof" Cartesian certainty. Furthermore, all of this is accomplished within conscious awareness itself in such a way as to neither require nor admit any further explanation or justification. All of this occurs within the charmed circle of my own ideas.

Materialism and the Standard Account For our purposes here, materialism about mind amounts to the thesis that all of our mental events, their properties, and their contents are, in the last analysis, either *nothing but* purely physical states, events, and processes occurring in the brain or are *wholly dependent* for their existence and character on states (etc.) of this kind. By calling these physical states, events, and processes *purely* physical, I mean to say that these states (etc.) consist *solely* of physical constituents (such as atoms, electrons, and so on), possess *only* quantitative physical attributes and are related to other physical states, etc. only in ways that can be exhaustively described and predicted in accordance with the fundamental laws governing force and motion. This, of course, is merely an idealization inasmuch as we currently have no way of modeling any of our mental phenomena in this way. Nevertheless, many people remain thoroughly convinced that there is nothing more to the matter than this, and remain confident that science will someday show this to be case, at least in principle.

I contend that the widely accepted materialist position outlined above is incompatible with what I have been calling the standard view about my knowledge of my own mental states, their qualitative attributes, and their contents. The standard view, as we have seen, holds that it is *sufficient* for me to know what I am thinking that I directly apprehend my own mental states, their qualitative attributes, and their contents and that it is both *possibly* and on many occasions *actually* the case that I grasp those states (etc.) with incorrigible certainty. Thus, I need do no more in order to *know* what my mental states, their qualitative attributes, and their contents are than to be directly aware of those states, properties, and contents. Further, given that my awareness of those contents is *immediate*, I grasp those subjective facts with greater certainty than I grasp any other facts, including those foundational for natural science.

This view must surely be false if materialism is true. On that view, my putative apprehension, even if real, plays no role at all in constituting what my judgments concerning my present mental state, its qualitative attributes, and contents happens to be – that is simply the consequence of the operation of my brain, and what brain state that operation has happened to produce. The basic problem is this: if materialism as I have characterized it is true, then what causally determines what my judgments concerning my mental states are, their qualitative attributes, and contents will be is something purely physical (a brain state) which I do not apprehend *as such* at all. This being the case, any judgment concerning what I directly apprehend is wholly causally dependent on and explained by physical facts that lie beyond my putative apprehensions themselves and exercise their causal influence independently of them, so that no reference to them is needed in order to explain why I judge the way I do. It follows, then, that my reflective awareness or apprehension of my own mental states (etc.) does *not* play any essential role in forming my judgments concerning my mental states (etc.) after all. To the contrary, its influence has been preempted from playing any such role by the causal operation of physical brain states, which wholly explain the formation of our judgments in terms of physically necessary and sufficient causal conditions that transcend conscious awareness and exercise their causal influence independently of it.

More than this – and for the same reason – those putative apprehensions will be powerless to *justify* those judgments considered as objects of *belief*. If materialism is true, my beliefs, no less than my judgments, will be the product of the necessary and sufficient causal conditions in my brain that produce them. Thus, my belief that my judgments concerning my own mental states, their qualitative attributes, and their contents are true given the evidence provided by my putative apprehension of those states, their qualitative attributes, and their contents is itself the causal product of the operation of purely physical brain states that in fact I do not apprehend *as such*. Further, the real (physical) explanation of why I hold this belief makes no essential mention of, hence excludes the influence of, those putative apprehensions in the formation of these beliefs. As such, the presence of those putative apprehensions in conscious awareness means little or nothing with regard to the beliefs that take them as their objects. These results will hold regardless of whether we actually do apprehend our mental states, their qualitative attributes, and contents and regardless of whether those apprehensions would in fact justify those judgments and their associated beliefs.

We can put this point, then, in the form of a dilemma. First, suppose that my apprehension of my mental states, their properties, and contents is knowable independently of the operation of my brain entirely on the basis of evidence drawn from conscious awareness. In that case, my brain states and their properties have no essential role to play in either explaining or justifying my judgments concerning my mental states, their qualitative attributes, and contents and materialism as characterized above is false. On the other hand, suppose that my judgments and beliefs concerning my mental states, their qualitative attributes, and contents are in fact fully and completely explicable in terms of my brain states in such a way that does not refer in any indispensible way to my putative apprehensions of those states in conscious awareness. In that case, my putative apprehension of my mental states, their properties, and their contents will play no role in the formation of those judgments and those beliefs, which have a complete, exhaustive causal explanation in terms of purely physical brain states. Nor will we be able to alter or decline any belief on the basis of the putative evidence provided by our putative apprehensions; we will have no choice but to believe what we have been caused to believe by purely physical states of our brain. On this alternative, neither will they play any role in explaining or justifying those judgments or beliefs.

Nor does it seem that we could somehow confirm the truth of our beliefs about own mental states, their qualitative attributes, and their contents through *comparing* them with the putative apprehensions that they apparently take as their objects. Again, either our doing so is the exercise of a purely mental power exercised independently of my brain or it is not. If it is, then materialism is false *so far forth*. If it is not, then both the fact that I make the comparison and the result I arrive at is the product some purely physical process occurring in my brain which makes no essential reference either to what is being compared or to the comparison itself, considered as mental acts or contents. Once again, these play no role in the process, which is wholly determined, from first to last, by purely physical events occurring in the brain.

Supposing materialism to be true, then, it turns out, then, that I do not know what I am thinking after all, at least as the standard account has it. Indeed, even my claim that it *seems* to me that I am thinking such-and-such, since this reports the putative content of a mental state putatively directly apprehended by me, casually depends on some state of my brain that I do not apprehend as such. In that case, I do not know even so much as the fact *that* I am thinking, *even if* and *even when* I am. Neither, then, do I possess the certainty about these subjective facts that they appear to me to possess, or the immunity from error I suppose them to grant me when I apprehend them clearly and distinctly.

On the other hand, it is *simply a fact* that I do know what I am thinking, and thus that I am thinking, with incorrigible certainty when I clearly and distinctly apprehend my own acts of thought, and thus know this with greater certainty than I could know *any* empirical, scientific theory no matter how apparently well-confirmed. Given this, any conflict between the standard picture I have sketched above and the supposed results of, say, neuroscience, have to be resolved in *favor* of the standard picture, given its greater certainty and evidence, and thus those results accommodated to the standard picture rather than taken as proof against it, even if it cannot be justified from public evidence apprehended from the objective, third-person point of view.[35]

Further Inconveniences of Materialism I suspect that few committed to materialism are likely to agree with the conclusion I drew in the last sentence, and are likely to claim that, if the standard picture conflicts with the apparent results of neuroscientific investigation, it is the standard picture, not neuroscience, that must be put aside. What is it, after all, but a palpable bit of introspective "folk psychology" of the sort that a truly scientific approach to consciousness, the mind, and cognition is intended to supersede? Whatever difficulties appear to attend the materialist program at the current moment, we can continue to look forward to that day (which never seems to get any closer) when it will finally triumph. However, if the argument of this paper is correct, these sanguine hopes have no prospect of realization *at all.*

First, a few home truths. If we are scientific realists, we suppose that natural science is concerned to investigate the natural world, a realm of real things existing independently of our awareness of it. The goal of natural science is to acquire substantive truths about this realm of externally existing objects. These truths are contingent truths, and so cannot be acquired *a priori*, through some sort of armchair reflection. Instead, we investigate the natural world through observation guided by something like the classic scientific method, formulating and testing hypotheses through guided observation and, when possible, controlled experiment. In this way, we arrive at knowledge of, or at least well-confirmed beliefs about, the natural world. Natural science, then, also involves the exercise of discursive reason, including constructive imagination, memory, and deductive and inductive inference. Since its results are not knowable in advance, natural science requires, and is an example of, theoretical inquiry and thus presupposes the cognitively necessary conditions for the possibility of such an enterprise.

---

[35] See Chapter Five below.

The role of the aforementioned cognitive faculties, especially sense perception, is crucially important in the project of theoretical inquiry. Science can neither proceed nor succeed without the use of these cognitive faculties. More than this, these faculties have to be *reliable*, i.e. have a general tendency, when properly employed within their proper limits, to lead to the goal of theoretical inquiry – objective truth for its own sake. Sense perception, memory, judgment, and inference are all required for natural science and must be reliable if we are to be even so much as capable of theoretical inquiry, whether scientific or otherwise. Indeed, in a certain sense, we have to take the reliability of our cognitive faculties for granted. This is something that we cannot do if we believe that Materialism is true except by believing in the teeth of the evidence in violation of all of our doxastic obligations.

Further, we are justified in doing so, since any challenge to the reliability of these cognitive faculties would have to employ them, and thus suppose them to be reliable so far forth, which would thereby undermine any such challenge before it was even formulated. *Pace* Hume, it is not possible for there to be any rational argument that undermines reason since any such argument undermines itself in undermining the very faculties we have to use in order to evaluate it. Therefore, we cannot seriously entertain any such argument in any event, since to do presupposes that it might be the case that we are in no position to do just precisely that. As such, we could never have compelling reason to accept its conclusion, even if the argument was sound and its conclusion true.

Of course, it does not follow from this that this assumption is itself *substantively* true. A lunatic must make the same assumption if he is to think at all, yet in his case, because he is mad, this assumption is after all false and none of his substantive beliefs either justified or justifiable given that fact. Still, neither he, nor we, can do any better.

Nor does it follow from this, however, that our cognitive faculties are thereby made immune from every possible challenge. In some cases, substantive beliefs, apparently confirmed by theoretical inquiry, are such as to make the required employment of our cognitive faculties impossible for us if taken to be substantively true. In those cases, it is those apparently well-confirmed beliefs, not our cognitive faculties, that must give way, and the evidence for them accommodated to the necessary assumption that our cognitive faculties are reliable. For, unless those faculties are reliable, then none of our beliefs can count as well-confirmed, and thus neither can the substantive beliefs that, if true, would undermine the reliability of the cognitive faculties that produce them. Unless we are to countenance the possibility that reason could undermine itself, by arriving at beliefs that would make its employment in the pursuit of truth impossible or otiose, which as we have seen cannot obtain, we have to draw the line whenever we discover any such tendency in thought, and reassess its putative foundations in the evidence. To persist in these beliefs in the face of the fact that, given their truth, no one could have reason at all for believing that they were so would be to commit the fallacy of *special pleading* – exempting a cherished belief from the sort of critical scrutiny that one would recognize to be perfectly legitimate in any relevantly similar case.

We have already seen that materialism, as characterized above, is problematic in this regard. Where our putative apprehension of our individual mental states, their qualitative attributes, and their contents are concerned, materialism severs the connection between those putative apprehensions and the production of our subsequent judgments and beliefs concerning their objects. This leaves them no role to play in explaining those judgments, this being fully accounted by the operation of purely physical causes operating in the brain. In the same way, it rules out our putative apprehensions from playing any role the justification of those beliefs as well, by leaving no room for those apprehensions to have any influence, as such, on the acquisition or retention of those beliefs through rational assent to judgment.

More than this, it fragments what seem to be an extended series of related thoughts (such as those involved in making inferences or interpreting data and experimental results) into merely accidental collocations of such thoughts when taken in relation to their non-mental, purely physical causes existing in the brain. What we experience as content-relevant, logically structured, continuous, and internally related lines of reflection in thought turn out to be merely the correlates of non-mental, purely physical causes existing in the brain, related if at all by logically contingent, external relations of efficient causality governed solely by mechanical forces and the laws of motion.

If materialism as I have characterized it is true, the aforementioned experience is surely an illusion in relation to the proffered explanation. Our conviction, which forms a significant part of the standard account of what rational thought and theoretical inquiry consist in, i.e. it is the relations of content-relevance and logical relations between propositions that guide our thought toward the theoretical truth, must be regarded as false if materialism is true. The real, neurophysiological explanation of what is going on when we reason (etc.) involves only the operation of non-mental, purely physical causes existing in the brain (etc.) making no essential reference to anything else in its explanation of my line of thought. Given this explanation, none of those features of my thoughts that I take so seriously have any role at all to play in the explanation of my reasoning, or on what in the end I believe. Therefore, if materialism is actually true, no one ever has, or ever could, have a belief that was actually based in any significant way on any apprehension, judgment, inference, or empirical evidence. That is to say, no one ever has, or ever could, have a rational belief of any kind.

The implications of these results for natural science, conceived of as a form of theoretical inquiry, are obvious and very serious indeed. Science recommends itself to us on the authority of its capacity to provide us with objective truth about the natural world. Yet, if materialism is true, we are at a loss to either know or justify that claim on the basis of any sort of proof or rational evidence. After all, our ability to know or justify *any* claim must ultimately depend on our ability to apprehend the presence or absence of the relevant sort of rational support on the part of any reasons or evidence that may be offered in favor of any claim and the claim they are intended to justify. Given the truth of materialism, however, such apprehensions can play no essential role as such in the production of any of our beliefs, this being wholly the consequence of the operation of purely physical causes existing in our brains. At best, they merely attend or supervene upon the brain states to which they are to associated and possess no powers of their own by means of which they could contribute either to the formation, direction, or justification of the beliefs we are thereby caused to acquire.

If materialism is true this same account, of course, has to be applied to science itself and to neuroscience as well as one of the branches of science. On that account, no scientist, or even neuroscientist, has ever held any belief on the basis of observation, reasoning, or the use of rational procedures such as experimentation. Instead, purely physical processes occurring in their brains, processes that have led to the production of certain brain states correlated with what the standard picture would call occurrent beliefs, have produced all of their scientific beliefs. However, neither these beliefs themselves, nor any of their conscious antecedents, owe anything to the putative apprehensions and mental processes of observation, inference, and experimental confirmation that preceded them in conscious awareness considered as such. Considered in relation to the purely physical causal processes occurring in the brain to which materialists suppose them to be either reducible or wholly dependent upon considered as such, that we experience these processes as episodes of scientific investigation and discovery is neither here nor there. Indeed, as far as we can know (or even have any reason to believe on the standard picture) the connection here is purely fortuitous and accidental.

One might want to challenge this seemingly deadly conclusion on the ground that physical processes of this kind occurring in the brain could *physically realize* valid deductive reasoning or the proper scientific procedure for arriving at the objective truth about the natural world. While this is perhaps conceivable (if anything can count as conceivable if materialism is true – a difficulty I will not pursue here), this could only be a contingent fact about any brain process, one that could not be revealed by the investigation of the brain, its structures, or processes considered as such.

Only some sort of correlation between certain kinds of brain processes and the corresponding mental processes could possibly establish this, and there are insuperable difficulties of an *a priori*, conceptual sort that prevent us from even making the attempt if materialism is true. First of all, in order for us to make these correlations, it is required that we both apprehend our mental processes and states as well as their qualitative attributes and contents, and that this apprehension play some *independent* role in the formation of our judgments and beliefs about what those processes, states, properties, and contents are. As we have seen, however, the operation of purely physical causal processes in the brain preempts any such influence if materialism is true. So no such correlation could be securely established on the subjective side of the equation.

Second, if materialism is true, the scientific project of attempting to investigate and confirm the existence of such a correlation, itself an example of theoretical inquiry, must be physically realized by some purely physical process occurring in the brains of the researchers themselves. This purely physical process will have a complete description according to which each stage in the that process and each of its elements – the brain events and states composing it – will have been the product of previous stages in that process in accordance with the laws of physics. From the perspective of this description, its outcome will have been completely determined by, and thus predictable from, its antecedents, which provide the physically necessary and sufficient conditions for its occurring/existing. In that case, on the assumption that materialism is true, the relation of this process of inquiry (as understood in terms of the standard picture) will be just as accidental and fortuitous in relation to the physical processes that supposedly realize it as that of any other exercise of theoretical inquiry. Its putative results, regardless of how well confirmed they may appear to us to be (and this appearance, after all, will simply be the consequence of the operation of physical causes as well, rather than the exercise of reason as such) will be no more well-grounded than any other putative exercise of reason in theoretical inquiry. There will thus be no way to know that this example of theoretical inquiry "physically realizes" a rationally justified result.

Thirdly and finally, we have no direct access to the physical world, its processes, states, or quantitative attributes. All of our musings about the world of nature, understood as a realm of physical objects, is mediated by sense perception, imagination, memory, and inductive and deductive reasoning. In turn, mental states and processes occurring in conscious awareness constitute each of these cognitive faculties. If we are even to investigate the brain, for example, we have to do so using the senses, imagination, memory, and reasoning, since these are the sources of our data and the very faculties that we must use in order to interpret and arrive at well-confirmed beliefs about the brain. However, as we have seen, if materialism is true, there is no role for any of these to play in the production or justification of any of our beliefs, including our scientific beliefs about the brain. Once again, the production of these beliefs will have a complete explanation in terms of the operation of purely physical causes existing in the brain wholly subject to the laws of physics. As such, if materialism is true, it will not be possible for us even to know anything about the brain itself, if knowledge is anything like what the standard account takes it to be. In that case, the correlation will not be possible even on the side of its supposed object.

The Autonomy of Reason and the Need for an Immaterialist Alternative Unless the apprehension of our own mental states, their qualitative attributes, and their contents is able to play some role in the production of our judgments and the justification of our beliefs, rational belief and knowledge, including substantive knowledge of the truths about the natural world will not be possible. If materialism is true, however, it appears that there is no prospect of this; not even knowledge of the brain itself is possible if thought is nothing but, or wholly dependent on, purely physical processes occurring in the brain. The lesson we must learn, then, is that knowledge of substantive truth, of whatever kind, is only possible if my apprehension of my own mental states, their qualitative attributes, and their contents *as such* are capable of contributing to the production of my judgments and the justification of my beliefs. In other words, materialism (as I defined it above) must be false if knowledge is to be possible. However, since knowledge, and in particular knowledge of my own mental states, their properties, and their contents is *actual,* so too is it possible. Therefore, materialism is actually false. Either that, or rational discourse and theoretical inquiry are not possible – not even the inquiry that I have been engaged in here.

To put it another way, one of the necessary conditions for knowledge is the *autonomy of reason* in theoretical inquiry, which rules out any sort of naturalistic, efficient causal explanation of its functioning, and in particular, in the explanation and justification of our beliefs. Instead, reason must be capable of directly apprehending our mental states, their qualitative attributes, and contents. Among these properties are those logical properties by means of which mental states and their contents are related to each other in a manner relevant to their truth, evoking spontaneous judgment, deductive and inductive inference, and by means of these arriving at justified, true beliefs about substantive matters of fact.

Since this autonomous use of reason requires that it operate, in its functioning, independently of the influence of non-rational causes, such as those involved in the production of brain states and processes considered just as such, mind must be so conceived, at least in its cognitive operations. If that is so, mental states (etc.) cannot be conceived as either nothing but or as wholly dependent on the brain states with which they are associated. The mind, then, cannot be the brain, or something wholly dependent for its operations on the brain. It must be something more than this, something with its own characteristic operation that it exercises independently of anything going on in the physical world. In other words, if there is knowledge, then some form of mind/body dualism must be true. But there is knowledge. Therefore, some form of dualism, emergentism, or idealism must be true and, at any rate, materialism as characterized above must surely be false.

Chapter Five

Could Introspection be Unreliable

– Even in Principle?[36]

Many philosophers and psychologists give little credence to claims based on introspection. On the one hand, we hear the charge that such claims, since based on the supposed "hidden" contents of individual streams of consciousness, are not scientifically testable, hence not scientifically verifiable and thus cannot count as evidence for (scientific) psychologists. On the other, we are assured by psychologists that our introspective reports are frequently false or inaccurate, so that psychology can in fact prove that the putative evidence of such reports is no such thing, but are simply an act of "confabulation" on the part of experimental subjects.[37]

Now I must admit that I find these claims incredible and preposterous; I cannot conceive of them as being true. My attitude toward these claims is at one with Hume's attitude toward claims concerning miracles: they are so absurd that they do not even deserve to be investigated and can be quite reasonably rejected out of hand. This I have done, and not even bothered to acquaint myself with the supposed empirical evidence for

---

[36] I would like to thank Richard Curtis for his comments on an earlier draft of this paper.

[37] Of course, it cannot be the case that both of these claims are true, since if the first is true, the second cannot be and, for the same reason, if we can prove the second then the first must be false. Clearly, something is wrong here. I shall argue that the first, while true as far as it goes, has no dire consequences, while the second, being inconsistent with the first, must rejected as false.

the unreliability of introspection. As such, I surely owe an apology to those who have endeavored to prove this claim by means of empirical evidence or accepted it on that basis. My apology shall take the form of an explanation of my reasons for denying these claims so cavalierly and contending that *no* empirical evidence, *even in principle*, could show them to be true, so that empirical evidence is not even relevant to their evaluation. However, I shall approach my target obliquely, by briefly considering two other, related issues: the reliability of sense perception and of eyewitness testimony, both of which have also been the target of skeptical scientific research. Having established the general pattern of argument I will use in these two cases, I will then be in a position to present the parallel argument against the in-principle possibility of anyone proving that introspection is unreliable.[38] I shall then briefly consider the notion of introspection itself and attempt to remove some of the misconceptions surrounding that notion.

Could Science prove that Sense Perception is Unreliable? Descartes famously begins his critique of the senses in *Meditation* I by adumbrating the hoary *argument from perceptual error*, the skeptic's stock in trade from the time of Protagoras.[39] When I was a young man, the argument was always interpreted as a stand-alone proof that the senses were unreliable, and reconstructed as the thesis that since the senses are sometimes deceptive they might always be so, or at any rate, might be so at any moment that I might raise that question.[40] Contemporary Descartes scholars, however, have revised that contention. A more subtle reading of the text suggests that Descartes does not after all believe this argument sufficient to show that the senses are unreliable. In fact, the conclusion that he actually draws, that we should never altogether trust a faculty that has once misled us, is remarkably modest. More than this, Descartes immediately softens the blow by noting certain further facts about perception. We are, he admits, only very infrequently subject to perceptual error, and what errors we are subject to are generally corrected in short order by subsequent sense-experience, so that our faculty of sense perception, like our capacity to do arithmetic, is

---

[38] "Unreliable" means "not dependable, liable to mislead or deceive, and thus beneath rational credence." One should not claim that, e.g. introspection is unreliable unless one intends to assert that it is not dependable, liable to mislead or deceive us, and is thus beneath rational credence.

[39] *CSM*, Vol. II, 12.

[40] For a classic presentation of this interpretation, see Jay Rosenberg, *The Practice of Philosophy*, Englewood Cliffs, NJ, 1978, 17-20.

fallible but self-correcting.[41]

Descartes thus tacitly (and I think knowingly) admits something that is often urged as a criticism of the argument from perceptual error. The claim that we are subject to occasional perceptual errors is itself a contingent, empirical claim that can be known to be true only on the basis of experience, and indeed, sense-experience. Thus, our confident claim to know that there are perceptual errors actually *presupposes* that the senses are not systematically misleading or unreliable about the nature of the external world. If they were, we would be in no position to assert this fact based on sense-experience, since sense-experience would not be capable of providing evidence for any claim, no matter what its content, and we could trust it no further than sensible people trust the claims of fortunetellers. Thus, either sense perception is not reliable as a source of knowledge about the world, in which case we cannot justify this claim using the argument from perceptual error, or sense perception does in fact provide us with adequate evidence for the factual premises of that argument, in which case we must suppose sense-perception to be generally reliable. We can thus have no reason to doubt the in- principle reliability of the senses based on the argument from perceptual error. The most that follows is that sense perception is *fallible*, which we already knew and from which no obvious dire consequences follow – or are drawn by Descartes.

Now, suppose that a scientist were to argue, by reference to well-known optical illusions such as the Muller-Lyer diagram and similar devices developed by psychologists, that sense perception (specifically in this case, *visual* perception) was not a reliable source of knowledge about the external world. In the first place, we should note that psychologists developed these devices on the basis of prior knowledge of the physics and geometry of vision, and more specifically that they were deliberately designed in order to evoke erroneous judgments in response to questions about what we see. These illusions exploit well-known features of visual perception (such as perspective) that ordinarily provide accurate perceptual information but which in the artificial, experimental circumstances of this experiment evoke, and ire intended to evoke, false spontaneous judgments precisely because

---

[41] I develop the analogy between the senses and arithmetic calculation in my paper "Being Mistaken and Being Deceived," read to the Northwest Conference on Philosophy held in Moscow, Idaho in 1982.

they are operating in their usual, and generally reliable, way. As such, these experiments are from the very first a set-up job. Such experiments are possible only due to what we already knew pre-scientifically based on ordinary sense perception. Therefore, *they actually confirm*, rather than refute, the reliability of sense perception by providing, by means of sense perception, supplementary evidence for what we already believed on perfectly adequate grounds.

If one were to balk at this, however, one could further enforce this result by noting that the experimenter, in reporting his or her results needs to depend on sense perception in order to report accurately what his subjects say and do in response to his or her questions. More than this, the experimenter needs to use visual perception in order to confirm that the judgments made by the subjects in question really are erroneous. However, if the point of the experiment is to establish that visual perception is not a reliable source of knowledge about the external world, then there is no way for the psychologist to establish this on the basis of his or her visual experience without indulging in a cognitive version of the fallacy of special pleading. In this case, the truth of the thesis makes the evidence used to establish it worthless as proof. To adopt such a research program, then, is surely self-defeating. For the same reason, any book intended to establish such a thesis based on such evidence could not possibly succeed, and one could safely neglect its conclusion even though it might contain much useful information on other topics.

Could Science prove that Eyewitness Testimony is Unreliable? It is often confidently reported that both science and the empirical evidence acquired from court cases proves that people are generally poor observers of the world around them and that, for this reason, eyewitness testimony is unreliable and not to be trusted.[42] No one, of course, questions the fact that eyewitness testimony is fallible, and that claims based on eyewitness testimony can be and sometimes are defeated by other evidence. However, admitting this claim is perfectly consistent with maintaining that eyewitness testimony is generally reliable, just as the fact of perceptual error is perfectly consistent with the possibility of perceptual error. Oftentimes, the claim that eyewitness testimony is unreliable simply intends to suggest that we

---

[42] People really do say this; see *C. A. J. Coady, Testimony: A Philosophical Study*, Oxford at the Clarendon Press, 1995,. 264-5, so the position I am criticizing is not, after all, a straw man.

should never accept eyewitness testimony at face value, but always demand some other sort of additional evidence before accepting any such claim. However, even so modest a claim as this seems impossible to sustain. Ultimately, *all* empirical evidence of *any* sort is derived from and epistemically dependent upon, eyewitness testimony. If eyewitness testimony *as such* is unreliable, even in principle, then no empirical claim can ultimately be sustained and that will include any claim to the effect that eyewitness testimony is beneath rational credence.

It is often pointed out that nearly everything that we believe is derived from the testimony of others, so that if we were restricted in our beliefs only to those things that we could confirm for ourselves, there would be very little that we could claim to know. Newman, for example, famously used the proposition "Great Britain is an island" as an example of such a fact, accepted by us not on direct evidence, but rather on the consent of all men and the weight of authority.[43] Newman also supposes that to do this is eminently rational – a procedure that we rightly follow in countless other cases. Very few, I think, would want to interpret Clifford's dictum that to believe on insufficient evidence is always morally wrong in so strict a way as to exclude such empirical claims as the belief that Great Britain is an island from the class of rational beliefs. As such, no sensible epistemology can afford to dispense with testimony as a source of rational belief. Even casual reflection reveals many manifest "inconveniences" of such a consequence, an exercise I am here content to leave to the reader.

In this case, however, the rub is that *all* testimony ultimately relies for its *provenance* on eyewitness testimony, the substantive empirical content of which was originally derived, not from the testimony of others, but from someone who simply witnessed the relevant events. Any claim based on testimony, no matter how second-hand, must terminate in an original witness or witnesses who actually experienced the relevant events or states of affairs that ultimately anchor the entire chain of testifiers. Indeed, any testamentary claim that does not so terminate is, no matter how ancient and how distinguished may be its transmitters, rightly seen to have no basis at all. It follows straightaway that unless eyewitness testimony is reliable, no testamentary claim, no matter how apparently well-grounded, could be

---

[43] John Henry Newman, *Essay in Aid of a Grammar of Assent*, Notre Dame, IN, University of Notre Dame Press, 1979, 234-5; originally published in 1870.

rationally credible.

Nor would it do at all to turn away from testimony and insist on confirming all substantive claims on one's own. Even if this were possible (as it obviously is not) even here, we would not be able to escape from the tyranny of eyewitness testimony: for one to insist on one's own observations, trained or otherwise, is precisely to insist on the reliability of eyewitness testimony – namely, *one's own*. To see this point is to realize, at the same time, that *all substantive, empirical claims of whatever sort ultimately rest on eyewitness testimony*, and to call eyewitness testimony into question is ultimately to call into question all of our empirical beliefs, of whatever sort. This, of course, would include the results of any supposed scientific experiments intended to demonstrate its unreliability. We need never fear, then, that science will be able to establish any such contention, since for it to do so would completely undermine the very possibility of empirical evidence for any claim, including scientific ones, and especially the claims currently under discussion.

If any scientist writes a book claiming that eyewitness testimony is unreliable, he expects us to accept that claim based on his cognitive authority. That authority, in turn, is grounded in the empirical evidence, such as a set of experimental results that provide the justification for his or her claim that eyewitness testimony is unreliable. The scientist in question claims to have performed these experiments and observed the results or to be reliably reporting the work of other scientists who have done so. In any event, we are being offered an argument from testimony, and one that terminates in the eyewitness reports of scientists, whether his or her own or those of others. At the same time, all of this evidence is supposed to support the claim that eyewitness testimony is unreliable. If that is so, then this raises serious questions about the very possibility of there being scientific evidence for such a claim, given that all such evidence ultimately rests on the very sort of evidence, (i.e. eyewitness testimony) that is being called into question.

Once again, we face a dilemma. If the thesis of the envisaged book is in fact true in the unqualified, unrestricted sense in which it is stated, then we could have no reason to believe that thesis based on the proffered evidence. On the other hand, if we accept the proffered evidence, we thus are prevented from accepting that thesis, because to accept that evidence as evidence *for any thesis at all* presupposes the falsity of the very thesis the evidence was put forward to justify. There may be good reasons for reading such a book, but no one ought seriously to entertain the idea that its thesis might turn out to be correct.

I am really rather doubtful that anyone supposes that eyewitness testimony *as such* is unreliable. Instead, I suppose that what was really intended was to assert that eyewitness testimony is typically unreliable in certain circumstances or in certain situations, or liable to certain distortions due to the influence of memory, suggestion, or the demand for detailed observation that goes beyond what most of us ordinarily muster, thus inviting "confabulation" and the evocation of putative memories that contain false elements. Indeed, most of the psychological experiments that I have heard about intended to establish this thesis, like the ones used to construct optical illusions, have the character of a set-up job, exploiting the limitations on human observation that are already well known to common sense and ordinary experience in order to scientifically "prove" a foregone conclusion.

We can add to this the further point that, since all information derived from the senses ultimately depends on the reliability of eyewitness testimony, the question concerning the general reliability of eyewitness testimony cannot be altogether be separated from that of sense experience generally. Indeed, it is precisely by reliance on sense-experience, which itself presupposes the reliability of eyewitness testimony for every claim at which it arrives, that we have discovered these weaknesses and limitations. On the other hand, to the extent that we believe based on sense-experience (hence on the basis of eyewitness testimony) that perceptual errors (such as those to which eyewitness testimony is prone) are few and capable of correction from within sense-experience, we must likewise hold the same about eyewitness testimony, since these two claims ultimately rise or fall together. Thus, the strategy of using information derived from sense perception to discredit eyewitness testimony, then, is a mug's game, since to undermine the reliability of eyewitness testimony in this way equally undermines the reliability of sense experience, and with it, empirical science as well.

At the same time, the common dismissive attitude toward

eyewitness testimony evinced by many intellectuals, especially when used to discount any claim that one does not want to take seriously, teeters dangerously on the brink of unreasonable (because self-refuting) skepticism.

Private Experience and Private Language Before turning to introspection proper, I want to consider one last preliminary. As I already mentioned, one of the constant objections offered to the legitimacy of introspective evidence is that introspective evidence is "private" or "subjective" and thus "unverifiable." It is therefore regarded either as not evidence at all or as at best second-rate evidence to be relied on only in the extremity. Psychology nowadays scorns the older, "introspective" approach to the study of the mind as "unscientific" and generally holds that any reference to the supposed "inner workings" of the mind is irrelevant to the explanation of "behavior." Instead, we are told that science has to be about the "publicly observable," the "quantifiable," the "testable," or the "verifiable." Since introspective reports are none of these, they are taken to be scientifically irrelevant, and many look forward to the day when all such appeals will have been superseded and bypassed by a truly scientific psychology that regards the mind wholly from the objective, "third person point of view" that is thought to be the characteristically scientific perspective on reality.

Among philosophers, appeal to introspection meets a different sort of challenge, one grounded in the philosophy of language and which questions the very meaningfulness of terms referring to "private" mental contents. According to an influential argument descending from Wittgenstein, linguistic reference to private objects constitutes a "private language" that must somehow establish reference on the basis of purely "internal" criteria rather than the external, "public" criteria that establish the meaning of all other terms. Given this, how can anyone *really* know that he or she is using these terms correctly, even in his or her own case? The very idea of such a language, they tell us, is somehow incoherent.

Both of these critiques seem to suppose that there is a fundamental difference between our experience of our supposed "inner states," such as a sensation of pain, and "outer experience" of material things, like a tree. This view, however, seems to me not only to be wrong, but rather obviously wrong. *All* experience, including "outer experience," is private and subjective in *the same sense* that "inner experience" is. All *experience* (considered *as such* whether we call it "inner" or "outer") is constituted phenomenologically by the unique stream of inner states and their contents existing in and for each individual conscious subject. It is thus *subjective*, in the intended sense, i.e., occurring in an individual conscious subject taken from a unique and incommunicable point of view. In every instance, each person's apprehension of an "external" object or state-of-affairs is perspectivally unique, and while its content may qualitatively overlap with other, similar experiences had by others at the same time in the same place, it remains uniquely that person's and, no matter how exhaustively described, *incommunicable* as lived by the subject – thus, in the intended sense, *private*. This holds for all subjects, so that while there may be *shared* experiences, but there are no *public* experiences.[44] As such, if the privacy and subjectivity of the immediate contents of conscious awareness is sufficient to constitute any discourse about them a private language, then *all language is private* and there can be no other kind.[45]

For the same reasons, it is clear that there no objective "third person" perspective or point of view *on lived experience*. In this context, the use of the terms "perspective" and "point of view" when they are attached to "third person" are systematically misleading, suggesting that "third person" refers to some sort of alternate phenomenological stance (distinct from the "first person" perspective) that we can adopt *within* experience, perhaps even switching back and forth between them at will. However, it seems clear enough that all experience is lived *ineluctably* from the first person point of view and there is no other even imaginable. (Just ask yourself, "What would it be like to live your life from the third person perspective?") The third person stance – and it is precisely a *stance* – is neither a perspective nor a point of view on experience, but rather a theoretical construct that we imaginatively adopt in order to get some

---

[44] See next footnote.

[45] While the notion of private language is constantly excoriated, we never hear anyone talking about "public language." Indeed, what could a *public* language even be or be about, in the intended sense of "public" that somehow contrasts with the intended sense of "private" used here?" It would seem that it could only be a language that somehow was learned and used without being processed through the subjective, private streams of conscious awareness of individual language speakers aware of what they were saying and what they are saying means. What would that be like? Unless and until this is somehow specified, the oft-used notion of a "public criterion for the use of words" is and remains just as empty and mysterious – one is tempted to say that it is meaningless as well.

purchase on the nature of things or reality as it exists independently of experience. It therefore can neither compete with the first person perspective from within experience nor exclude that perspective in principle as a source of hard data that needs to be recognized *as such* and to which our psychological theories must accommodate themselves, regardless of one's naturalistic "druthers." Indeed, without the data provided for us by experience from the first person point of view on lived experience, the third person point of view would not even be conceivable, let alone constructible, by anyone – not even a scientist.

Could Introspection be Unreliable, even in Principle? As we have seen, all substantive empirical claims, including scientific ones, are based on evidence apprehended from the first person point of view or perspective on lived experience. If there even is to be empirical knowledge of any sort, scientific or otherwise, then it must be possible for us to rely on lived experience for the materials from which theoretical constructs such as those employed in philosophy and natural science can successfully arise. At the same time, as we have seen there is no difference *in kind* between "inner" and "outer" experience – *all* of our lived experience is constituted by a stream of subjective, private mental contents apprehended from the first person point of view by individual conscious subjects, describable to others but nevertheless incommunicable as part of lived experience. As such, these materials will not be available to us unless it is possible for us directly and immediately to apprehend, clearly and distinctly, our own mental contents.[46]

Even so, given that those mental contents are subjective, private, and are (considered *in themselves* or *as such*) nothing but pure appearances there seems no reason, in principle, why this should not only be possible, but actually be the case. Ideally, then, we ought to be able to grasp these contents with incorrigible certainty *when we apprehend them clearly and distinctly.* Nothing more than this is necessary to make introspection possible, nothing more needed to make introspection actual than that we should engage in it, and no reason why it cannot be (as it surely is) an important source of substantive knowledge about the human mind. More to the point,

---

[46]Again, as I have argued elsewhere, not everything can be apprehended mediately or indirectly by means of having first apprehended something else; if experience is to be possible at all, there must be something that is apprehended *simpliciter* – a *de facto* foundation for human thought, experience, and knowledge. That there be mental contents that are directly apprehended is unavoidable, on pain of irrationality. See Chapter 3 above.

since the necessary conditions for lived experience are the same conditions for the reliability of introspection, to call introspection into question is to call lived experience into question as well, and with it the very possibility of empirical knowledge.

Further, just as the reliability of sense perception ineluctably rests on the reliability of eyewitness testimony, so too does the reliability of eyewitness testimony rely on our being able to directly and immediately apprehend the subjective, private contents of my individual stream of conscious awareness. Eyewitness testimony, after all, is *mediated* by such contents, and unless I can reliably apprehend them, I cannot after all have any reason to suppose that I am in fact capable of reliably witnessing and reporting anything about the external world. Due to this fact, any scientific experiment that casts doubt on our ability to apprehend the subjective, private contents of our own minds (which is essentially to introspect them, as we shall see, though introspection proper is deliberate and involves concentration of attention on those contents as such) will also undermine the reliability of eyewitness testimony and thus, in turn, sense perception as well. As such, it will also undermine itself as a reliable source of knowledge about the external world.

To illustrate this point further, suppose someone were to write a book calling introspection into question on scientific grounds. The writer's claims will be based on empirical evidence derived from psychological experiments that he (or she) has performed or reliably reported to have been done by others. That writer will have apprehended this experimental evidence by means of his (or her) private, subjective stream of consciousness in which those results are represented by mental contents of which that person is directly and immediately aware. Those results, then, will only constitute evidence for that person if he or she can rely on that private, subjective stream of conscious awareness for information about the results of scientific experiments. If that person can rely on his or her private, subjective stream of conscious awareness in that way, then as I have argued all of the conditions for the possibility of the accurate introspection of our mental contents are in place. On the other hand, if what these results are intended to show is that introspection is not reliable, these grounds will likewise undermine the claim that one's private, subjective stream of consciousness is apprehended reliably in such a way as to be a source of information about the external world, such as the results of scientific experiments.

In that case, I cannot be sure of any experimental results, or of anything else. One cannot even reasonably believe that one can reliably apprehend one's own thoughts, hence that what one is writing expresses those thoughts, especially when one believes that one is composing the book that denies that introspection is reliable. (And for that matter, how could such a person even know *that*?) In that case, it is difficult to see how one could think, or write at all. The very existence of the book, then, is the very best evidence that we could have that its intended thesis is false. Now, if the author of such a book thinks that he or she has been ill used, feels resentment of my apparently flippant criticisms, certain that they are merely sophisms, etc., he or she can know this only through being directly and immediately aware of his or her mental contents. For it is only by means of these that he or she apprehends what I have written as well as his or her reactions to it. To the extent that he or she is so and is quite certain about this then, to paraphrase Hume, he or she can read in this the downfall of his or her principles.

Having made this point, the main argument of this paper is completed, and a negative answer given to the question that serves as its title. I wish I could leave it at that. However, there are currently a number of false ideas about what introspection is, how we do it, how we ought to do it, and under which circumstances it is trustworthy. Although I cannot discuss all of this here, I feel the need to provide the outline of a general account of the nature of introspection in order to dispel some of the common objections that have been raised to the use of this cognitive faculty. I shall begin by considering the vexed issues concerning privileged access and incorrigibility.

Privileged Access and Incorrigibility A major set of misconceptions about introspection arise from the doctrines of privileged access and incorrigibility. Given the foregoing, both of these doctrines have strong credentials to be true. If introspection is possible, then it is also possible for me to apprehend my mental contents as such. Since my steam of lived experience is private, only I have direct and immediate access to its contents and thus only I have the authority definitively to pronounce on what those contents are. Further, since mental contents are pure appearances, and thus are nothing more than what they appear to be, there is no appearance reality/distinction that can be applied within lived, conscious experience considered just as such. While I may be in doubt as to whether this is a dagger I see before me, I cannot doubt that I am "appeared-to daggerly." Surely, then, my mental contents are capable of being incorrigibly apprehended by me, so that what I say about my mental life always trumps what anyone else, including a neuroscientist, may want to claim about my thoughts or experiences based on "external" observation of my brain, at least when they are clearly and distinctly perceived.

However, it is also important to note that the nonnegotiable basic reliability of introspection, like that of sense perception, memory, discursive reasoning, Hume's inductive habit, and so on, does not confer infallibility on my judgments with regard to my own mental states any more than it does in the parallel cases involving other cognitive powers. We have no reason to believe, in the first place, that all (arguably) mental processes of interest to psychologists and philosophers are accompanied by conscious mental contents and are thus introspectable. Second, there is foreground and background, center and periphery in my intentional field of consciousness. I am not aware of all of my mental contents to the same degree or even in the same way. Attention will tend to concentrate on certain salient features of one's conscious awareness at any one time and thus some contents rather than others, with the result that those other contents will receive a reduced share of my attention or drop out of occurrent conscious awareness in virtue of the fact, while present to me in my intentional field of awareness not such that I am attending to them presently. It is also the case that some mental contents are difficult to apprehend in a sustained manner and may thus resist being perceived clearly and distinctly. More than this, some of my mental states are so confused, complex, or affectively overwhelming that it is impossible for me to constitute the psychic distance necessary to get an analytic perspective – as we say, "I was too close to the situation, too involved to be of any help, even to myself." Such mental contents may resist any sort of direct apprehension or analysis, and thus be better explored through other means, such as literary expressions of those states that "externalize" them in affective language.[47]

We should not therefore suppose that the use of introspection, despite its promise of incorrigible certainty with regard to some of its objects under ideal conditions, as well as having the last word with regard to states of that sort, is incapable of falling into error. Like our other reliable-in-principle cognitive faculties, introspection is both finite and fallible. At the same time, by analogy to these other cases, we have the same good reason to believe that introspection is capable of being corrected from within experience as we do for thinking that sense-perception and eyewitness testimony are. At least, we had better hope so. Empirical science is not possible unless sense perception is a generally reliable cognitive faculty. In turn, sense perception cannot be a reliable cognitive faculty unless eyewitness testimony is, since all information derived from sense experience ultimately depends for its provenance on eyewitness testimony. At the same time, eyewitness testimony will only be trustworthy if it is the case that I have reliable, direct and immediate awareness of the contents of my subjective, private stream of conscious awareness, which as we have seen, is all that is required in order for introspection to be possible. If introspection is not reliable then neither are these other cognitive faculties.

We add to this that, since there is no third person perspective on lived experience, there is no way for any psychologist to empirically "investigate" the claims on behalf of introspection from an external, non-subjective, third person point of view on experience and thereby verify or falsify introspective reports. Since the subject's inner states are subjective, private, and incommunicable as lived, there is no way for any scientist to compare the claims made by the subject to the facts, since the only facts relevant to assessing those judgments are subjective facts about the subject's mental contents, facts in principle beyond observation from the external, objective (thus "scientific") point of view. There is only one way to discover the pitfalls and limits of introspection, and that is by the use of introspection, which presupposes that introspection is a reliable, self-correcting cognitive faculty. As such, if I have good reasons to believe that introspection is sometimes wrong, that is only because I have discovered that this is so introspectively, and this positive result will not be possible unless I am taking introspection to be a generally reliable, hence self-

---

[47] I have heard people say this sort of thing about "psychological" novelists like Henry James, Tolstoy, and Proust, though I am in no position to verify these claims myself.

correcting, cognitive faculty. For the same reason, to the extent that I believe that such errors undermine the validity of introspective claims, at the same time I am disqualifying introspection as a source of evidence for any claim, including claims concerning its own reliability.

Psychologists who construct experiments intended to show that introspection is unreliable, like those who construct optical illusions or simulations intended to test the limits of eyewitness testimony, are really relying on tacit knowledge of the pitfalls and limitations of introspection acquired by means of that very faculty. That they can do this at all thereby presupposes, and in turn experimentally confirms, the reliability of introspection as a source of knowledge about the mind rather than undermining it, since it confirms that this faculty is self-correcting. As such, it will not be surprising if psychologists, exploiting the already well-known limitations and weaknesses of this cognitive faculty discovered from within conscious awareness by means of introspection itself, are able to produce experimental "set-ups jobs" intended to confirm a foregone conclusion. However, these experiments prove no more than the similar "set up jobs" that might be used to discredit sense perception or eyewitness testimony as reliable sources of knowledge about the external world and which we have already seen we have sufficient reason to dismiss. Further, given the interdependence of sense perception, eyewitness testimony, and direct and immediate apprehension of one's own private, subjective mental states, any such experiments would be self-undermining, since nothing can count as empirical evidence or prove anything unless these faculties are reliable and so no scientific experiment could ever confirm such a result, even if it were true. All that would follow is that empirical science is incompetent to establish any conclusions at all, including this one. Given this, the only response to claims concerning introspective errors, controversies, and disagreements (to the extent that they admit of resolution at all) is that what is needed is simply more, or more careful, introspection.

How do we Introspect? Ordinarily, of course, we "think past" our immediate mental contents toward their putative originals in the world and discourse about those things. We do not think about our own subjective states and contents, but instead about their intentional objects – the independently existing external things that our mental states putatively represent by means of their intentionality. We only rarely advert to our mental contents and their features *as such*, and only philosophers and some old-fashioned psychologists ever do so in a sustained fashion. This fact naturally leads to the notion that introspection is some strange "reflexive," self-transcending act that converts subjective mental *contents* into a realm of subjective mental *objects*, such as ideas or sense-data. This notion often is thought to lead to some sort of reductionist phenomenalism, such as we encounter in a consistent empiricism, like that of Berkeley or Carnap. A proponent of this sort of view infers from the (true) thesis that all lived experience is apprehended from the first person point of view by means of private, subjective mental contents to the (false) thesis that we are never aware of anything at all in any fashion but our own ideas. Having made this initial error, such a person is further led to believe that ideas or complexes of ideas are the only objects that are conceivable for us, and that nothing can be meaningful for us unless it can be expressed in phenomenally reductive terms or verified by "sense-data," as phenomenalists would interpret this notion.

To the contrary, if there is to be any such thing as conscious awareness at all, there has to be what I have been calling lived experience. Lived experience, in turn, is always from the first person point of view — even the third person perspective on reality, as it enters into the lived experience of any person, including a neuroscientist, is adopted and apprehended from the first person point of view, the only perspective on lived experience there is or can be. It can never be outflanked by any science, can never be naturalized, and it can never superseded by any scientific discovery, since for us to apprehend any such discovery as a part of lived experience requires that we be conscious of it *in* and *through* lived experience; otherwise, we do not apprehend it *at all.*

The first person perspective is ineluctable and inescapable and in every case trumps the claims of all theoretical constructs such as scientific theories, which we can call "perspectives" only in a metaphorical sense that does not constitute them as alternatives or competitors to the literal, first person perspective of lived experience.[48] In turn, lived experience itself, so far as the direct and immediate apprehension without which conscious

---

[48] Of course, there are as many individual perspectives on lived experience as there are individual conscious subjects. This raises important philosophical questions that, unfortunately, I have no space to explore here.

experience is not possible is concerned, consists of private, subjective mental contents immediately present *in* and *to* conscious awareness as its modes. If I am aware of anything mediately or indirectly (such as the external world), I am so only through being directly and immediately aware of my own private, subjective mental contents. Indeed, even if some version of direct realism is true, and somehow the contents of my perceptual acts are material things themselves *via* their perceptible surface qualities, so that my perceptual act somehow terminates in an apprehension of the surfaces of individual material things, it remains that my apprehension of that thing is always partial, unique, and incommunicable *as lived*. More than this, my apprehension of external objects, even if they in some sense appear in and to conscious awareness, is nevertheless always a mediate apprehension, never a phenomenological fact that is given *in* consciousness, and thus must either be inferentially justified by a philosophical argument or asserted dogmatically as something to be affirmed as the only alternative to idealism and skepticism. This last is a strategy of evasion, not an argument. The inescapable primacy of the private thus remains.

From this perspective, the Platonic/Augustinian/Cartesian admonition to turn away from the senses and turn inward to seek the truth, at least as often interpreted, can be seen to rest on a false dichotomy. It is not as though there are two experiential realms, one of which consists of external, objective, public objects and another that consists of another, distinct set of subjective, private objects – ideas, sense-data, and so on: there is only one realm, that of lived experience and the subjective, private contents that constitute it. There is, then, no need to turn inward, or anywhere else, in order to introspect – the subject matter of introspection is already present to us in every moment of lived experience. It is not a matter of identifying some special class of entities or objects to which all conscious awareness can be reduced or out of which it is constructed, but simply in our appreciation of mental contents *as such* – as modes of awareness to which only the individual conscious subject in his own case has access in lived experience.

To introspect is not to make these contents into a distinct class of theoretical objects by a special act of apprehension, but simply to resist and arrest, in a cool, safe hour for a specific purpose, the natural and no doubt evolutionarily useful habit of thinking past those contents to the intentional objects to which they naturally convey our attention and, by doing so, our thought. In that case, our attention can rest on those contents (of which we were already immediately and primarily aware in the first place) just as such, and permit our appreciation of their properties and relations considered independently of their role in subserving the "outer awareness" of material things. Nor does this require any sort of precisive abstraction, reduction to some special class of entities, or any phenomenological *epoche* that prescinds either from the intentionality of those contents or the existence of their intentional objects. It is simply a matter of shifting our attention from one aspect of lived experience (my apprehension of the external world and material things by means of mental contents) to another (the contents themselves by means of which that very apprehension is possible for us) *within* lived experience. This at most involves a voluntary shift in foreground and background, center and periphery in consciousness, not its falsification by being flattened into a "parti-colored plane" of externally related, Humean simple ideas from which lived experience becomes a theoretical construct.

While our ability to accomplish this in fact is limited both by our inherent finitude, individual talent, and by other extraneous factors, it can be improved with practice. One can become a trained observer of the "inner" world of consciousness just as one can become a trained observer of external nature or other human beings. What the actual limits of introspection consist in, and the degree to which they can be mitigated, is an open question, one that can be resolved solely through the use of the very faculty we are investigating – an investigation that will not even be possible unless introspection is a reliable cognitive faculty. There is nothing for it but to try – let the chips fall where they may! Wherever they fall, however, the desired thesis that introspection is unreliable cannot be established by scientific experiments. Not all empirical questions, after all, are scientific ones.

Chapter Six

The Inescapable Self

Berkeley notoriously claimed that, while we have no *idea* of the self, we nevertheless have a *notion* of the self as a spiritual substance.[49] Hume and modern scholars of British empiricism have ridiculed Berkeley for this factitious, *ad hoc* device, claiming that Berkeley was vainly attempting to evade the critique of his commitment to spiritual substance implicit in his attack on Locke's transcendent material substance. Hume, of course, did not stint to apply the same arguments to Berkeley's notion of spiritual substance that Berkeley applied to Locke's notion of material substance, with the same result. Terms like "spirit," "self," and "soul," Hume concludes, are meaningless because they are not traceable to any ideas originating from sense impressions.[50] That Berkeley is defenseless in the face of this criticism is still the generally received opinion among philosophers. With few exceptions, Hume's objection is regarded as a crushing refutation of Berkeley's metaphysics of minds and ideas and the natural prelude to Hume's fully consistent empiricism that dispenses with substance altogether and reduces all aspects of mind to ideas and relations between ideas.[51]

---

[49] Berkeley, *Principles of Human Knowledge*, I, 27 – in Ayers (1975), 85.

[50] Hume, *Treatise*, I, IV, V – in Selby-Bigge, 132-133 and I, IV, VI, 251.

[51] For some dissenting views, see Ian Ramsey, "Berkeley and the Possibility of an Empirical Metaphysics," in Warren Steinkraus, ed., *New Studies in Berkeley's Philosophy*, New York, Harcourt, Brace, and Winston, 1966, 17-31, and I. C. Tipton, "Berkeley's View of Spirit," 59-70 in the same volume.

Hume, in turn, rejects the very notion of the self as something over and above said ideas and their relations. In a famous passage, which I will discuss at length below, he reports that nothing imaginable/conceivable corresponds to the term "self". No mental image or element of such an image comes to mind when Hume utters the word "self" internally, no mental content comes into view when I turn the introspective beam inward to take stock of my mental inventory. In accordance with the hard but sound empiricist principle of meaningfulness that the meaning of a term is the idea from which it is derived and which in turn rests on an impression of sense, Hume concludes that the term "self" is meaningless. Instead, he offers us an account of the self according to which what we *call* the self is nothing but the aggregate of associated ideas that constitutes a distinct stream of consciousness. The self, then, is reduced to a series of self-existent, intrinsically conscious sense-data, held together by relations of association, neither having nor needing any principle outside themselves in order to exist or interact. Hume is thus resolved to explain all mental phenomena on these principles, arriving at a kind of reductive psychological atomism; the self he rejects as superfluous, and hence as an illusion. Although Hume later reconsidered his reasons for rejecting the self, he denied that the difficulties that he had discovered were sufficient to call that view itself into question, instead choosing to exercise the "skeptic's privilege" of pleading ignorance concerning such an abstruse question.[52]

Hume blinked. Had he examined the notion of the self in more detail – thereby tacitly admitting that he perfectly well knew that there was such a thing and that he was one such – he might have come to recognize how fundamentally wrongheaded his reductionist psychology is. In a true exposition of the self, which I hope to present in this chapter, I intend to show what everyone, including Hume, knows about the self. Having done this, I will show that Hume's discussion of the self constitutes a

---

[52] Hume, *Appendix* to the *Treatise* – Selby-Bigge, 633-636, especially the second to last paragraph on 636. The difficulty Hume identifies arises from two of his own (apparently ungiveupable) principles, i.e., each mental event is a distinct existence and between distinct existences we can perceive no connections, and is precisely the problem of the unity of consciousness, which even he sees is necessary in order for the illusion of the self to be possible. In passing, we may note that, although he never read the *Treatise*, Kant seems to have divined that the issue of the unity of consciousness was a major problem that any psychology adequate to the facts of conscious awareness as lived must face and solve; whether he managed to solve it is a question I cannot discuss here.

performative self-refutation of his own reductionist account of the self. This, in turn, will show that Hume's account of the self is too limited to account for everything we know (and he knew) about the self. I also hope to clear up some misconceptions about the nature of the self, and by doing so certain popular misunderstandings concerning then nature of our knowledge of the self.

What is the Self? By "self" here I mean "a self-conscious, rational subject," what Descartes called a *res cogitans*.[53] To be a self is, first, to be conscious, i.e. possess occurrent awareness in its active exercise, not merely as a capacity. Awareness is thus act, both in the sense that it is something real or actual, as opposed to merely potential, and in the sense that it is the actualization or realization of a potency as what Aristotle calls *second act*.[54] However, not every conscious being is a self – non-human animals, for example, who are conscious but are not conscious selves. Thus, mere conscious awareness by itself is not sufficient for selfhood.

To be a self requires, second, that one also possess self-awareness, i.e. for one to be conscious in such a way that the *fact* that one is conscious is given along with, or *disclosed*, along with one's merely being conscious, i.e., awareness of the sort we share with other sentient creatures who are not selves.[55] It is due to this feature of the sort of awareness that human beings (at any rate) naturally possess that we are able to distinguish conscious awareness, which is endurant/ongoing, from its contents, which come and go, succeeding each other with dizzying rapidity. Further, to say that the self is given or disclosed in this way in and by the form of conscious awareness enjoyed by human beings is to say that it is a permanent feature of that form of conscious awareness, not the product of some special "reflex act"

---

[53] Descartes, *Meditation* II (in *CSM*, Vol. II, 19); there are a number of different meanings attaching to the term "self," all of which are important but not all of which concern us here.
[54] In traditional Aristotelian terminology, first potency is pure potency or capacity, not yet realized in any way, as when we say that a baby in the crib is potentially a language-user. Second potency/first act is the realization of a potency consisting in the possession of a skill or ability that one is not currently exercising; the same person as a young man is a language user, but having taken a vow of silence is not currently exercising that skill or ability. The same person, released from his vow and currently engaged in animated conversation, is a language-user in second act, one who both possesses and is presently exercising that skill or ability.
[55] The term "disclosed" is Ramsey's – see his "The Elusive Self" in his *Christian Empiricism*, London, The Sheldon Press, 1974, 159-76. (Reprinted by James Clarke, with an introduction by Jerry Gill, in 2009).The name of this essay was inspired by the title of Ramsey's article.

on our parts, as many philosophers have claimed.[56] Although we do not often attend to awareness-as-such as an element of our conscious life, it remains, like the fact of our own existence, something that we can advert to at will whenever we like, simply by directing our attention to it. Further, since only a rational being is capable of the intellectual apprehension of facts *as such*, only rational beings can be occurrently self-conscious.

The notion of self as I am using it here is associated with a singular way in which we use the personal pronoun "I" to refer to oneself as a conscious subject. Kant called this the "I" that accompanies all my representations. The "I" in this case the self-conscious subject, which is not a content of consciousness, but rather that which *has* those contents of consciousness as part of the stream of conscious contents passing through the intentional field of awareness that constitutes conscious awareness of the basic sort we share with non-rational creatures, possessing a continuity over time that cannot be constituted by merely external relations. We thus apprehend it as something in addition to what we ordinarily classify as contents of consciousness: sensations, perceptions, memories, thoughts, and so on, even if we also recognize how they are related to one another by resemblance, contiguity, and cause and effect.

It is the "I" in this sense that is given along with or disclosed in ordinary human consciousness, though not typically adverted to in everyday experience, as a simple, endurant subject exercising an (on its part) undifferentiated act of awareness/attention. However, there are extraordinary circumstances in which the I that accompanies all our representations *does* come into the center of experience, not as a content of conscious awareness but precisely as the conscious subject to which a particular predicate applies. She loves *me*, *I* am the one who embarrassed the entire company by telling that inappropriate joke, *I* and not *you* am afflicted with an incurable, fatal illness, and so on. In these cases, replacing the personal pronoun with a proper name does not convey the full

---

[56] In particular, nineteenth and early twentieth century thinkers, such as Tetens, Brentano and the phenomenologists, as well as introspective psychologists such as E. B. Titchener routinely held such a view. This led to the largely unsuccessful attempt to base a scientific, observational psychology on introspection, intended to simultaneously live and observe our conscious episodes. For some of the difficulties with this approach, see John Paul Sartre, *The Transcendence of the Ego*, New York, Farrar, Strauss, and Giroux, 1957 (originally published in 1936) and H. J. Paton, *Kant's Metaphysics of Experience*, New York, MacMillan, 1936. 233-238.

significance of the propositions, which is in no way "cashable" from the third-person point of view.

As Kant saw, we cannot account for the unity of consciousness by supposing that the independently-existing elements of consciousness become externally related to one another by principles of association. Such complexes, considered in themselves, have no more unity than a pile or sand or a random collection of books sitting on my desk. Nor are Kant's transcendental rules of constitution and synthesis sufficient to supply this lack. As Kant himself avers, only the presence to those complexes of a continuously existing subject – the I that accompanies all my representations – can provide a true principle of unity for consciousness over time, by being singular, self-identical, and distinct from the contents of consciousness that it enter its intentional field of awareness.

Moreover, this "I" or self is *incorrigibly* given to me in consciousness through my apprehension of the distinction between what I am aware of and my awareness of it as a conscious subject. Although this fact is not given to me prior to experience of the contents of consciousness, once given, I apprehend my subjectivity with extrinsic certainty, so long as I am capable of any thought at all. Even an amnesiac is a self, in the sense of a self-conscious, rational subject and capable of distinguishing between himself and the contents of his stream of conscious awareness, even though he does not know who he is. In the same way, Avicenna's flying man, whose consciousness is, for a time, miraculously deprived of all sensuous contents and is thus perceptually "empty," is and knows himself to be a self-conscious rational subject despite that fact merely in contemplating that very fact in being aware that his conscious awareness is currently devoid of any perceptual content.[57] Even if awareness of the self is not normally possible apart from the presence of some content – at the very least, reflective thought – it is clearly there independently of, and thus neither

---

[57] One version of this argument is found in his treatise *al Shifa*, as quoted in Seyyed Hossain Nasr and Oliver Leaman, *A History of Islamic Philosophy*, London, Routledge, 1997, 1022-1023. This is apparently one of three different versions of the argument. Avicenna's claim is that we do in fact have an apprehension of the self independently of sensuous intuition, though we do not ordinarily advert to it. If successful, this thought-experiment shows that the soul is an immaterial self-conscious subject in no way dependent for its activity, hence its existence, on the body. It also refutes Hume's contention (discussed below) that we are never conscious of anything except perceptions.

identical with nor reducible to, any particular content or collection of such contents. I thus know that I am a self-conscious rational subject, i.e., a self, simply through being one, as a fact given along with experience as I actually live it every waking moment; this is a direct consequence of the kind of conscious awareness I possess by nature. Beyond this, there is really nothing more that can or needs to be said here, though I won't let that stop me from trying![58]

The Self as Subject Since the self in this sense is the *thing* that *has* the contents of conscious awareness as its modes, it is not itself (and could not be) one of the contents of conscious awareness and thus does not appear in the intentional field of consciousness as one of those contents. The self, then, is always a subject and never an object for itself. It is something given along with the intentional field of awareness as one of its Kantian *formal* features without appearing in that field *as such* or by being represented there by any of the contents of that field. In this way, the self functions in conscious awareness in a manner similar to that assigned by Kant to space and time.

When Kant claims that we do not perceive space and time, he is perhaps best understood as claiming that, unlike the phenomenal objects and events that are organized and ordered in phenomenal space and time, space and time themselves are not represented there as distinguishable contents. Rather, Kant calls them *forms* of intuition, and supposes that they are disclosed, i.e. *given along with* those objects and events. Although Kant regards space and time as *a priori* – in his special sense which means given prior to and as necessary for the possibility of experience as we actually live it – he should not be thought to hold that space and time are present in conscious awareness prior to the reception of phenomenal objects or events. Indeed, he seems to hold to the contrary that space and time are merely virtual, existing prior to the appearance of phenomenal objects and events in conscious awareness as merely structural capacities for experience. Even so, once the phenomenal world is actually constituted within

---

[58] Elsewhere, I have identified the self with the soul as occupying the *now*, from which the soul exercises its sole operation as the proximate *per se* cause of the body's operation, at the interface of which with the body the immaterial intentional field of conscious awareness arises by means of which the soul becomes a mind. The now is thus the sole vestige of the soul in conscious awareness as that from which the individual perspective of the self is ontically grounded, launched, and from which the self as subject emanates.

conscious awareness, it becomes possible for us to distinguish space and time as forms of intuition from the objects and events that are organized and ordered in space and time, by the use of non-precisive abstraction.[59]

We are thereby able to arrive at the *concepts* of space and time *as such*, despite their being inseparable in experience from the phenomena they organize and order. More than this, *once* we have these concepts, it becomes possible for us to use precisive abstraction to *imagine* empty space and empty time and explore their mathematical properties, even though these are not, and never could be objects of (perceptual) experience for us. However, since whatever we do experience can only be apprehended by us through its appearance in space and time, what we know to be true about space and time through mathematical investigation as forms of intuition must inevitably contribute to the structure and organization of phenomena in experience. Due to this, we are thereby able to arrive at *a priori* synthetic truths about the phenomenal (if not the noumenal) world. For Kant, there can be no question of space and time as forms of intuition representing noumenal space and time; further, they are the only space and time we can coherently conceive.[60]

In a similar way, we can arrive at the notion of *consciousness as such*, i.e. awareness-as-activity as given/disclosed within and by experience, by means of the same sort of two-stage abstractive process, as follows. We apprehend the fact that we are conscious by non-precisively distinguishing, from within conscious awareness itself, between our awareness, on the one hand, and that of which we are aware of on the other. Having done this, we are thereby able to arrive at the concept of consciousness understood as *awareness-as-such*. Since this operation initially involves a non-precise abstraction that simply highlights different elements of conscious experience, we can accomplish it within conscious awareness itself. Indeed, to apprehend the fact that one is conscious – grounded in the ability to distinguish, by non-precisive abstraction from within conscious awareness itself, between one's being aware and that of which one is aware (= the contents of consciousness, properly so called) – *is* already the apprehension

---

[59] Nor, in passing, is it possible for us to reduce space and time to relations between phenomena, since these relations can only be characterized as external, contingent, spatial and temporal relations between them, thus constituted independently of, hence prior to, those phenomena themselves.

[60] Kant was clearly wrong about this, but I will not go into this matter here.

of the self as subject. However, this apprehension does not become clear and distinct until we further distinguish, through precisive abstraction, between awareness-as-such and the contents of consciousness and identify the self-as-subject with the former as instantiated by and perspectivally individuated in one's own case.

Nevertheless, our having distinguished non-precisively between awareness and that of which we are aware in experience makes possible and facilitates our subsequent, imaginative apprehension, through precisive abstraction, of consciousness *as such*, i.e. *awareness-as-such* as distinct from the *contents* of consciousness. We can thus use precisive abstraction in order to imaginatively apprehend and investigate consciousness independently of its relation to its contents. Whatever features we discover to belong to consciousness so considered (i.e. as awareness-as-such) will be features possessed by consciousness over and above those contributed to it by its contents and the relations between them and will thus be irreducible to them. Consciousness reflectively apprehended in this way will also reveal the intrinsic features of awareness-as-such by the manner in which phenomena appear within the intentional field of awareness beyond what they themselves contribute to it (as mere contents of conscious awareness) by means of their intrinsic features.

From the Empirical to the Substantial Self At the same time, to isolate awareness-as-such considered in contrast to its contents is not yet to give a complete account of the self. Although, in apprehending awareness-as-such we also apprehend the self as subject, there is clearly more to the self than what we apprehend in consciousness itself simply as pure awareness-as-such. Intuitively, the self is more than just pure awareness; rather, it is that which *has* or *exercises* awareness-as-such. To conceive of awareness-as-such as somehow *ownerless*, as awareness without a subject to be aware of, in, and by means of it, is analogous to the notion of existence without relation to an existent – and just as meaningless. The self, then, has to be something more than just the intentional field of awareness considered as such. That something more is the substantial self that becomes an empirical self through becoming a conscious subject in such a field.

However, our apprehension of the self in this further, substantial sense stops well short of an apprehension of the essence or nature of the self considered as that which becomes a self-conscious rational subject. Since awareness-as-such is not conceivable apart from some substance in which to ground it, we must infer that the self is also a substance. However, it does not follow that this substantial self is transparent to itself, so that its nature or essence *qua* substance is available to introspection.

Thus, in a sense, Kant was right and Descartes was wrong. Descartes supposed that, since consciousness is essential to personhood, that it is also essential to the substance that is a self. This is an error; that which becomes conscious, and thus a self-conscious subject, may be so only accidentally or incidentally.[61] At the same time, in another way Descartes was right and Kant was wrong. There is not another, noumenal self, operating independently of conscious awareness, possessing a distinct consciousness of its own inaccessible to us and of which the empirical self is a mere appearance or representation to "inner sense."[62] There is only one self, the empirical self that each one of us is; whatever it is that becomes conscious and thus a self-conscious subject does so in and as an empirical self/consciousness, not through possessing some noumenal consciousness behind or beyond that which we actually live. At the same time, that thing that becomes conscious is something existing prior to and independently of consciousness. It is thus, in that sense, a noumenal being – a thing-in-itself – transcending consciousness in such a way that it is not even represented there as that which becomes conscious, even when it is conscious. This substantial self is thus known, as Aquinas says, only through its acts by means of its effects in conscious awareness, and therefore is for us only comprehended as a theoretical posit.[63]

---

[61] For this, Descartes was taken to task by Malebranche; see (e.g.) Nicholas Jolley, "Malebranche on the Soul," in Stephen Nadler, ed., *The Cambridge Companion to Malebranche*, New York, Cambridge University Press, 2000, 31-58, and references. It is to be noted that I have left the nature of this substance an open question; substance dualism, idealism, and emergent materialism are available for all I say here as possible accounts of the relation of mind and body; however, reductive materialism and physicalism are not.

[62] Not all Kant scholars read Kant as asserting this; Paton, for example, suggests that there is the noumenal and phenomenal selves are not two selves, but simply a single self viewed from two points of view; see his (1949), 273-275. In response to this, we need merely ask, "Viewed by whom?" No matter how we answer this question, we come back to the self as a self-conscious subject, which is neither Kant's noumenal self nor his phenomenal self *qua* appearance to "inner sense."

[63] See Aquinas, *ST*, I, I, 84 a. 1-4. This is my own interpretation, rejected by some Aquinas scholars, especially those who regard Aquinas as a materialist who denies that we are conscious of our mental states and acts; see Pasnau, *Aquinas on Human Nature*, New York,

Contributions of the Substantial Self to Consciousness For Locke, substance was literally *substans*, that which "stands under" and the sole function of which is to provide the principle of unity for collections of sense-qualities through being that in which they inhere. Berkeley incessantly attacked this notion of substance – which he identified with Locke's material substance – as something inert, immobile, unconceiving, and inconceivable. His primary objection to this notion of substance was not that it transcended sense experience and was therefore unknowable, but rather that material substance, as characterized by its proponents, was purely passive, lacking any active powers. Instead, Locke's material substance is capable only of being moved by external forces themselves already in motion. Berkeley thus joins a long line of philosophers, both before and since his time, who have identified substance with the exercise of an *activity* intrinsic to it and thus as a source of existence and change through its own immanent operation.

This is the kind of substantiality Berkeley attributes to spirit, one that makes all the difference between the useless, inconceivable material substance posited by Locke as a substratum for secondary qualities and the active spiritual substances (the soul and God) Berkeley posits in his own theory. Since spirit is an active substance, and not merely passive and inert, it *is* knowable through its activity in and on conscious awareness as displayed in those features possessed by it that we cannot plausibly account for by reference to the contents of conscious awareness, and the relations between them, alone.[64]

Kant is a good, if unwitting, guide to some of these. First among these are space and time as features of conscious awareness, which we have already discussed. The intentional field of consciousness, in which the contents of consciousness appear, is uniform and homogenous – a *continuum*, Kant calls it, indefinite in extension and thus neither finite nor infinite considered in itself. Further, space and time have intrinsic

---

Cambridge University Press, 2002. Pasnau and other recent Thomist scholars, eager to evade the problems they perceive to be associated with Cartesianism, ultimately end up attributing views to Aquinas that are obviously self-refuting.

[64] Hume, of course, disputes this, claiming that if we restrict ourselves to the contents of consciousness and the relations between them, then mind is no more active than Locke's matter, and is itself wholly passive. I shall argue that Hume is wrong to restrict us in this way, and in so doing falls into performative self-refutation. See section III below.

mathematical properties, ones that they possess independently of their contents, though those properties are revealed to us only by reflection on those contents as we encounter them in experience. The spatial and temporal relations between those contents considered in themselves, however, are merely external and accidental to them, as Locke and Hume insist. They are thus insufficient to constitute space and time as these are revealed to us in lived experience, even as mere forms of intuition existing only in and for conscious awareness. Space and time are thus *a priori* (i.e., innate structures of consciousness), the pre-conscious contribution of the operation of the substantial self that, like conscious awareness itself, is the actualization of a potency in that substance. We are thus rationally justified in positing that substantial self as a necessary condition for the possibility of experience as we actually live it in and through conscious awareness.[65]

A second way in which the substantial self affects conscious awareness is through the activity of *synthesis* by means of which the intentional field of conscious awareness is constituted as what Kant calls a manifold of sensuous intuition. Locke, Berkeley, and Hume are at one in their insistence that the contents of conscious awareness are mental images as opposed to external material things. Hume, for his part, insists that the "atoms" of conscious awareness are simple ideas – shapes, colors, smells, tastes, textures, and so on. Being both simple and basic, Hume contends that they must be regarded as "original existences" incapable of further explanation or cause. Kant seems to follow Hume in thinking that these simple sense qualities are the fundamental elements of conscious awareness and the sole contribution of noumena to conscious experience, one given in such a way as to provide no information about their causal source other

---

[65] As has been pointed out many times, Kant's strictures on our knowledge of noumena, if consistently embraced, would make his own transcendental investigation of the necessary conditions of the possibility of experience impossible. The categories, the various forms of synthesis, and the transcendental unity of apperception cannot be understood to be features of consciousness or as reducible to such features. They are pre-conscious structures, processes, and realities that transcend consciousness, the positing of which is the entire point of transcendental argumentation. Given the success of that argumentation, we are surely justified in positing these pre-conscious structures (etc.), and thus positing them precisely *as real* in the full-blooded sense, i.e., as things-in-themselves. If so, then we are also warranted in claiming to know that they exist, on the ground that experience as we actually live it in and through consciousness would be impossible unless they existed as its (partial) cause. We are thus justified in claiming to know that they exist, and to make various claims about them. All of this is to know things-in-themselves, contrary to Kant's official strictures on knowledge of this kind.

than (at most) its bare existence as a theoretical posit, something that Hume the skeptic is unwilling to do. Hume then proposes to construct the complex contents of the intentional field of conscious awareness using his three principles of association: resemblance, contiguity, and regular, repeated succession in time ("cause and effect.") Kant, however, maintains that these principles alone are insufficient to account for our experience as we actually live it in and through conscious awareness, for among the following reasons.

First, we experience the phenomenal contents of consciousness as a *manifold*, i.e. a single whole composed of disparate but intimately related parts or elements, as what Kant calls the *phenomenal world*. Further, that we should experience phenomenal contents in this way is a necessary condition for unity of consciousness. If there were no structure or order to experience, if periods of time or areas of space were to be completely discontinuous, or run backwards, repeat themselves, or switch attributes willy-nilly, we would be unable to make sense of what we experience, and experience itself would make no sense to us. Conscious experience would be no more coherent or intelligible than a dream or an acid trip. Hume has no way of showing, and does not even attempt to show, that his principles of association are capable of insuring, or even being very likely to produce, let alone sustain as a going concern, the phenomenal world that we actually live in and through our conscious awareness.

Kant proposes his own system of categories as necessary conditions for the possibility of such a manifold, and of his schematized categories as principles of synthesis in the imagination responsible for the creation of mental images in our intentional field of conscious awareness. With these in place, we are guaranteed that, given that we have experience at all, experience will constitute a manifold and conscious awareness will be unified so far forth. The very existence of a phenomenal world in consciousness, then, supposes the operation of a substantial self that constructs it from its atomic constituents through some pre-conscious process. Whether or not we agree with Kant's particular account of these principles of construction, his central point stands. The contents of conscious awareness and the relations between them are insufficient to account for the existence of a phenomenal world existing as a manifold of sensuous intuition.

More than this, Kant notes that we routinely distinguish between subjective and objective in experience, explaining some features of the phenomenal world by reference to facts about the subject that experiences it and others by reference to facts about the objects represented by the contents of consciousness, of which we take those contents to be the appearances. Thus, we take some changing, temporally ordered series of conscious experiences to be different views of one, unchanging object whereas we take others to be a series of temporally ordered events. My serial inspection of the outside of a house represents an example of the first, whereas my observation of a ship travelling down river represents the second. Were we not able to make this distinction, we could not classify experiential episodes as regular sequences of events as distinct from merely subjective sequences of views of a single, unchanging thing. However, there are no certain marks in experience (if we limit ourselves to the contents of conscious awareness as such) to distinguish these two, as Hume himself admits without quite grasping the implications of this admission.

Indeed, on Hume's own principles, we have no reason to believe or expect that there should even be able to *recognize* repeated, regular sequences in experience *as such*, let alone for such sequences to be capable of producing habits of expectation that are routinely gratified in experience. As we travel down the road, objects appear to travel by us at a great rate of speed while we remain stationary, yet it is we, not they, that actually move in the ordinary sense of that term, in which to move means "change of place" involving continuous passage through space without occupying any of the places through which one passes. As I walk down the long hallway toward the front door every morning, I observe the same items in the same temporal sequence, fully anticipating what I will see, the order in which I will see them, and find those anticipations uniformly gratified. Yet I have no tendency to posit any causal connection between any of these events or to regard the sequence as a causal one, despite the fact that it conforms to the conditions postulated by Hume's regularity theory of causation.

The difference between sequences of these kinds, though given along with experience, is not explicable in terms of experiential contents themselves considered as such. In this case, we can perhaps do no better than to suppose, with Kant, that what is given along with the contents of experience in the case of those sequences we classify as *causal* is an apprehension that the events composing them occur in accordance with a rule strictly dictating the order of their occurrence. Further, rather than being immanent in experience, this rule or law takes the form of an external imposition on those contents. On this view, the objectivity of such sequences is solely a consequence of their subsumption under a casual law, which explains why we cannot "see" causal connections. The imposition of this law on experience is, in turn, to be explained in terms of the pre-conscious operation of the substantial self that produces the manifold of sensuous intuition in accordance with the category of cause and effect. This pre-conscious operation constitutes that sequence as a series of causally related events rather than as merely successive states of/occurring in experience. Once again, the substantial self shows itself to be present *in* consciousness by means of its effects on its contents without being present *to* consciousness as an object represented by any of its contents.

Having gleaned what we can from Kant, let us move on. We may note, for example, that identically one and the same mental content (the complex idea of a red ball, say) may either be either a percept, a memory, something imagined, dreamed, or an hallucination. In principle, the contents of each of these distinct mental states could be numerically the same, or at least qualitatively indistinguishable in each appearance in conscious awareness. In that case, what state I am in is neither constituted by, nor explicable by reference to, any facts about that particular content. Hume, of course, wants to claim precisely this, insisting that impressions, for example, are distinguished from ideas by means of their "force," "vivacity," and so on. However, there are at least two obvious problems with this proposal. First, it is simply false to the phenomenological facts. Impressions are *not* always more lively than ideas – memories, dreams, hallucinations, even images produced by the willful imagination can be as clear, distinct, and compelling as percepts. Nevertheless, we are generally in no doubt as to how to classify particular mental contents with regard to their type and could not even accomplish this much unless we were able to classify these contents independently of our awareness of these sorts of qualitative attributes, as we shall see.

Second, and more importantly, there is simply no necessary or explanatory connection between different degrees of "force" or "vivacity" accompanying different mental states considered as types and their being the types they are. It is purely a contingent matter of fact that, e.g., percepts strike us with more "force" and "vivacity" than memory images typically do. Therefore, even if "force" and "vivacity" provide a criterion for distinguishing percepts from other mental contents in most cases, it is insufficient to constitute percepts *as such*, as opposed to memories, hallucinations, dream-images or willful products of the imagination. Only if I am already able to distinguish percepts from memories, dream-images, hallucinations, or products of willful imagination can I notice that certain features intrinsic to the contents as such generally accompany contents of that type. Indeed, were this not so, I could not classify the contents of consciousness according to type in the first place, and thus would not be able to notice these accidental correspondences.

My ability to distinguish different types of mental states (perception, memories, dreams, hallucinations, willful imaginings, etc.) from one another, then, belongs not to what, following Kant, we can call the *matter* of conscious awareness (i.e. its contents) but instead to its *form*. Thus, just as space and time are given along with consciousness of the contents of consciousness, and thus *in* consciousness, without being present *to* consciousness as a representational content capable of becoming an object of conscious awareness, so too are individual mental states as non-voluntary *operations* over those contents. That a given content is a perception, as opposed to a memory, a dream, an hallucination, or an image willfully produced by the imagination is a consequence of the mental state containing that content rather than any feature of the content itself. It thus bids fair to be another contribution to conscious awareness of the pre-conscious operation of the substantial self that produces, not merely the manifold of sensuous intuition in space and time, along with the order and organization of its contents, but also operates over those contents, constituting and presenting them according to their types. For us as self-conscious rational subjects, our awareness of these states is a basic, given fact of consciousness – a Humean "original existence" neither needing nor being capable of further analysis within consciousness itself.

To this point, I have characterized the substantial self as present in consciousness only in its effects, noting the various features of consciousness neither reducible to nor explicable in terms of the contents of consciousness and the relations between them. However, the substantial self, though initially a theoretical posit made by reference to its effects on, and thus in, consciousness, is clearly and obviously present in consciousness in another way, one that has been staring us in the face all along. The substantial self is also present in consciousness as the empirical self, as that which is occurrently aware of the products of its own pre-conscious operations in conscious experience. The substantial self, that which becomes conscious in the intentional field of awareness produced by its pre-conscious activity, is as a result also that which is conscious in that intentional field of awareness and *to which* its contents appear as the matter of its mental states. This, of course, is precisely the empirical self, i.e. the individual, self-conscious rational subject in second act or *res cogitans*. Again, the substantial self as I have characterized it is not a noumenal self that wholly transcends consciousness and about which we can know nothing. The substantial self is the empirical self, and is not merely present in consciousness but immanently and ubiquitously present there through its simple, uniform, and (on its side) undifferentiated act of awareness/attention.

At the same time, the substantial self, *qua* substance, is more than simply the intentional field of consciousness, with its forms of intuition, contents, and various kinds of mental states. The substantial self includes the empirical self but is not exhausted by it: *qua* substance, the self exists as a thing-in-itself despite its being the case that it is only as the empirical self that it actually, as opposed to merely potentially, a self and so self-aware. In the same way, the empirical self thus knows its own nature *qua* substantial self only indirectly, as something to be discursively comprehended as a theoretical entity rather than something intuitively apprehended as or by means of a mental content that represents it as an object in consciousness. Nevertheless, because of its pre-conscious synthetic and constitutive activity, the substantial self affects itself *qua* conscious, empirical self and can be thus indirectly apprehended by itself *qua* empirical self by means of its effects in consciousness as their transcendental cause or principle. Since the substantial self is so by means of its pre-conscious operations over the inputs that are thereby constituted as contents of consciousness, it is a substance in the active, rather than merely passive, sense. It is thus no mere passive substratum as Locke imagined material substance to be. To the contrary, the substantial self exercises an immanent activity by means of which it becomes an empirical self and thus qualifies to be a Berkeleyan spiritual substance so far forth.

The final point is this. As empirical self, the substantial self acquires further powers that it exercises as a conscious subject within consciousness itself, hence with full, intentional awareness. The substantial self, *qua* empirical self, thus reveals itself as not just the subject of its own mental states, but also the self-conscious principle of its own mental *acts*. The substantial self thus becomes, *qua* empirical self, a self-conscious agent capable of directing the course of its own mental life. In this way, it thereby becomes capable of explicitly rational thought and theoretical inquiry. The empirical self, then, is no mere passive spectator of the phenomenal world constituted by pre-conscious processes over which it has no control. As conscious subject, the self both *reacts* to what it experiences and also *acts*, first in relation to its own mental contents, then as well in relation to the intentional objects those contents represent them in consciousness. The empirical self is thus an *agent*, and thus active in the full and proper sense.[66]

Just as qualitatively indistinguishable mental contents can serve as the matter of formally different mental states – perception, memory, imagination – so too can one and the same propositional content in thought serve as the matter for distinct propositional attitudes. Thus, one may know that Caesar is dead, or merely believe this, fear this, doubt this, hope this, wish this, entertain its possibility, fantasize about it, and so on. These mental acts are self-conscious, willful operations over propositional contents, voluntary inasmuch as we can resist or refuse assent to the spontaneous judgments that arise in the face of sense perception and other sources of information about the world. It is only because of this that theoretical inquiry – and thus rational thought and discourse – of the sort I am engaging in right now is even possible. In theoretical inquiry, I am active in regard to my own mental contents taken, not just as contents, but as representative of non-mental intentional objects constituted independently of my awareness of them. This concerns not just facts about "external" objects that transcend consciousness, but about myself *qua* thinking thing insofar as facts about myself (such as that I exist), though revealed to me in

---

[66] Again, we must reject Kant's idea that the empirical self is an appearance to "inner sense" that represents a noumenal self that is really calling the shots prior to and without our consent and which itself is just the reflection of the noumenal self's activity. If that is the case, then I am not a self at all *qua* empirical self and my agency is merely an illusion.

consciousness, are nevertheless not merely truths about appearances but instead objectively true about the world.

In the same way, when confronted with competing potential beliefs on theoretical topics or alternative possible actions, I exercise my agency in reflection, deliberation, and choice concerning what I will believe or do. I thus exercise my rational agency in gathering and examining the evidence, considering the pros and cons of each alternative, reasoning, and drawing a conclusion about what is likely to be true or best to be done under the circumstances. I thus experience myself, *qua* empirical self, as an agent. Finally, in full-blown intentional, purposive action the self as agent apprehends itself as *cause*, affecting first the self's own body, a material thing, and through that influence acting as a cause in the world and producing effects there.[67] Since only a substance can be a source of activity in this way, the existence of the substantial self is thus further confirmed through the apprehension of the agency exercised by the empirical self.

This, then, completes my phenomenological survey of our knowledge of the self as revealed in conscious awareness, not as present in consciousness in the form of a content that represents an object, but instead as self-conscious subject affected by and affecting conscious awareness in various ways, and through its own immanent conscious acts affecting the world. The substantial self is thus knowable, and known by us in reflection, by means of its effects in conscious awareness, consisting in all those features of consciousness that cannot be accounted for by reference to the Aristotelian matter of consciousness, i.e. the contents of consciousness and the relations between them considered just as such. Since it is known only reflectively in and by its effects, rather than being directly apprehended like the contents of consciousness, the self can be overlooked or treated as merely a passive spectator of those contents. However, a closer look reveals that nearly everything that makes conscious experience possible is the product of the activity of the self, whether this is the pre-conscious activity of the substantial self as such or as exercised by that self as the occurrently conscious empirical self, the Cartesian *res cogitans*.

Could the Self be an Illusion? Why have so many philosophers rejected

---

[67] For an account of how this is possible on a Cartesian substance dualist account of the person, see my *How Free Will Works*, Eugene, OR., Wipf and Stock, 2011, 51-70.

the existence of a substantial self and dismissed the empirical self as merely an illusion? Although questions of this kind are often merely rhetorical, in this case I think we have a clear and obvious answer.[68] Philosophers have supposed that, if there is a self that can be investigated and talked about, then it must be an *object* of some kind that can be apprehended and viewed from point of view external to itself. Given the otherwise sound contention that in order for anything to be an object for us it must be represented in conscious awareness by a particular set of mental contents, our inability to identify the self with anything that *appears* in the intentional field of conscious awareness naturally leads many philosophers to suppose that there is no such thing.

The most notorious case of this sort of reasoning is found in Hume. In his famous chapter "Of Personal Identity" in the *Treatise*, Hume explicitly attacks the notion of the self I have presented in this chapter. There is, he claims, no "spectator self" or Dennetian "homunculus" inhabiting the intentional field of awareness, no one who is aware of its contents. Although Dennett calls the traditional conception of consciousness the "Cartesian theater," it is Hume, rather than Descartes, who first used the image of a theater to describe the stream of consciousness as a series of merely successive, externally related events jointly constituting the totality of one's conscious life.[69] However, he hastens to correct, this image has a fatal flaw insofar as it suggests that there is anyone actually watching the show. The theater is empty; there is no audience, and no one is home. He thus rejects the question concerning the basis of personal identity by denying that there is any such thing.

Lumbered with the contention that ideas are mental images and that the meaning of a term is the mental image that arises before the mind's eye when we utter the term internally, Hume is easily persuaded that we have no idea, and therefore no concept, of the self:

> For my part, when I enter most intimately into what I call myself, I
> always stumble on some particular perception or other, of heat or
> cold, light or shade, love or hatred, pain or pleasure. I never can

---

[68] Of course, it might not be the complete answer – there may well be other motives for denying the self. However, I will not speculate about this here.

[69] See David Hume, *A Treatise of Human Nature*, I, IV, VI, L. A. Selby-Bigge, ed., Oxford at the Clarendon Press, 1888., 253.

catch myself at any time without a perception, and never can observe any thing but the perception. When my perceptions are removed for any time, as by sound sleep, so long am I insensible of myself, and may truly be said not to exist. And were all my perceptions removed by death, and could I neither think, nor feel, nor see, nor love, nor hate, after the dissolution of my body, I should be entirely annihilated, nor do I conceive what is further requisite to make me a perfect nonentity. If any one, upon serious and unprejudiced reflection, thinks he has a different notion of himself, I must confess I can reason no longer with him. All I can allow him is, that he may be in the right as well as I, and that we are essentially different in this particular. He may, perhaps, perceive something simple and continued, which he calls himself; though I am certain there is no such principle in me.[70]

Of course, this entire chapter has been an attempt show that I, at least, have a different notion of my self than that offered by Hume, according to whom I am merely a series of externally related sense-data that thereby constitute a unified, albeit temporary and perishing, stream of conscious awareness. More than this, I contend that everyone else, including Hume, knows the self in the exactly the same way and possesses what Berkeley calls a notion, and today we call a concept, of the self as a self-conscious, rational subject or *res cogitans*.[71] Hume is thus either badly misled by his preconceived ideas or simply being disingenuous.

In the famous passage just quoted, Hume uses the personal pronoun "I" twelve times, "me" and "my" once each, and "myself" twice.[72] In each instance, Hume uses the term substantively in reference to his own self, but the irony of this seems lost on the ever-ironic Hume. If Hume *qua* self was nothing more than a series of externally related mental contents, the "I" could legitimately refer only to that stream of conscious contents

---

[70] Hume, *Treatise*, I, IV, VI; in Selby-Bigge, 252.

[71] Berkeley, since he accepted the empiricist account of the meaningfulness of words, used the term notion for what we would today call a concept; given the empiricist strictures of his philosophy, however, Hume .as right to point out that Berkeley has no right to the use "notion" in this way. Since we have seen past this limited perspective, however, that no longer need trouble us today.

[72] Actually, he uses "my" three times, but in two of these cases, the use of the pronoun is possessive, modifying "perceptions."

taken as a whole. Yet "I," "me," and "myself" function throughout the passage to refer, not to any particular perception – the only things, according to Hume, of which I can be aware – nor even to the sum total of my perceptions, but instead to the thing that *has* these perceptions, i.e. the self-conscious subject that is both aware of those contents as the matter of his mental states and that over which his mental acts operate. On Hume's own supposition, the mental acts he performs, the judgments he arrives at, and the propositions he claims to know on their basis could themselves be nothing more than externally related, successive mental contents occurring as part of that series without any subject to perform, draw, or affirm them. They could not be what Hume himself takes them to be – acts, judgments, and well-confirmed truths – and must take them to be if they are to function as philosophical arguments, something Hume clearly intends they should do. We can confirm this by a detailed analysis of the passage.

When Hume "enters most intimately into what he calls himself," what is he doing?[73] He is performing the mental act of introspection, turning his attention inward in order to contemplate the contents of his own mind, thus constituting those contents, *as such*, to be the matter of that act and thus at the same time the object contemplated in that act. Hume can only actually succeed in doing this if he is a self-conscious subject of the sort I have been characterizing in the earlier sections of this chapter. On his own account of the self, the most he can do is state that certain externally related mental contents are succeeding each other in the stream of consciousness that constitutes him *qua* self.

Actually, even this is too much, as we can see if we merely ask the question "*Who* is reporting that this series of events is occurring in Hume's stream of consciousness?" If not Hume *qua* self-conscious subject, then it is not the product of introspection, and thus not a report of the contents of Hume's stream of consciousness, since there is neither a self-conscious subject to introspect nor to report on the contents of that stream of

---

[73] William Barrett successfully parodies Hume's procedure here by comparing Hume to a man who, sitting in his armchair, wonders if he is presently at home and decides to resolve this question by going outside and looking the window of his house – if he sees himself, he will conclude that he is in fact home and, if not, he will conclude that he must be somewhere else! Notice that this procedure would be perfectly sensible if one was asking this question about someone other than oneself. See Barrett's *The Death of the Soul*, New York, Doubleday Anchor Books, 1986, 46.

consciousness. There is just the stream of consciousness itself, a series of contents/events occurring without a conscious subject distinct from it. In that case, the propositional content to the effect that a certain series of events is occurring in that stream of consciousness is itself just another content/event in the sequence of contents/events occurring in the stream of consciousness that Hume identifies with his self. This content/event is only externally related to those that went before and at best accidentally about the mental events that came before it; nor, on Hume's view, can there be any self-conscious subject in a position to judge that this is so. After all, any such judgment would simply be another content/event in the sequence, only externally related to those that went before it and at best accidentally about the mind…and so on. If Hume is able to introspect or make judgments about his mental contents at all, then he is a self *qua* self-conscious rational subject and his claim to the contrary absurd. Certainly, unless he is such a subject there is no way that he could ever be in a position to apprehend any phenomenological facts about his own inner life capable of demonstrating the contrary. In that case, there is absurdity in even attempting such an investigation.

Nevertheless, let us consider Hume's report that, when he introspects, he does not find any self. Instead, he says, he finds only particular mental contents – perceptions – consisting in simple sense qualities such as heat or cold, pleasure or pain, or feelings like anger. Further, he says, he never perceives anything but sensations and feelings and for all he knows would cease to exist without them. The evident conclusion he wishes to draw is that he is nothing but the sum total of his perceptions and the relations between them and nothing more. However, let us consider Hume's claim that we never perceive anything but sense-qualities. This claim seems obviously false on the face of it, unless we are *assuming* that in order for something to be perceived it has to be, or be constituted by sense qualities, in which case, a claim that we have seen ample ground to doubt in the case of the self. I am aware of the self that I am by being a self and, in this case, by my awareness of myself as a *perceiver*, engaged in the activity of perceiving those contents of my intentional field of conscious awareness through introspection and thereby as endowed with perceptual states, of which what Hume calls perceptions are the contents. Unless there were such states and acts, there would not be perceptions at all, but merely dissociated sense-data which were neither perceptions, memories, dream-images, nor products of the exercise of the imagination. If Hume is a perceiver at all, then he is also a self-conscious, rational subject – a self as I have defined it. The mere fact that he can classify the contents of his stream of consciousness by type shows that he is aware of more than those contents as such, but also of his mental states and acts.

Undoubtedly, Hume would want to supplement his claim that he has no concept of the self by appealing to the empiricist criterion for meaningfulness, common property of all British empiricists from Hobbes onward. According to this claim, the meaning of a term is the idea corresponding to that term. Since, for Hume, ideas arise from impressions, it is the original impression that is the source of the meaning of a term, so that all substantively meaningful terms arise from sense-experience. This gives us a simple, straightforward test for the meaningfulness of any term, one constantly employed by Hume, usually preceded by the admonition to "consult your own experience." One simply utters the word inwardly to oneself and then waits to see if a corresponding mental image arises in the imagination; if one does, then the term is meaningful; if not, then it is meaningless. If I want to know whether "redness" is a meaningful term, I say "red" to myself and then observe that a red patch appears in the perceptual space of the imagination. Again, if I want to know whether "giraffe" is a meaningful term, then I utter "giraffe" to myself and observe that a mental image of a giraffe, perhaps of a drawing of a giraffe taken from a children's dictionary, appears before the mind's eye. However, when I utter the words "self," "soul," or "God" inwardly in the same fashion, I observe that nothing (or at any rate, nothing suitable) corresponding to these terms arises as a mental image in my intentional field of imaginative awareness. This, then, is taken to prove that, since I have no idea deriving from an impression of this putative object of awareness, that I altogether lack a concept ("notion") of it as well.

Again, I believe that I have already made a sufficient positive case for knowledge of the self (*qua* self-conscious rational subject) to establish the fact that I am a self, and so, too, is everyone else capable of following that positive case, including David Hume, deny it as he might. If the empiricist criterion for meaningfulness is incapable of confirming that fact by means of its peculiar method of consulting one's own experience, then that is simply a *reductio* on that particular test for meaningfulness. Indeed, if

Hume is even capable of applying this test and reporting its supposedly negative results, or even so much as denying that he is a self *qua* self-conscious rational subject, then he is such a self by that very fact. One needs just ask, "Who is consulting his own experience? Who is reporting these results? Who is denying that he is a self?" Clearly, the answer is that it is David Hume, *qua* self-conscious rational subject, that is doing so, and who has no plausible alternate explanation of this consistent with his own account of the self as merely an externally related series of discrete mental contents. If we consult our own experience, or are even capable of doing so in accordance with Hume's own admonition, the palpable absurdity of such an account must surely be evident to us.

Let us now, in the next place, note that Hume does not simply report his claims about the self as merely his own opinions about these matters, he presents them as arguments, addressed to other inquirers, intended to persuade them that there is no such thing as a self or soul. Thus, Hume, the self-conscious subject, addresses other self-conscious subjects through his writings, in an attempt to persuade them that they are not, after all, precisely what they would have to be in order for that activity, and that address, to make any sense at all – i.e., self-conscious rational subjects. Once again, we need only ask, "Who is making this appeal? To whom is this appeal addressed? If this is not an appeal by one self-conscious rational subject to another, then how are we to describe what is going on here? Even if we could describe it, could we do so in such a way that the activity had any point as an exercise as part of the project of theoretical inquiry?" Once again, if Hume is any position to make this appeal to others, and for them to be able to consider, let alone accept, it then the conclusions he wishes to draw based on those arguments cannot be true. The reader may easily ask the same questions in his or her own case – as Hume says, "consult your own experience." Do so, and I think that you will agree that Hume's account of the self cannot be correct; indeed, the very possibility of your doing this proves its falsity.

In the rest of the chapter from which the above excerpt is drawn, Hume goes on to claim that the notion of the self as anything endurant, simple, and unchanging is utterly false. He then attempts to reduce the self to the stream of consciousness, and to explain how it is that the illusion that there is a self arises, though once again we have to ask, "If there is no self, why do we need to explain the illusion that there is a self?" Only self-conscious rational subjects are subject to illusions, delusions, or false beliefs. If there are no self-conscious rational subjects, there is literally no one capable of being subject to such an illusion. Again, just ask yourself, "Who is it that is subject to this illusion, if there are no selves?" Once again, if there is anything at all to explain here, such as how some benighted people ("metaphysicians," Hume calls them) get the false idea that they are selves, i.e. self-conscious rational subjects, then there clearly are selves, and our apprehension of ourselves as such, described earlier, is not and cannot be an illusion. The only one who could possibly be laboring under an illusion here is Hume himself; while this may be remarkable, it is by no means mysterious in the way it would be if Hume's view were such as to be conceivably true. Upon reflection, it just seems quite obviously impossible for the notion of the self, *qua* self-conscious rational subject, to be an illusion.

Hume ends the quoted paragraph with a series of remarkable statements. He claims that if anyone, upon reflection, thinks he has a different notion of himself, then Hume can no longer reason with him. Perhaps, he avers, some people are different from himself in this respect; he admits the possibility, but firmly reasserts that there is no such principle in himself. Once again, unless Hume were a self, in the sense of a self-conscious rational subject, it would not be possible for him to even so much as formulate these possibilities, let alone confirm one of them, either introspectively or on the basis of argument. Only a self-conscious rational subject could do anything like this, so it is quite impossible for Hume not to possess the concept of such a subject or to plausibly deny that he is one, however much he may refuse to acknowledge this. Indeed, were it not for Hume's explicit claims and statements in this chapter of his *Treatise*, one would never attribute such a view to him, given that he clearly does assume throughout the *Treatise* and indeed all of his writings that both he and his readers are self-conscious rational subjects. That this is so is not surprising, since no other supposition is rational discourse even coherently conceivable. On the other hand, that his official doctrine forces him to deny this unavoidable supposition simply shows that Hume's philosophy is deeply incoherent, at least as far as its results are concerned. In this, to quote Hume against himself, he may read the downfall of his principles.

Hume's entire discussion in this chapter of the *Treatise* is an exercise in *performative* self-refutation. Throughout this text, Hume constantly engages in activities – introspection, judgment, argument, and so on – that would not be possible for him to engage in if his official doctrine of the self were true. Like someone who sings, in good tune and with perfect pitch, "I can't sing, can't sing a note..." his very performance refutes his theoretical contentions. At the same time, these very performances illustrate that Hume is precisely what he claims to *know* himself, on their basis, not to be, namely, a self-conscious rational subject, or self, distinct as such from his stream of conscious awareness considered simply as a set of externally related mental contents. The same holds for everyone reading these words. No matter how one twists or turns, one cannot escape the self. Indeed, even to try to do so proves its inescapability, since only a self as I have characterized it could undertake such a project to begin with. It is thus useless to even try. Only when we accept this fact can a true philosophy of the human person.

Chapter Seven

Objections to Dualism

In his excellent recent defense of Hylomorphism, James D. Madden discusses a number of theoretical objections to Substance Dualism.[74] While he concedes that none of these objections are "deal-breakers," he does contend that these objections make Substance Dualism an unattractive theory in relation to Hylomorphism. In this paper, I want to make the best reply I can on behalf of at least one kind of substance dualism, albeit one that makes some significant concessions to the Hylomorphist position. First, I will briefly sketch the Dualist position that I propose to defend, Next, I will consider the classic objections to Substance Dualism in relation to the position that I have outlined, concluding that these objections are much less formidable than they are usually taken to be.[75] I will conclude

---

[74] James D. Madden, *Mind, Matter & Nature*, Washington, DC, Catholic University of America Press, 2013, 60-88.

[75] For reasons that will emerge, and for others that I have discussed elsewhere, I am persuaded that "no consciousness" views are certainly "flat-out" false and the reductive materialism is *almost* certainly false i.e., even if true, such that we could never, even in principle, have any rational justification for believing it. Beyond that, although I have a marked (and rationally defensible) preference for Substance Dualism, I have to admit that other views, such as Emergent Materialism, Panpsychism, Idealism, and so on are at least possibly true. Perhaps even some form of Non-Reductive Materialism could turn out to be true. At any rate, these other views are still in the running, so I am somewhat less dogmatic in this area than perhaps I am in others. Since, as I have argued elsewhere, Hylomorphism really amounts to no distinct, substantive view of its own (see my essay, "Could Sensation be a Bodily Act?" - on the *Philpapers* website) it will easily accommodate itself to whichever of these views proves to be correct at the end of the day, so that as long as any of them is in the field so is Hylomorphism.

that, while the Substance Dualist position I have sketched here is not perfect, it bids fair to be closer to the correct view about the relation between mind and body than any of its rivals and so deserves to be affirmed in preference to them, despite its as yet unresolved difficulties and problems.

What is Substance Dualism?

There are many versions of Substance Dualism, both ancient and modern, so it is appropriate to begin with a brief sketch of the dualist view that I intend to make a case for, without talking too much space contrasting it with related views. On the view that I am defending here, a human being is a *living organism*, a compound substance consisting of two substances, soul and body, each of which possesses its own distinct and contrary nature and its own act of existence. At the same time, each is by nature naturally dependent on the other for the exercise of its characteristic operation, so that the two form a single mutually interdependent complex of operations. Considered in itself, the body of an organism is a material thing like any other material thing: it is a compound substance consisting of many parts, both proper and constitutive, that can be scientifically analyzed on several levels: organic, biochemical, chemical, and physical. *Qua* material thing, the substantial form of the body or *forma corporeitatis*, encoded in its DNA, is both educed from its physical microstructure and strongly supervenient on it. At the same time, this substantial form dictates the standard pattern of organic development and endows that body with all of its qualitative attributes, including its dispositional ones, such as its causal powers and liabilities for change. Nevertheless, the body *qua* material thing possesses no properties different in kind from any other material thing; to this extent, it is a "machine," though as we shall see a "machine" is not exactly what we have typically taken it to be.

By contrast, the soul is a simple, immaterial, sempiternal substance existing without a natural material component. It inherently possesses a single, undifferentiated act of *per se* causation by means of which it serves as the substantial form of the body, not *qua* material thing, but rather *qua* living organism, through being the proximate *per se* cause of its continuous existence and operation as a living thing. The soul is thus the principle of the life of the body, exercising an act that, in relation to itself, shrinks to a single, zero-dimensional point but which in relation to the body *qua* material thing whose operations it sustains, is temporally and spatially extended as that sustaining act terminates in the spatially and temporally extended body that is the object of that act and through which that act achieves its effect of sustaining its operations.

Conscious awareness arises at the interface between soul and body, constituted by space and time as forms of intuition constituting an intentional field of awareness in which various contents - sensations, feelings, passions, emotions, mental images, concepts, thoughts, judgments, beliefs, inferences and so on, spontaneously arise in various ways from various sources and are immediately apprehended by the self. Just as the body is alive through the power of the soul to sustain its operations as a living organism, so too is the soul conscious through its association with the body, although consciousness belongs to the soul and is in no way a bodily act of any kind.

A soul that has become conscious is a mind. As mind, the soul acquires a number of additional powers by means of which the immaterial contents of consciousness come to be present in its intentional field of awareness. While those contents are immediately apprehended by us and capable of being introspected, the acts and processes by means of which the mind produces those contents are not and can only be the subject of transcendental analysis and investigation. A mind that possesses self-conscious rational agency (and not all minds do) is a *self* and, in addition to its mental contents also apprehends itself as an ongoing subject of awareness, not as one content among others (as Hume assumes would have to be the case) but rather as that which apprehends those contents. A soul that is *by nature* a self-conscious rational subject (or *rational soul*) is *eo ipso* an individual substance of a rational nature, or *person*. So too, then, will be the organism (for example, a *human being*) of which such a soul is the substantial form, and this status will attach to both that soul and the organism whose substantial form it is regardless of whether that person is, or is even physically capable of, being an actual conscious subject so long as the soul and the body are still joined.

I have discussed the details of this account in other places.[76] This

---

[76] See my essays "Mind, Body, Space, and Time," and "From Private Experience to Public

sketch will have to suffice for the present as well as the many questions that it doubt brings to the reader's mind. Let us instead turn to the standard objections to dualism and see how it fares in relation to them.

The Interaction Problem

The most commonly heard objection to Substance Dualism is the interaction problem, first raised by Princess Elizabeth of Bohemia in her correspondence with Descartes.[77] Dualism says that the soul and the body are substances of contrary natures yet that they somehow causally influence each other. *Prima facie*, it is difficult to understand how an immaterial, sempiternal substance like a soul could in any way exert efficient causal influence in the spatio-temporal physical world. In the same way, it seems equally mysterious that any purely material body could exercise any sort of causal influence over an immaterial substance like a soul. In response to Elizabeth, Descartes frankly owns that this is a mystery, but one that we must accept and live with given that the natural light of reason informs us in no uncertain terms that we are both minds and have bodies. Despite what others may think he should have said, I think that this response by Descartes is well taken.

Substance Dualism is arguably the default position on the mind/body problem; it is the most natural view to take on the grounds of ordinary, everyday lived experience.[78] Monistic views, whether Idealist or Materialist, require us to regard our experience as systematically misleading, though this is easier for the Idealist to make out than the Materialist. Now, of course, if some other theory about the relation between mind and body were able to successfully explain that relation, it might be preferable to Substance Dualism. In fact, however, every theory about the mind has its own analogue of the interaction problem that crops up precisely at the point where the precise relation between the mind and the body has to be explained.

Language," on the *Philpapers* website.

[77] See Lisa Shapiro, ed. and trans., *The Correspondence between Princess Elizabeth of Bohemia and Rene Descartes*, Chicago, IL, Chicago University Press, 2007, 61-73.

[78] See Tomas Bogardus, "Undefeated Dualism," *Philosophical Studies* 165 (2), (2013), 445-466.

Idealists deny the existence of the body, whereas Eliminative Materialists deny the existence of consciousness *as experienced*. Neither of these views is plausible given the fact of that experience and what we experience when we advert to it; indeed the latter is simply obviously false in relation to lived experience. Reductive materialists and identity theorists have no way to explain how conscious awareness as we experience it could be *nothing but* some purely physical process going on in the brain when these two things are so obviously different from one another. Panpsychists, Emergentists, and Constitutionalists have the difficulty of analyzing the relevant relations in such a way as to make them both clear and relevant to the explaining the relation between mind and body. Property Dualists, Double Aspect theorists, and Neutral Monists have the difficulty of explaining what this thing that is neither mind nor body but somehow both mind and body and neither mind nor body exclusively is supposed to be...and so on. Even if the Interaction Problem is a problem for dualism, there is a cognate problem for every other theory that has been tried so far – the mystery of mind, which in the case of dualism is articulated as the Interaction Problem, remains unsolved and is thus provides no reason for us to abandon Substance Dualism in favor of some other theory. Dualism remains the *prima facie* best explanation of the relation between mind and body on the basis of our common, everyday experience. As such, the presumption in favor of that view is not yet overcome and Descartes' refusal to be baited on that score vindicated.

However, the defense of dualism need not depend solely on this merely negative argument. I honestly believe that the Interaction problem can be solved, though not perhaps in the way that it was put to Descartes, either in the context of his own theoretical commitments or those likely to be taken for granted by those opposed to dualism on extra-philosophical grounds. At any rate, the idea that there is something *incoherent* about Dualism can, I think, be laid to rest by in a fairly straightforward way on the view I have sketched above. Let me discuss mind/body interaction from both aspects: mind to body and body to mind. Let us begin with the relation of body to mind.

How the Body Influences the Mind Descartes and Princess Elizabeth's common commitment to Galilean physicalism made the problem of body/mind interaction insoluble for them. In particular, their rejection of substantial forms, non-physical structural features of external bodies existing as global emergent properties of those bodies, which while strongly supervenient on their physical microstructure serve as the ontological principle of all of that body's qualitative and dispositional attributes, leads to the problem of the external world and, ultimately, to Humean skepticism.

The first step on the way to a solution to the mind/body problem is the rejection of Galilean physicalism and the acceptance of a neo-Aristotelian ontology of material things, for which the constituents of a thing's physical microstructure constitutes merely the noumenal matter of that material thing, not its entire reality. Material things are compound substances consisting of matter and form and for which form is the principle of intelligibility existing in that thing as its nature - its individualized, concrete essence.

Matter, understood as the modern scientific tradition understands it, is never present to us as something experienced by us - it is a theoretical entity, something posited to explain something else of which we are immediately aware in experience. As such, matter is only indirectly intelligible to us and cannot even be conceived of by us unless there is something else of which we are directly or immediately aware. Since matter cannot be present to us in conscious awareness as such, it is necessary that there be something else that conveys the nature and reality of the external world to us in order for us to even so much as conceive, let alone posit the existence of matter as modern science conceives it. However, if Galilean physicalism is true, there is nothing external to conscious awareness except matter in motion. Galileo, Descartes, and Locke suppose that causal interaction between our bodies and external things, all of which are constructed from simple material substances, somehow gives rise to sensation and perceptual experience in consciousness, but the difficulties in spelling this out simply reflect another aspect of the mind/body problem and ultimately undermine the New Science of matter in motion itself.

On the ontology of material things, however, it is possible for external objects to be present in and to consciousness by means of their substantial forms that, being non-physical, are potentially contents of conscious awareness. On the traditional account, numerically one and the same substantial form can simultaneously exist in an external object as its nature or concrete essence and also in a different way ("formally and intentionally") in the mind as an intelligible species or concept. The story of how the substantial form of a material thing comes to be present in the mind as an intelligible species is one I have told elsewhere.[79] In this context, I just want to consider a couple of aspects of this account.

While the term "species" as used in the Scholastic (and for that matter the neo-Scholastic) tradition is somewhat vague, to call a substantial form a species is to say that it exists in some medium of transmission (a wave-packet, a state of a sensory organ, a brain state, etc.) without becoming the nature of that medium which it informs. Instead, the medium simply possesses that substantial form as an extraneous structural feature that "piggybacks" on that medium without changing its nature. Although it is the qualitative forms (which are merely perceptible surface properties of the material things that we experience in sense-perception) that are actually received in the act of sensory stimulation the brain, which has evolved to subserve conscious awareness, its needs and ends, acts as a kind of "common sense" that organizes all of this disparate inFORMation in such a way that its substantial form is present in conscious awareness, first as the principle of structural unity in the phantasm (roughly, "mental image") and then in the intellect as a concept, indifferently applicable to many particulars.

This concept, existing in the mind as a universal, when imposed by the intellect as on a mental image or phantasm makes that collection of sense-data a *representation* of an extramental particular, something that both exists and instantiates a nature capable in principle of being multiply instantiated by other particulars as well. From this information the physical microstructure of that material thing can be theoretically reconstructed by natural science through analogical modelling. In this way, genuine knowledge of external, material things becomes possible and, on its basis, the sort of theoretical inquiry that natural science engages in. Thus, both knowledge of the external world and scientific realism find a genuine basis and prospect in this theory, one denied to a Galilean physicalist picture of things.

---

[79] In the aforementioned essay, "From Private Experience to Public Language" on *Philpapers*.

How the Mind Influences the Body One of the most pervasive features of our ordinary everyday experience is the fact of *personal agency* and its efficacy in producing change in the world by means of bodily activity. To use the hackneyed example yet again: I will that my arm should rise and subsequently observe that it does. The most natural description of this situation is that my act of will, a mental event occurring in conscious awareness, caused the rising of my arm, an act of my body, a material thing in the external, physical world. Yet how can we make sense of this otherwise unshakeable conviction? The most natural supposition, the only one apparently conceivable to Descartes and Princess Elizabeth, and for that manner many people today, is that in order to direct the body, the mind must somehow enter the order of horizontal efficient causes, as occurs in the case of body-body interaction. As such, the soul must somehow generate and insert some sort of *influxus physicus* into the physical world, either in the form of physical energy or exert some sort of influence that moves physical energy around in the brain in order to guide and control bodily behavior. However, on the model of mind and brain/body interaction I have offered elsewhere,[80] since the soul acts as the *per se* cause of the body's operation rather than as an efficient cause, it need not enter the order of efficient causes in order to influence the course of events in the physical world.

Instead, since the soul's act of sustaining the body's operations is a necessary condition for the occurrence of those operations, the soul can simply withhold its sustaining act from those proposed actions that it does not choose to acquiesce in, thus removing one of the necessary conditions for them to proceed into full realization or enactment. Since that sustaining act is present to me in conscious awareness as the general awareness or apprehension that accompanies all mental contents of whatever sort I can exert immediate, voluntary control over those contents by *concentration of attention*, i.e. by simply disattending from those proposals for action (realized in the brain and central nervous system as physical *action-patterns*) that I elect not to enact. Of course, this supposes that the physical body/brain is not a closed system that altogether excludes the possibility of vertical non-physical causal influence. To see whether this is true requires that we now

---

[80] See my *How Free Will Works: A Dualist Theory of Human Action*, Eugene, OR, Wipf and Stock, 2011, 51-70.

turn to some further objections to Substance Dualism.

Causal Closure and the Conservation Principles

A second objection often urged against Substance Dualism is that it is unscientific for some reason and cannot be accommodated to the known facts of neurophysiology. In particular, dualism is taken to violate a thesis known as the Causal Closure Principle: According to this principle, all physical systems are causally closed, such that only physical causes can be admitted for physical events. This principle is typically stated as a well-known or unassailable dogma of modern science, sufficient by itself to exclude Substance Dualism. However, this "Principle" is vague and difficult to interpret in such a way as to be both true and empirically significant. On the one hand, it is sometimes treated as a methodological principle that bids us seek physical causes for physical events. Methodological principles, however, are merely prescriptions guiding theoretical inquiry and do not provide an *a priori* guarantee of their universal applicability. Such a principle is either open to the possibility that there may be non-physical causes for some physical events or it simply expresses a general, dogmatic refusal to entertain any but physical explanations for physical events, regardless of what the empirical evidence of lived experience indicates. This principle, then, is not strong enough by itself to exclude Substance Dualism from serious consideration.

A more substantive version of the principle claims that physical processes are "gapless," i.e. are spatio-temporally continuous and (*qua* physical) contain no breaks between the physically necessary and sufficient conditions for the production of any physical effect that require us to postulate any other causes to explain how the behavior of organisms are elicited. In particular, it is claimed that human neurophysiology is "gapless," which seems to exclude either the need or the possibility that there is some sort of role for something called the soul or mind to contribute to the production of human action, such as introducing energy into the brain or moving the energy in the brain around. However, the sort of influence that I have supposed that the soul or mind exercises over the brain does not depend on there being any such gaps at the level of horizontal, efficient causation in order to affect human action. Instead, the mind, through concentration of attention, acquiesces in the full realization of some action-patterns in the brain and withholds its acquiescence from others, which therefore fail to reach fruition. No matter what I choose, the result will be something that, when viewed from the third-person point of view available to the neurophysiologist, will look as though it were completely self-explanatory on the horizontal level of efficient causation. As such, this "gaplessness" is not sufficient to show that the physical order is somehow closed to the influence of immaterial substances like the soul or mind.

Nor does the notion of causal necessity justify the belief that, so far as the production of human behavior is concerned, the physical universe is closed to any non-physical causes or influences. As I have argued elsewhere, Hume's critique of the notion of causation and causal necessity as understood according to the Philosophy of Nature associated with the New Science ought to be accepted as sound, so that in principle there can be no empirical evidence for the existence of such causes or of such necessary connections in nature. However, I have proposed a different, more traditional account of causality according to which causal necessity is conditional and all physical processes in principle interruptible, so that even if all of the physically necessary and sufficient conditions for the production of some effect, B at T+n are actual and operating at T, that guarantees that B will actually arise or occur only if nothing intervenes to prevent that effect from arising or occurring by interfering with the currently operating process that would, if not interfered with, naturally give rise to B.[81] The operation of the soul or mind would thus be one factor capable of interfering with any such process occurring in the brain that achieves its end through conscious awareness, in the way that intentional actions do. On this view, there is no fatalistic necessary operating anywhere in nature, only natural processes with natural outcomes that nevertheless can be prevented from being actualized through outside interference.

The same holds of the conservation laws, which are sometimes held up as a scientific barrier to the possibility of non-physical influence in the production of human intentional action. On my view these laws, like all natural laws, are only conditionally necessary. Further, if dualism is true, then the mind and brain operate together as a single system in the production of human action, and thus the brain considered in itself is not a

---

[81] See my *Determinism and Causality*, Amazon CreateSpace, 2017, 108-128.

closed system after all insofar as the production of intentional action is concerned, even if it appears to be physically closed when looked at from the external point of view taken by the neurophysiologist. While the amount of energy in the brain and the angular momentum of its parts remain constant, since according to dualism there is more to the production of intentional action than what happens in the brain as such, these principles in no way rule out the possibility of a non-physical influence in the production of human action.[82]

The Apparent Dependence of Consciousness on the Brain

Another common claim made by critics of dualism is that both the existence and the character of consciousness appears to be dependent on the brain in serious and important ways that seem contrary to what we would expect to be the case if consciousness were a purely non-physical affair. Many well-known facts and a mountain of anecdotal evidence attest to the fact that damage or injury to the brain can lead to the cessation of consciousness as well as affecting all of its functions, including perception and rationality. To many, this strongly suggests that consciousness, as such, must be completely dependent on the brain and so strongly supervenient on its operation. From here, it seems just a short hop, skip, and jump to some version of epiphenomenalist materialism.

As I said earlier, the soul is a simple, immaterial, sempiternal substance exercising a single, simple, and undifferentiated activity, by means of which it serves as the vertical, *per se* cause of the operation of the body qua living organism. Apart from the body, this activity conceived of as intrinsic to the soul itself shrinks to a single, zero-dimensional point experientially constituted for a self-conscious rational subject as a sempiternal *duree* I call the *now*. As such, the soul is not capable of any

---

[82] I note in passing that Hylomorphists who push these objections to Dualism (as does Madden, op. cit. 65-69) are generally silent about how their own view avoids these difficulties. In Madden's case, it appears that he ultimately denies that the body exists as a material thing, a collection of externally related *mikra* captured in fields of force and operating in accordance with the laws of motion. Instead, these entities are merely "virtually present" in the body and no longer possess their proper natures, much as chemicals lose their observable properties when they combine in reactions. Such a view is almost certainly empirically false unless formulated in such a way that it is intolerably vague and obscure. Nor can it be used to evade facing the problem of the conservation laws, which so far as we know apply to the human body in exactly the same way as any other physical system.

contentful conscious experience apart from the body in relation to which it exercises its characteristic operation. Again, the intentional field of conscious awareness, characterized by 3D space and the A-theory time in which a stream of conscious contents arises at the *interface* between body and soul and constitutes that soul as a mind, a conscious subject. Conscious awareness thus depends both on the body and the soul for its existence. Without the soul, the body is not alive and contentful conscious awareness cannot even arise since the non-physical intentional field of awareness, which properly belongs to the immaterial soul, cannot exist. In the same way, the body *qua* living organism is the source of our mental contents, either directly through the soul's presence to the body as the terminus of its characteristic activity as the vertical, *per se* cause of its continued existence and operation or indirectly through the species conveyed from external objects to the brain where the agent intellect extracts them and conveys them to the mind. When the body *qua* material thing ceases to function, this spells the death of the body *qua* living organism as well, since the soul in that case is no longer capable of exercising its characteristic operation in relation to the body. At this point, the soul becomes separated from the body and ceases to exercise its characteristic activity as *per se* sustaining cause in relation to it. For the same reason, it ceases to possess an intentional field of awareness and a contentful stream of consciousness, at which point conscious experience ceases. At most, the *now* that serves as the mark of its presence in and to consciousness remains.

I think it is much more plausible to suppose that the brain evolves to serve the needs of consciousness, which are focused not merely on reproductive success but simply on the enjoyment of further experience and new varieties of conscious awareness than to suppose that the process of brain development is purely organic and the growth of consciousness merely an accidental, fortuitous consequence of a process in which it plays no part. In that case, when the brain and the sensory organs are operating properly, they successfully convey us to the ends to which consciousness directs us. However, the body *qua* material thing is a highly complex "machine" with many moving parts and a finite window of operation, so that many things can go wrong. In some cases, the dependence of the mind on the proper working of its "machinery" can lead to a loss of functioning, robbing the mind of both the raw materials and the operative capacities necessary for rational thought or for a proper human "superego" to control its appetites and emotions. None of this is, or should be, unexpected on the basis of the dualism I have sketched here.

Animal Minds

For Descartes, the body *qua* material thing is a self-operating machine that neither admits nor needs the soul as the sustaining cause of its operation. Instead, "animal spirits" in the blood are or contain the "life-force" that distinguishes living from non-living bodies. Even so, purely mechanical explanations are possible for all bodily behavior considered as such. For this reason, Descartes dispenses with animal souls, on the ground that they are explanatorily superfluous. Everything that animals do, according to Descartes, can be explained on mechanical principles in the same way as the movements made by *automata*, machines made by human beings that partially imitate the behaviors of persons and animals. For this reason, Descartes notoriously denied that animals are conscious or feel pain, a thesis in which he was followed by Malebranche and his school, such as the English Malebranchian, John Norris of Bemerton.[83] Norris's defense of this Cartesian thesis is by far the most challenging presentation of the difficulties involved in the imputation of immaterial souls to beasts. I frankly own that I have no ready response to it.

At the same time, since I find it inconceivable both that animals altogether lack consciousness and that a body could be conscious without the presence of a soul, I have no choice but to affirm that animals possess immaterial souls. These souls are limited in their powers relative to human souls if for no other reason than that the brains of animals are less complex. Animal consciousness is mostly limited to sensation, appetition, and primitive fear and anger. Further, these limited conscious reactions are both triggered by and trigger innate, instinctive patterns of behavior that animals enact in a more or less automatic manner. Non-human animals altogether lack abstract concepts. Because of this, they are incapable of thought, language, judgment, reasoning, knowledge, or rational belief. For the same

---

[83] See Descartes' Letter to Henry More, 5 February 1649, in *The Philosophical Writings of Descartes, Volume III,* London, Cambridge University Press, 1991, 365-367 - known more familiarly as CSMK - Nicolas Malebranche, *The Search After Truth,* Thomas Lennon and Paul J. Olscamp, eds., London, Cambridge University Press, 1997, 98, 323-325, and John Norris, *An Essay Towards The Theory of the Ideal or Intelligible World,* Vol. II, London, Edmund Parker, 1722 (facsimile reprint by Kessinger, 2006), 58-100.

reason, they altogether lack self-consciousness and personhood. Although they exist as temporally continuous conscious subjects through time they lack any awareness of this fact, so can neither dwell on the past nor anticipate the future.

Their natural capacity to learn is also extremely limited. This is not surprising, since learning is of little use to non-human animals because, lacking language or any other medium of transmission they cannot preserve or pass down whatever they may have learned from their limited experience to others of their kind. There is thus no evolutionary "payoff" to animal learning and so no selective pressure for developing it. Animal learning manufactured in the lab through various forms of conditioning engendered in an artificial environment is strongly redolent of the "Clever Hans" phenomenon. Anecdotal reports of amazing animal feats of memory, judgment, and so on are just that, occasional and generally unrepeatable incidents that are merely aberrant rather than indications of significant "hidden assets" inherent in animal "intelligence" and just waiting to be liberated and expressed by a human researcher who has found the magic key needed to access them.

This is not to deny that animals exhibit remarkable, if limited, abilities to navigate through the world, respond to environmental challenges and to simulate complex social and even engineering behavior as result of mere evolutionary conditioning, such as those exhibited by spiders, ants, and bees. The point is simply that these feats are neither the product of intelligence nor evidence of it. Animals do not *think*. As such, we have to understand their apparently intelligent behavior on the basis of other principles than those that would be used to interpret the behavior of a self-conscious rational agent like a human being. Human beings can learn from and appreciate the beauty, efficiency, and complexity of a beehive or a spider's web; bees and spiders do not and cannot since their behaviors and the complex structures they build are purely the result of instinct produced either by natural selection or the wise provision of a beneficent Creator.

As Descartes and Malebranche point out, our natural tendency toward anthropomorphism makes it almost impossible for us not to suppose that dogs have beliefs ("Master is home"), know things, reason, and both recognize and have affection for their owners of a sort analogous (and in the eyes of many, superior) to that of which rational beings are capable in relation to each other. For the same reason, it is very difficult for us not to be misled by anecdotal evidence into supposing that non-human animals have much more interesting and complex inner lives than they actually do, rather than one that simply subserves the stereotypical, limited stock of standard life-tasks that one sees endlessly repeated in nature documentaries on PBS and *Animal Planet*.

In the same vein, even though animals almost certainly feel and react to pain, as I have argued elsewhere it is doubtful whether animals can *suffer* if this means anything like what it does in the case of a rational human being.[84] Non-human animals are not persons or selves, and have no capacity for living outside the present moment. As such, they lack the necessary conditions for suffering; in their case, then, pain serves a merely epistemic function that is largely beneficial to them and that it is hard to see could have been replaced by any less painful mechanism.[85]

Even despite the differences between human and non-human animals in terms of the character and quality of their mental lives, I think we must credit non-human animals with immaterial souls for two reasons. First, animals are *living organisms*, not just machines or *automata*, and thus not reducible simply to bodies *qua* material things. Modern medical science no longer recognizes any quasi-physical *tertium quid*, like animal spirits, *elan vital*, or *chi* existing in the body as a "life-force" that distinguishes living bodies from inanimate things. If we are to make this intuitively obvious distinction, we shall have to make reference to something non-physical - the soul - in order to do so. Secondly, animals are conscious subjects, albeit in a way very different from the way in which we are. Since, as I have suggested elsewhere, sensation cannot be understood as a merely bodily act, only a being with an immaterial soul could be conscious in even in minimal way.[86] I can thus see no alternative to conceding that any plausible form of Substance Dualism must attribute immaterial souls to non-human animals, despite the apparently unanswerable questions and inconveniences that this <u>admission seems to entail:</u> e.g., Why so many souls? How are they

[84] See my essay "Pain and Evil," on the *Philpapers* website.

[85] As I have argued in my aforementioned essay.

[86] See appendix I, "What Does it Mean to Say that the Soul is the Form of the Body?"

individuated? Are animal souls immortal? If so, where do they go when animals die? Do plants have souls as well? And so on. Even in the worst case, however, the price does not seem to me to be too high to pay. Perhaps all dogs *do* go to Heaven. Who knows?

The Resurrection of the Body

Classical Platonic Dualism, which sees embodiment as a punishment, dependence on the senses a limitation of the soul's powers, and the liberation of the soul from the body as the return of the soul to its natural home, explicitly denies both the necessity and desirability of the bodily resurrection. Christianity, however, teaches in no uncertain terms that there will be a general resurrection of the dead prior to the last judgment. The imagery used in the Christian Scriptures and the Hebrew Bible leave little room to doubt that this involves a literal rising from the dead and the reunification of the soul with the body. Heaven is not just the soul's return to God; the body, albeit a glorified one, must come along as well.

According to Platonic dualism, the soul is a complete substance in the sense that it depends on the body neither for its existence nor for its characteristic operation, which is purely intellectual and contemplative. Indeed, according to Plato, association with the body simply hampers the soul's operation and death is the positive liberation of the soul from the limitations imposed by sensuous embodiment. Heaven is thus conceived of as a place of spiritual communion without bodies of any kind. The sort of dualism defended here, however, does not go this far, claiming that the soul is independent in existence but not operation from the body, so that the soul *by nature* has no scope for its characteristic operation apart from its unity with the body – only special divine intervention can bring it about that the soul continues to have contentful conscious experience in the disembodied state. Thus, on the dualist view presented here, the bodily resurrection is not superfluous. Indeed, in accordance with what Aquinas teaches, unless some divine creative act intervenes to maintain my contentful consciousness after the death of the body, the death of my body is also *my* death. This is not because I am a body but rather because without the body the soul cannot naturally have any contentful conscious awareness, and I cannot exist *qua* self-conscious rational agent unless my soul is conscious in this way. The immortality of the soul, then, is not sufficient by itself for the survival of the conscious self after death.

Does the soul continue to have contentful conscious awareness after death? Many contemporary Christian philosophers, both materialist and dualist, doubt or deny this contending that human beings, like plays, are "gap-inclusive," and thus wholly cease to exist at the death of the body only to be alive again at some later time.[87] Indeed, those who believe that persons are bodies or strongly supervenient on bodies can hardly hold any other position. While such views avoid some obvious difficulties, this is not at all consonant with many traditional Catholic views, such as the belief in purgatory, prayer for the dead, and the Cult of the Saints. Catholic theology teaches that, in addition to the last judgment that precedes the resurrection, there is an individual judgment for each person immediately after death, as a result of which the dead even now either enjoy the bliss of heaven or experience the pains of Hell despite the fact that the Last Trumpet has yet to sound, while many others languish in Purgatory until the time of their purification is completed. Among these, despite all his vaunted materialism, is Aquinas himself, who claims that a special divine dispensation makes experience and thought possible for disembodied souls precisely for this end, complete with telepathic communication between distinct individuals. Still, complete restoration of human nature awaits the bodily resurrection of the dead. Non-Catholics, of course, will not feel themselves bound by the same teachings; here I will only say that the view I have put forward here is consistent with these teachings and so need not be a stumbling block acceptance on the part of Catholics.

In addition, the idea that persons are "gappy" leads to difficulties in its own right that that are not faced by the view that the soul and its conscious awareness continues to exist after the death of the body. Proponents of the memory criterion of personal identity must face the famous duplication argument, which seems to entail that memory is not, after all, a sufficient condition for personal identity across the gap.[88] Those who require bodily continuity as the criterion of personal identity, as does

[87] See, for example, R. T. Herbert, *Paradox and Identity in Theology*, Ithaca, NY, Cornell University Press, 1979, 127-75, especially 129-147.

[88] But see R. T. Herbert, op. cit. 162-170 and his article, "One Short Sleep Past?" *International Journal for Philosophy of Religion* 40 (2), 1996, 85 - 99.

Aquinas, have to insist that the glorified bodies of the resurrected be numerically identical to the ordinary human bodies that they possessed at death. This leads to a number of puzzle cases involving bodies that share the same matter at the moment of death, a problem by no means limited to the obvious case of cannibalism. It is very likely that each one of us possesses some of the atoms that belonged to other human beings at the point of death and even conceivable that there is someone who, at the point of death, is mostly or even entirely composed of such atoms upon whom other deceased persons have a prior claim. If resurrection requires that one get one's exact body back, how could such a person be resurrected at all? These objections are probably not insuperable, but they do need to be effectively answered. The dualist view scouted here is not troubled by them.

If neither memory nor bodily continuity are sufficient for personal identity, what will do? My suggestion, one made by other dualists, is that personal identity is ontologically constituted by *sameness of soul*. The matter of the body is constantly changing and the body itself constantly gaining and losing qualitative attributes. The metaphysical possibility of brain transplants, body-switching, and so on seems to undermine the claim that sameness of body is a necessary condition for personal identity. Yet, for the same reason, the possibility that someone could "scrub" my memory clean and replace it wholesale with a set of putative memories that were in fact completely fabricated seemingly gives the lie to the notion that continuity of memory is either necessary or sufficient for one's being the same person. On the dualism recommended here, however, the soul is a sempiternal entity not subject to temporal passage, and thus neither endurant nor perdurant considered in itself, but by nature "timeless," though in relation to time as its act terminates in its effect it can be described as endurant. It is thus intrinsically self-identical. Further, inasmuch as it is a substance, a simple substance and such as to possess its act of existence in a timeless manner, the soul is also naturally immortal in relation to the body. By contrast, both the body and the conscious self are passing things of this world, the former a compound substance consisting of many simple substances trapped in temporary collections by forces and efficient causes, and the latter something dependent for its existence on the continued existence and operation of the former. That both of these ordinarily cease with the death of the body is therefore what we would expect. However, since numerically one and the same soul continues to exist independently both from its body and its stream of conscious awareness, it is something that continues to exist through all the changes that befall a person, including death, and thus serves as the ontological criterion for personal identity.

Sameness of soul thus provides a metaphysical account of personal identity. Of course, there is no way for anyone to be absolutely certain that anyone, including ourselves, are the same soul today that they were yesterday, so one might question whether the sameness of sole criterion for personal identity is of any epistemic use to us. Certainly, as Swinburne argues, any such judgments would have to be based on indirect evidence, such as apparent bodily continuity, continuity of memory, similarity of appearance and similarity of personality.[89] However, one might well argue that this is the best we could expect under any circumstances and that the indirectness and corrigibility of such evidence is itself what we would expect to be the case if personal identity were constituted by sameness of soul. Nothing to which we have immediate access can make this to be the case.

On the version of dualism recommended here, I will be resurrected if my soul once again becomes conscious through the operation and influence of my body, just as it was prior to my death. For this it is not required that I possess numerically one and the same body that I had at the moment of death, only one that is qualitatively similar to that body in certain respects, especially with regard to the structure of its brain, so that I possess ongoing conscious experience relevantly connected to my previous experience as I remember it. If conscious experience is continuous between death and resurrection, then there will be no break in one's conscious experience, only the replacement of one, miraculous cause of contentful consciousness with another, the glorified body that will arise at the Last Trumpet. If the soul is dormant in the "intermission" that separates death from resurrection, then the body and its associated memory will supply the sort of continuity that it provides across gaps in experience during life, such as sleep and unconsciousness due to fainting, blows to the head, and anaesthesia. For as Reid points out, if as Locke claims "one thing cannot have two beginnings," then contentful consciousness, being gappy, cannot

---

[89] See his contribution to Sydney Shoemaker and Richard Swinburne, *Personal Identity*, London, Blackwell, 1984, 49-66. See also Richard Swinburne, *The Evolution of the Soul*, revised edition, Oxford, Clarendon Press, 1997, 147-173.

be the principle of personal identity and needs some further principle beyond itself, perhaps knowable only indirectly, as the ontological principle of its unity.[90]

Conclusion

None of the objections to substance dualism that we have considered here - and these appear to be the major ones - appear to be insuperable. As such, the dismissive view taken toward dualism by many philosophers and scientists seems largely without warrant, especially given that the lockstep conformity in favor of materialism appears to be weakening.[91] At the same time, the many alternatives to dualism do not seem to be motivated by any genuine theoretical impulse – they all have the look of *ad hoc* constructions devised primarily to admit the bankruptcy of materialism while avoiding the substance dualism that their own arguments seem to entail. Given that substance dualism is the default position in the philosophy of mind, the lack of a better theory behooves us to frankly admit what we all know to be true deep down: that there is a soul in addition to the body, existing not merely as a function, organ, or dependent part of that body, but in its own right, and that I *am* this soul while I only *have* this body, despite the fact that both soul and body are indispensable for contentful conscious awareness.

---

[90] Thomas Reid, *Essays on the Intellectual Powers of Man*, Charlestown, MA, Samuel Etheridge, Jr., 1813 (Facsimile reprint by MIT Press with an introduction by Baruch Brody, 1969), 356-362.

[91] See, for example, the papers in Robert C. Koons and George Bealer, eds., *The Waning of Materialism*, New York, Oxford, 2010 and Andrea Lavazza and Howard Robinson, *Contemporary Dualism: A Defense*, London, Routledge, 2013.

Appendix I: What does it mean to say that the Soul the Form of the Body? (or, Why I am a Dualist and not a Hylomorphist)

In 1312, the otherwise forgettable, and forgotten, Council of Vienne solemnly decreed that "In order that all may know the truth of the faith in its purity and all error may be excluded, we define that anyone who presumes henceforth to assert defend or hold stubbornly that the rational or intellectual soul is not the form of the human body of itself and essentially, is to be considered a heretic."[92] The apparent object of this decree was John Peter Olivi, a Franciscan theologian who maintained that, while the vegetative and animal souls were responsible for the life and operation of the body, the rational soul of the human person, capable of acting without either using or affecting a bodily organ, was not the substantial form of a human being. Although one and the same soul is both the form of the body and a self-conscious subject, according to Olivi that respect in which the soul is the form of the body (through the exercise of its vegetative and animal functions) is not that in which it is rational, free, and immortal. The rational element of the soul is the substantial form of the body, not *per se* or essentially, but merely accidentally in virtue of its unity with the other functions of the soul that govern its bodily operations.[93]

This conciliar decree counts as a solemn definition on a controverted theological point. Conciliar definition of this sort is attended

---

[92] Decrees of the Council of Vienne, 1, in Heinrich Denzinger, *The Sources of Catholic Dogma*, Karl Rahner, ed., Roy DeFerrari, trans., 30th Edition, Fitzwilliam, NH, Loreto publications, 1954, paragraph 481, page 190.

[93] Denzinger, op. cit., 189-191.

by the full weight of the charism of infallibility and becomes an irreversible articulation of the deposit of faith through the agency of the *magisterium* of the Church. Without regard to what theologians of previous times have thought or argued, it now becomes a *de fide* pronouncement of the Church to which all theological speculation must conform, a formula that cannot be denied either directly or by implication. At the same time, like most pronouncements of this sort, it is open to further, indeed continual, interpretation and specification. While the view being condemned was (in scholastic terms) fairly clear and the option it represented firmly rejected by the Church, the Council fathers made no attempt to solemnly define the relation between the soul and the body. Although the definition forecloses some options, it does not reduce the options to only one. New attempts to characterize the relation of soul to body are still possible. In this appendix, I will attempt to present such an attempt. However, instead of focusing on the soul, I will be focusing instead on the body, suggesting that perhaps the best solution to the problem may be in understanding how the body fits into the equation. Nor will I limit myself solely to Scholastic, let alone Thomistic, alternatives. Instead, I will freely seek the insights of both contemporary and ancient philosophers in developing my view. The alternative that I will offer is a form of substance dualism and inspired by Descartes, although deviating from Descartes' stated views at a couple of crucial points. If such a view needs a name, I think that Semi-Dualism might do, though I do not myself endorse this label.[94]

What is a Body *qua* Material Thing?

To begin with, out of deference to and in imitation of my scholastic forbears, I draw a distinction between the body *qua* material thing and the body *qua* living organism. In the first sense, the body is identical with a particular material thing, composed of various functionally differentiated organs and tissues which are in turn resolvable into a vast agglomeration of individual cells interacting in various ways. These, in turn, are resolvable from the scientific point of view first into chemical, and

---

[94] This contrasts with other recent attempts to articulate the soul/body relation, such as Moreland and Rea's Thomistic Realism (See J. P. Moreland and Scott Rae, *Body and Soul*, Downers Grove, IL, IVP, 3rd ed., 2000 and Robert Pasnau's Semi-Materialism, a view he attributes to Aquinas without endorsing it himself – See his *Theories of Cognition in the Later Middle Ages*, New York, Cambridge University Press, 1997. (The term is defined on pages 36-37.)

ultimately into physical agglomerations of atomic and subatomic particles governed solely by the (for all intents and purposes at the physical level of analysis) deterministic laws of nature. In this sense of the term, we can use "body" to refer indifferently both to a corpse and to a living body. It is a body in this sense that gets anatomized on an operating table by a medical student or that the police attempt to find when they suspect that a missing person has been murdered.

Is the body *qua* material thing a substance? To raise this question opens a big can of worms, since both the notion of substance and the question of whether material things are substances are controverted. Here I will limit myself to considering whether or not the body *qua* material thing is a substance in the Aristotelian sense. For Aristotle, not just anything identifiable by a single name counts as a substance. A pile of sticks, though identifiable and nameable as such, is not a substance despite the fact that the sticks are all spatially contiguous to one another and thus are related to one another in a number of ways. The same arguably holds for the side of a mountain or an artifact like a brick wall, though here intuitions may differ. Aristotle requires that a something that counts as a substance has to be more than merely a heap or a loose agglomeration of merely externally related things. Instead, what seems to be required is that the elements of anything we can designate as a substance need to be functionally integrated into a unified whole as its proper parts, i.e., as functionally differentiated parts of a whole characterized by an overall pattern of operation to which the functioning of those parts is ordered either as means or as partially constitutive and which is not the operation of any of those parts considered just as such. Each part, then, is integrated in the whole in such a way that it subserves and is ordered to an operation that is not the operation of any of its parts considered in itself but of the whole taken as such, and thus as a single thing despite being composed of many distinct parts and distinguishable elements.

Aristotle distinguishes both substantial and accidental forms. A substance is an ordered whole with integrated elements serving as its proper parts and whose operation is subordinated to the overall functioning of the whole. In order to be such a substance, the body *qua* material thing must have its own *substantial* form as the overall principle of its immanent operation, specifying the *general* pattern into which the parts and their operation are integrated and whose operation they subserve. This takes the form, in living things generally as Aristotle notes, of a stereotypical pattern of growth, development, maturity, and decline that appears to be governed by, or happen in accordance with, some internal principle (*dynamis* or *entelechy*) that organizes the parts and subordinates their operations to the production of the overall pattern to be realized in that body. In this way, the substantial form of a thing is the principle of all its qualitative properties and characteristics, whether these are inherent, relational, or dispositional. These subordinate forms rooted in and explained by reference to the substantial form are called *accidental* forms, since they can in principle be gained or lost without affecting either the existence or the nature of the thing that possesses them.

According to some of the later scholastics, the substantial forms of material things are *educed* from their matter[95] Although this technical term is left vague, we can perhaps approximate their meaning in modern terminology by suggesting that they are both *emergent* and *strongly supervenient* on their material substrate or (as we would say today) their physical microstructure. The substantial form of a material thing is essentially a *global* property of the matter out of which it arises, a property that qualifies the whole without belonging *as such* to any of its parts. It is the explanatory principle of all of the many qualitative and quantitative properties of the body *qua* material thing, which are generally *regional* rather than global properties of that material thing, properties that qualify the body only in one or another region, aspect, or non-essential respect. Because the substantial form of a material thing is a global property of that thing, we will detect no presence of that form through mere examination of that thing's physical microstructure by itself. Instead, we begin from what we are given as phenomenal data in sense-perception and seek theoretical explanation of these observable phenomena in the categories of physiological, chemical, and physical analysis. By establishing correlations between what we observe and processes occurring at each subsequent level

---

[95] On this point, see Dennis Deschene, *Physiologia: Natural Philosophy in Late Aristotelian and Cartesian Thought*, Ithaca, NY, Cornell University Press, 1996, 122-167; see especially 139-44. The rational soul is not educed from matter according to these figures, which is a reason for supposing that the rational soul is not the form of the body *qua* material thing. There is a good deal more to all this than I can discuss here and which I hope is irrelevant to the conclusions I want to draw. However, since I am not an expert in this area, I have to leave this question open.

of theoretical analysis, we show how what we posit at each level is dependent on (even if not reducible without remainder) the level below it, until we reach the level of the *mikra*, the ultimate level of physical analysis, whatever this may turn out to be.

In terms of theoretical explanation, we account for what occurs at higher levels by reference to what happens at lower levels by correlating processes occurring at the higher levels with ones occurring at the lower levels. In the order of this sort of explanation, the direction of flow is downward. However, since the lower levels of explanation carry with them no inkling of what is going on at the higher levels - there can be no licit "upward deduction" of what must happen on the higher level from knowledge of what is going on at the lower considered in itself - the order of intelligibility is the reverse of the order of explanation. What happens at the lower levels – in particular at the level of the *mikra* – will appear to an observer limited solely to that level and information about its elements, no matter how exhaustive, to be merely a random agglomeration of externally related objects, like a pile of sticks. The interactions between these elements and the processes those interactions constitute can only be apprehended as theoretically significant and meaningful by relating them to higher levels and the processes occurring there, something that requires independent access to those levels in order to be available to us. This is why the search for explanations must begin from sense-perception, which constitutes its objects as the appearances of material things, then proceed to an examination of its proper parts as perceptually apprehended, and only then proceed to the positing of imperceptible theoretical entities supposedly constituting the noumenal matter of material things. Even though we have a tendency to take these theoretical entities as more real than the material things whose matter they constitute, it remains that our only access to these entities is and remains sense-perception focused on material things that have both form and matter, and for which it is form, not matter, that is the principle of intelligibility. Our dual tendencies first, to confuse explanation with either theoretical or ontological reduction and second, to focus on the *mikra* to the exclusion of the other levels, dismissing them as mere phenomena without substantial reality, are perhaps understandable but nevertheless erroneous.

If the human body *qua* material thing is a substance, then it must have a substantial form, for which some late medievals coined the term *forma corporeitatis*.[96] Within the current paradigm, the natural place to locate this *forma* would be in the body's DNA as the master plan encoded there that governs every organic element, structure, stage of development, phenotypic expression, bodily disposition, and potentiality for change possessed by that body. The body *qua* material thing, as substance, would then unfold in actuality in accordance with that master plan, such that each action, property, and process occurring within it would be ultimately grounded in that plan insofar as these things either express or are conditioned by that thing's bodily states. The *forma corporeitatis*, then, constitutes the *nature* or *realized essence* of the body *qua* material thing. It is thus the principle of intelligibility for the body *qua* material thing and, as multiply exemplifiable by numerous individuals, constitutes both the abstract essence apprehended as in the form of a concept and the subject of nominal (i.e. qualitative) definition. In the same way, it is also the source of the truth-conditions for every true, descriptive/qualitative judgment about that body *qua* material thing. In the same way, it provides the non-propositional foundation for all sound inferences about the body *qua* material thing in accordance with the rules of material (as opposed to merely formal) logic. Some of these judgments and inferences concern the body as a whole, while others concern its perceptible proper parts. All of these find their content, objects, and justification at the level of sense-perception understood as the apprehension of the perceptible qualities of material things. Beginning from these empirically grounded judgments, we are then able to advance to the understanding of that body theoretically comprehended as a physical object.

The Body *qua* Material Thing and the Soul

I have just characterized the body *qua* material thing, as a substance with its own substantial form, the *forma corporeitatis*, the pattern of that body's organization and development encoded in its DNA. This *forma* is a global, emergent feature of the body *qua* material thing, one that is strongly supervenient upon its lower-level operations and processes, while nevertheless serving as the principle of all its other qualitative properties and so of its overall intelligibility as a phenomenal object – a material thing

[96] See Robert Pasnau, "Mind and Hylomorphism," in Jon Marenbon, ed. *Issues in Medieval Philosophy*, New York, Oxford University Press, 2008, 500-501.

as present in and to consciousness as a result of sense-perception. Does the *forma corporeitatis*, so understood, amount to the same thing as the soul, understood as the form of the body?

Pretty obviously not. Just because the *forma corporeitatis* is educed from matter, and is thus an emergent feature or global property of the body *qua* material thing, it is both emergent and strongly supervenient on the body understood as a physical object, an agglomeration of *mikra* constituting the noumenal matter from which that *forma* is educed. Like the observable intentional space of a mirror, a painting or a photograph, the *forma corporeitatis* is in this respect essentially a surface phenomenon, irreducible to its material substrate but nevertheless wholly dependent upon it, without causal powers of its own. The *forma*, then, is the principle of intelligibility in a thing without functioning as the cause either of its existence or its operation. Instead, on this picture, all of the efficient causal processes by means of which the various parts and properties of the body are developed and manifested are accounted for and referred to the lower levels of analysis, and ultimately, to the level of the *mikra*.

Aristotle, of course, assigned important management functions to the soul, especially in its vegetative and animal aspects.[97] It is the soul that makes the body live by being present in it as *dynamis*. It is the soul that brings about growth by converting outside matter and energy into the matter of the living thing, thus exercising the function of nutrition. The soul is also the principle of growth, movement and sensation in the bodies of plants and animals. And so on. Even latter-day Aristotelians have wanted to make claims like this on behalf of the soul.[98] However, modern medical science finds no "gaps" in the efficient causal processes occurring in the body for which we need to postulate something called "the soul" to account for or explain. All of the living functions that Aristotle once assigned to the soul, and later thinkers to some quasi-physical *tertium quid* such as animal spirits, *élan vital*, or *chi*, are now thoroughly understood to be governed by purely mechanical, chemical and physical processes occurring within the body, so that there seems to be no room, at the horizontal level

---

[97] See Aristotle, *De Anima* II, chapter 4-6, III, 3.

[98] James B. Reichmann, S.J, *The Philosophy of the Human Person*, Chicago, IL, Loyola University Press, 1985, 227-235.

of efficient causation, for input from any higher-level source in governing the day-to-day operation of the body. Like the intentional space of a mirror, picture, or painting, the *forma corporeitatis* seems to be causally inert.

Of course, there are also important differences between these two cases. As the body's nature *qua* material thing, the *forma corporeitatis* is also its principle of substantial unity (what makes this agglomeration of *mikra* a single thing) and the principle of all of its proper parts and qualitative properties insofar as these are functionally identified as such and integrated into the overall pattern and economy of the body's operation. The intentional field of a mirror (etc.), although it makes all the contents that appear there to be present in a single, non-physical space, itself is neither the principle of unity for the representational content of that field nor the principle of the contents that appear there. These must be referred, first to the picture *qua* material thing and then the picture *qua* physical object as reconstructed in the categories of theoretical natural science.[99] Even so, it seems that the *forma* can accomplish these significant tasks without possessing any powers of governance over the operation of the body *qua* material thing. The *forma corporeitatis*, then, cannot be thought of as the soul, or even as one of the aspects or elements of the soul. If we are to find a place for the soul as the substantial form of the body, we need to reconceive the body and to reconceive it in such a way that it is something more or other than simply what is revealed to us by medical research. To that task I now turn.

The Body *qua* Organism or Living Body

I already noted earlier in this appendix, there is another notion of body that we commonly employ in ordinary language; this is the notion of a body as a *living organism*, a sense in which we contrast the body with a corpse. When we conceive of the body as organic, or as a living organism, we conceive of it as actually operating as a living thing, exercising its various bodily organs and powers – something singularly absent in the case of a dead body or a corpse. The presence of DNA is not enough to explain the difference here; after all, even a dead body contains DNA. The singular difference between a living body or *organism* and a dead body is that in the

---

[99] V. C. Aldrich, "Mirrors, Pictures, Words and Perceptions," *Philosophy*, 55 (211): 39-56, 1979.

case of the former there is *operation*, the actual occurrence of change and development within the body in accordance with the master plan for that activity, the *forma corporeitatis* encoded in the DNA. In a corpse, all such activity has ceased, and the body is in a rapid state of decay into its elements.

Of course, there is nowadays strong resistance to the introduction of any principle extrinsic to the body in order to explain the difference between a living body and a corpse. Life, we are told, is a "chemical reaction," such that given the external and internal necessary conditions for the various physical and chemical processes that characterize living organisms to occur, they simply do so without further ado, in such a manner that no gaps appear that need to be explained by reference to a soul. However, the apparent self-sufficiency of this process may be only an illusion produced by a certain way of looking at the matter, one that is notoriously difficult to justify from the philosophical point of view. This story relies on the early modern conception of causation, which treats all causes as instances of what we now call efficient causation. According to this account of causation, causation is a relation between discrete events that are regularly ordered in time such that the first always precedes the second. On the basis of this constant conjunction, causal realists postulate a productive or "bringing about" relation between the prior and the posterior events in the sequence which necessitates, not merely the way in which we encounter that sequence in experience, but also reflects or represents some productive process occurring in nature itself, which in turn explains the regularity we experience and the necessity we attribute to its occurrence.

The problems with this view of causation are well known, though conveniently ignored by philosophers and scientists in most contexts. I refer, of course, to Hume's devastating critique of this account of causation in the *Treatise* and *First Enquiry*, which has never been refuted and has led many thinkers, most notably Kant, to reject causal realism in favor of some sort of anti-realism about natural causes. Indeed, this critique is so well known among philosophers that there is no need to review it here. Although everyone nods the head in Hume's direction when Hume's critique of the doctrines of the causal relation and the doctrine of the "necessary connexion" between cause and effect is mentioned, most philosophers and scientists continue to accept the truth of causal realism despite the fact that on their own naturalistic principles this belief can be at best an article of faith and at worst a mere scientistic prejudice.

On the one hand, as Hume points out, neither "the causal relation" nor the "necessary connexion" between cause and effect can be directly observed, merely posited as that which explains what we do observe. Yet, given that all knowledge depends on sense-experience, it seems that these notions are empty and vain, no more meaningful than the "powers" and "occult qualities" attributed to bodies by the Scholastics. Further, as he goes on to argue at great length, the real existence of causal connections between discrete events or of causal necessity in nature cannot be proven or justified either deductively or inductively. If we believe this, it is only because we cannot do otherwise due to the influence of custom and habit.

More than this, it needs to be noted that this difficulty about causation is the worm at the heart of the New Science itself, merely an aspect of the general epistemological problem generated by Galilean physicalism, the thesis that reality consists solely of the entities and properties posited by the New Science, all of which transcend the realm of sense-experience. Since these physically real things, and thus real causal connections between them, transcend sense-experience and are unobservable in principle, we can ultimately have no reason either to believe that they exist or that they are anything like what we imagine them to be. Inasmuch as the New Science cuts us off from reality and confines us to a realm of appearances, it also undermines scientific realism itself. The New Science, then, is epistemically self-refuting - even if it is true, we can never have any reason for supposing that it is.[100]

Of course, this does not stop us from inventing and positing hidden forces, mechanisms, and processes in order to constitute our perceptual objects as material things existing independently of our awareness of them, and even of taking the existence of these posited entities and processes to be "well-confirmed" by scientific investigation. However, whatever we posit to be the mechanism or entity serving as the "necessary connexion" between cause and effect itself needs to be

---

[100] See my book, *The Proof of the External World*, Eugene, OR., Wipf and Stock, 2008, Chapter 1. I have discussed the problems with Galilean physicalism in my *Physicalism and Scientific Realism* and *Reason and Illusion*, both published by Amazon CreateSpace, 2022 and in many other places.

connected to both cause and effect since it is itself, in its turn, just another discrete member of the causal series. In that case, there seems to be only two alternatives possible. First, we simply assert that some cases involving causal connection are simply basic and not further analyzable, involving some sort of immediate productive process incapable of further inspection or explanation. In that case, explanation just comes to an end and that end is simply a mystery that admits of no further investigation, so that not only is our search for an explanation is ultimately frustrated, but fatally undermined as well. On the one hand, we recognize the inadequacy of the explanatory mechanisms that we have so far, else we would not seek for further ones. Told that at some point we just have to stop without further possibility of illumination condemns us either to admit that, ultimately, we can explain nothing at all or to pretend to ourselves that our explanations are adequate and true, at least "so far as they go," a completely gratuitous assumption for which we have no warrant at all, however much we might be able to persuade ourselves that we are satisfied with it.

The other alternative is to attempt to close the gap by postulating further connecting mechanisms to unite the discrete causal connection to the discrete events it relates; here, of course, we are off on a vicious, infinite regress, since these connecting mechanisms, in turn, will need further connecting mechanisms to properly relate them to their *relata*, and so on, with the result that explanation will terminate only by exhaustion.[101] In practice, it is the latter course that natural science has followed, positing ever smaller and more exotic *mikra* whenever there is a felt need for a more fundamental level of explanation for phenomena, but never reaching "rock bottom." Once again, the search for explanation seems to be a pyrrhic quest. To postulate the horizontal array of efficient causes may be a dense ordering is both gratuitous and makes the search for explanations so as well.

To avoid these untoward results requires that we conceive of the causal relation in a different, and more traditional, way. Causation is not a relation between discrete, temporally ordered events each of which is conceivable without the other and thus in need of somehow being "connected" or "related" to one another by some *tertium quid*. Instead, we

---

[101] This is a version of "Bradley's Regress." See F. H. Bradley, *Appearance and Reality*, Oxford, Clarendon Press, 1893, 21-29.

must conceive of causation as a relation, not between discrete, temporally ordered events, but instead between *substances*, material things with substantial forms constituting their natures and thus endowing them with dispositional properties making them capable of affecting, and being affected by, each other. On this view, causation is an interaction between two things, one the agent and the other the patient, in which a dispositional property in the agent (a "power") is activated and expressed in relation to a dispositional property in the patient (a "potency") resulting in a real change in the patient. Genuine causation, then, is not a relation between two events, but instead between two things or substances constituting a single, temporally extended event, the production-of-the-change-in-the-patient-due-to-the-exercise-of-the-power-of-the-agent, in which the production of the effect (the change in the patient) is *simultaneous* with the exercise of the causal power of the agent and produced by it. This, then, is the starting point.

The next point is this. The medievals drew a distinction between *per se* and *per accidens* causation. The first roughly corresponds to the sort of causation that I have just done describing, and the second to the New Science's account of causation as a relation between events. Hume's critique of causation is devastating to the New Science's account of causation because of its inability to justify or explain how the causal relation can be something more than what we observe it to be – regular succession in time. Without such an account, neither causal nor scientific realism can be defended within the ambit of the New Science.

Per se causation, however, is different. Causal processes of this kind are visible, in a perfectly straightforward way.[102] When I see a child tracking mud on the rug, I see the child making the muddy footprints as he takes each step on the rug; the child's stepping and the making of the muddy footprint are not two events, but one. The child, as agent, produces the effect (the muddy footprint) by taking a step on the rug (the patient), resulting a change to that rug (its being muddied). In the same way, the math teacher as agent makes a diagram on the board by drawing it with chalk: the drawing of the figure using chalk (the cause) is the same event as

---

[102] I have argued this elsewhere in my essay "On Causation, with Special Reference to Hume," originally posted to *PhilPapers* and later Chapter 3 in my book *Determinism and Causality*, Amazon CreateSpace, 2017, 56-82.

the making of the diagram (the effect). At the same time, not all agents are persons: the fire, by heating the pan, fries the egg – the former is the cause, the latter the effect, a perceptual judgment we can easily confirm with simple empirical tests. In each case, the agent possesses and exercises the relevant power – to walk, to draw, to heat – as part of its nature. The exercise of that power is, in turn, the single, temporally extended event that is both cause in relation to the agent exercising that power (stepping on the rug, drawing with chalk, heating the pan) and productive of the effect in relation to the patient (the rug's being muddied, the board's being written on, the cooking of the egg) which changes as a result of the exercise of that power by the agent (becoming tracked with mud, having a diagram drawn on it, becoming fried).

The immediately foregoing suggests what is wrong the notion of causation as understood by the New Science and critiqued by Hume. By staying on the horizontal plane of *per accidens* efficient causes and trying to analyze causation as a horizontal relation between successive events, the New Science lacks the resources to explain how there can be any causal relation or "necessary connexion" between these discrete, temporally successive events. By focusing on examples of this kind, Hume keeps us spellbound by the New Science's picture of things, when we ought to be calling that picture into question. Medieval Scholasticism implicitly saw the implausibility of the modern view, insisting that in addition to *per accidens* causes, *per se* causes are also needed in order to make genuine, productive causality possible and thus to justify causal and scientific realism.

As Hume notes, when we conceive of causal sequences as a series of discrete, temporally ordered events each moment of which is external to all the others that precede and follow it, it is also perfectly conceivable that this series cease to exist for no cause or reason at any one of these moments without giving rise to any further events. The horizontal series determines, at most, the *content* of the next moment by reference to the contents of its temporal antecedents; it does not guarantee that any further such moment or moments will actually obtain.[103] We can find an explanation for the continued existence of such a series only in the operation of a *per se* cause that both *conserves* that series in being and *concurs*

---

[103] Indeed, it does not do even that, since in principle any sequence of such events could be interfered with and thus prevented from giving rise to their usual effect.

in the production of the contents of the next moment. Such a cause will not be part of the series of horizontal *per accidens* efficient causes, nor will its influence be detected there. Instead, it acts as a vertical cause of the series as a whole by the continuous application of the causal power to make that series continue to exist through time. Its effect, then, is the whole series itself, with all of its contents; it thus acts as the existence-cause of a whole rather than of any of the contents or the properties of those contents as such and does so by sustaining the operations of those contents across time.[104]

We seem to have wandered far from the ostensible topic of this appendix. However, there is an evident tie-in to my main topic. The difference between a dead body or corpse and a living body, or organism, resides precisely in the ongoing operation occurring the latter and notably absent in the former. The organism *lives*, and in living engages in all manner of activities and operations, such as growth, sensation, movement, and conscious, lived experience. Indeed, the body *qua* organism's being alive consists in its operating in this way. While the *forma corporeitatis* is the substantial form of the body *qua* material thing, like all such forms educed from matter it is strongly supervenient on the body's physical microstructure and thus possesses no distinct causal powers of its own. For this reason, it cannot be the principle of the body's operation as a living organism. Rather it simply dictates, in accordance with processes already occurring in the body at lower levels of analysis, the course and pattern of its development as a living thing and what qualitative properties it will possess as a result. *Qua* living organism, then, the body requires another, different substantial form, one not emergent from or strongly supervenient on the body as substantial forms educed from matter seem ineluctable to be. Therefore, since the body *qua* material thing by reference to its *forma corporietatis* does not account for the occurrence of these operations and processes and only determines what those operations are, in what order they will occur, and with what result (at least so long as nothing interferes), *that* they occur at all rather than not remains unaccounted for. It is here that

---

[104] To the extent that we attribute causal powers to the things and states-of-affairs that constitute the contents of those discrete, temporally successive moments, each of which has ceased before the other begins, such a cause will also have to be a *concurrent* cause as well, capable of preserving those causal powers in being across moments in time and applying them in the production of their effects in temporally successive moments. However, there is no room to discuss this here.

the notion of the soul, precisely as the Aristotelian principle of organic life, offers itself as the answer to our prayers.

The soul, conceived of as an immaterial substance distinct from the body *qua* material thing, can also be conceived of as the proximate *per se* cause of the body's operation and thus as the principle of bodily life.[105] Further, as a *per se* or vertical sustaining cause, it does so without entering the horizontal order of *per accidens* efficient causes as a "force" or principle of organization (*entelechy*). Rather, its influence is simply in directly sustaining the existence of the body *qua* material thing as a living organism and, by doing so, sustaining its continuous operation.

As Aristotle says, to be alive *is* for the body to exist. However, since the body *qua* material thing is evidently not the principle of its own continuous, organic operation for the body to be alive requires an external principle to serve this role. On the view presented here, the soul as agent immediately exercises a power as *per se* cause of the body's continuous operation in relation to the body *qua* material thing (as patient) resulting in an effect in that patient (continuous operation/existence through time as a living organism). As a result, the body becomes not merely a material thing, but a living thing, an organism. In turn, the body and the soul together form a single, albeit compound substance – the living body or organism – in which the soul functions as its substantial form (the principle of its continuous operation/existence as an organism) and the body *qua* material thing as its matter (as that which lives through the influence of the soul.) The body *qua* organism, then, is not just the body *qua* material thing considered as such, but the *product* of the union of that body and the soul joined to it as its principle of operation/life/continued existence. As we shall see, this product is no mere ghost in the machine, and this union no mere juxtaposition of disparate entities related merely by external causal interactions. Instead, as Descartes says, the relation between soul and body is much more intimate than the relation between a pilot and a ship.

On this view, soul and body are separate substances, opposed in nature and exercising separate acts of existence, but mutually dependent on

---

[105] Thus, Descartes' remark that substantial forms seem to him like "little souls" seems to be incorrect, at least if what he was talking about are such forms understood as the later Scholastics conceived of them.

each other for the exercise of their characteristic operations. Soul and body are thus made for each other, capable of exemplifying their natures only when joined together in such a way as to constitute a living organism. Are soul and body then to be classified as "incomplete substances?" No less a source than the *Catholic Encyclopedia* notes that this phrase is, if taken literally, self-contradictory.[106] In a different, innocuous sense, as I have pointed out elsewhere, every finite substance is an incomplete substance since every such finite substance is extrinsically dependent on something outside of itself if it is to operate at all – at the very least, according to the traditional view, on God the First Cause. However, the description can pass muster, not as the suggestion that the soul or the body lack something necessary for bare existence in principle as immaterial substance and material thing, but simply as noting the apparently unique relation of dependence that exists between them in the exercise of their characteristic operations.

Whither the Soul?

Of course, the soul is naturally much more interesting than the body, inasmuch as it is more mysterious and more difficult to know since (despite what Kant thinks) the soul does not appear in conscious awareness as a phenomenal object and can be apprehended by us, but rather only in act as the self-conscious rational subject that apprehends and engages in mental operations over phenomenal contents. According to Robert Pasnau, at least by the time of Descartes the later Scholastics had arrived at the notion that, in addition to being the substantial form of the body, the soul is also a *mind*, the principle of consciousness, intellect, will, and personhood.[107] Yet for the soul to be a mind and capable of all of these things is a poor fit with the Aristotelian conception of the soul as the substantial form of the

---

[106] See the article, "Man", first heading "Nature of Man" in the New Catholic Encyclopedia online - http://www.newadvent.org/cathen/09580c.htm The account I have given appears to me to capture the Council's intent, though it does not correspond to the letter of the NCE account of the relation of soul to body. A human being consisting of a distinct soul and body is no more two individuals than a human body is a set of countless individuals because it is composed of countless atoms, each of which is a simple substance in its own right. The notion that atoms, as components of the body, have only a virtual presence there and exist only in the same manner as two chemicals that become a third after a chemical reaction, just seems to be empirically false - atoms do not undergo any substantial change either in chemical reactions or in the body of which they are members.

[107] Pasnau, op. cit. 486 and passim.

body, especially if we identify that principle with what I earlier characterized as the *forma corporeitatis*. By and large, the Scholastic response to this difficulty appears to have been, and to be, to treat conscious awareness and the data to be derived from it as of no intrinsic interest, and instead to hew to Aristotle's view on the matter.

On this view, sensation is a bodily act, and so too are all the "mental" operations, such as perception, memory, and imagination, that operate with sensory images and are impossible apart from the body. Only the agent intellect, which performs an operation independently of any bodily organ, is fully immaterial and thus capable of surviving the death of the body. However, this is neither the survival of a person nor even the survival of the soul *as such*; on the Thomist view, for example, the immortality of the soul is merely the survival of a part of the soul that lacks even the power to be occurrently conscious in its separated state and, though still a separate entity in some sense, is no longer individuated.[108] For this reason, most Thomists have contended that in order for the resurrection to be possible, the glorified body we receive after death must be *numerically* identical to the body at the moment of death, a view attended with great, if perhaps not insurmountable, difficulties.[109]

I have discussed both the semi-materialist view and the problem of the Resurrection for dualists in other places.[110] Here I want to suggest how, from a substance dualist point of view, we can unite these two notions in a single account. Much more work needs to be done than I can undertake here; what follows is merely a sketch.[111]

---

[108] Aquinas ties himself in knots attempting to square his Aristotelianism about the soul with the doctrine of the soul's immortality, which comes to a head in his confrontation with "Averroism;" see his *The Trinity and the Unicity of the Intellect*, trans. by Rose Emmanuella Brennan, S.H.N.,New York, B. Herder Book Company, 1948, 201-283.Aquinas tries to argue that, in the period between the death of the body and the resurrection on the last day, the soul retains a distinct existence without however being individuated, something that he thinks only the body can supply. I do not find this persuasive – straightforward dualism seems an intuitively superior point of view.

[109] Patrick Lee and Robert P. George, *Self-Body Dualism in Contemporary Ethics and Politics*, Cambridge, Cambridge University Press, 2008, 74-81.

[110] See Chapter 3 above.

[111] I have dealt with all this in greater length in my Four-Volume series *The Nature of Inquiry*, Amazon CreateSpace, 2020, especially volumes IIA, IIB, and III.

First of all, the soul is a simple, immaterial substance. By "simple" I mean "not compound"; the soul is a unique kind of substantial form, not a form/matter compound. While needing a body in order to exercise its characteristic activity as proximate *per se* cause of the operation of the body *qua* organism and thus operating as a unique kind of substantial form, it is not itself a form/matter compound. As such, it is no mere component of the body and does not depend on the body for its existence or for its individuation as a substance.[112] Further, since the soul is a spiritual substance, it is simple in the further sense that it has neither spatial nor temporal parts. The soul, considered in itself, is a sempiternal being without any intrinsic location in space or time; it is present there in a manner similar to that in which God is present in power and knowledge to every element of the created world, except in a limited, finite, and dependent fashion. Conceived of without relation to the body, the soul's conscious life shrinks to a single point, an extensionless, zero-dimensional, contentless moment of pure *duree*. We can approximate this state in those cases in which our subjective awareness of time seems to "stand still" and becomes dissociated from any conventional measure of time as the passage of events, although in the case of the soul when not linked to body, this moment of pure *duree* has no content, no differentiation, and no diachronic extension. For the self-conscious subject in that case, *time stands still* – there is no awareness of the passage of time, even if time passes from some external perspective in time. In this case, the soul thus exemplifies the "consciousness without an object" that mystics sometimes attain through "minding-blowing" meditative practices, which may best be understood as) an apprehension of the now as such.[113]

While the soul as a spiritual substance is intrinsically conscious by nature, apart from its relation to the body it does not have any conscious

---

[112] On my view, since each soul is individually created by and conserved by God, the divine intention in creating that soul ought to be sufficient to constitute each soul as an individual substance. Further, each soul *qua* mind has, as an intrinsic feature, its own unique, incommunicable self-awareness capable of surviving body switches, amnesia, memory wipes, etc. See my paper "Problems for Dualism," forthcoming, for further discussion of this issue.

[113] For an alternative explanation of this see Jacques Maritain, "Natural Mystical Experience and the Void," in Joseph W. Evans and Leo R. Ward, eds., Challenges and Renewals, Notre Dame, IN, Notre Dame University Press, 1966, 86-100, where Maritain explains natural mystical experience induced by breathing, the repetition of mantras, and in some cases by the use of drugs, as the apprehension of one's own act of existence.

experience.[114] Unlike God, whose nature is transparent to His intellect in such a way that He is capable of knowing all things through contemplating His own essence and to know created things through His act of creating them, the human intellect is not the cause of what it knows. Instead, it is passive to and receptive of external influences without which neither contentful conscious experience nor knowledge would be possible. It is precisely by means of its relation to the body that the soul becomes conscious in this way.

On the side of the soul, the exercise of its activity as *per se* cause shrinks to a single, zero-dimensional point, corresponding to the dimensionless *duree* which is the soul's awareness of that act apart from the body, which in this terminates in nothing. However, in relation to the body, as its act of *per se* causality terminates in the body as patient and produces its effect in the body by sustaining its vital operations, it is present to the body at each point in space and moment of time during which it exists as an organism.

In relation to that process, that point of emanation or *duree* becomes the *now* – the point from which the soul as self-conscious rational subject acquires a perspective on the external world mediated by the body to which it is related as proximate *per se* cause.[115] Like the radii of the circle,

---

[114] What I have just said here contradicts, at least verbally, a claim that I made in an earlier paper, "Body, Mind, Space, and Time," where I contended that the soul was not intrinsically conscious, and that Descartes was wrong to hold this view. I believe I have seen more deeply into this matter and am now prepared to concede Descartes' thesis, though perhaps not in the way he meant it. When I denied that the soul was intrinsically conscious, I was thinking of the Platonic thesis that the soul is conscious under its own power and fully capable of contentful conscious experience on its own puff, so to speak. I still think that this is wrong - the soul is not intrinsically conscious in that sense. The thesis I am affirming here is that to be conscious does, after all, belong to the essence of the soul, so that it is never wholly without consciousness, even when separated from the body. However, apart from the body the consciousness enjoyed by the soul is nothing but a sempiternal, dimensionless *duree*. At the time I wrote that paper, I still did not envisage any relation between consciousness, on the one hand, and the soul's operation as the *per se* cause of the body's vital operation, though I think that such a view was already implicit in what I was writing at that time. I now think that consciousness is the subjective awareness of the exercise of that act, as I shall now go on to explain. I am hopeful that this will clarify my view and absolve me of any fatal error. *Mea culpa, mea maxima culpa.*

[115] Since the soul is a finite rather than a necessary being, it also needs both a *causa in fieri* that exercises *per se* causality in relation to it in virtue of which it exists sempiternally. This cause, of course, is God Himself, a metaphysically necessary being acting as first cause of the soul's

all of which emanate from a single point at its center but terminate in every point on its circumference so that center point is thereby related to the entire circle, so too does the soul's activity become extended in act as it terminates in spatially and temporally extended body in relation to which that act is exercised. At the same time, just as the center point of a circle remains unchanged in itself as a result of its being related to the points on its circumference, so too does the soul remain unchanged in being related to the extended body as the *per se* cause of its operation. It is thus remains immaterial, sempiternal, and unchanged by the body to which it is related. Nevertheless, as conscious being, the soul when related to the body becomes a mind, the subject of contentful mental states.

Consciousness, which in this case takes the form of the subjective awareness or apprehension of the soul's act of *per se* causality as it terminates in the production of its effect in the body *qua* patient, itself becomes extended as an *intentional field of awareness* characterized by Euclidean 3D space and A-theory time as Kantian forms of intuition, which may or may not resemble space and time considered as noumenal realities. In beings for whom that intentional field of awareness is also an intentional field of apprehension, in which mental contents function not just as "triggers" for inbuilt instinctive reactions or mechanically acquired behavioral reactions, conscious subjects are capable of distinguishing between content and object and thus of apprehending themselves as the subjects in which those contents inhere. Subjects of this sort thus become self-conscious subjects or *selves*. In our own case, we are also self-conscious *rational* subjects, capable not just of mental states (sensation, perception, imagination, and so on) but of mental acts that possessing and beginning from abstract concepts are capable of judgment, inference, belief, theoretical inquiry, and so on. Any distinct thing that is by nature a self-conscious rational subject is also a person, which Boethius defines as an *individual substance of a rational nature*.[116] Human beings, I contend, are such beings.

---

existence. In turn, in sustaining the existence of the soul, which acts as a secondary cause of the continuous existence and operation of the body, God is also the *ultimate per se* cause of the body's operation.

[116] Boethius, "A Treatise against Eutyches and Nestorius," in H. F. Stewart, E. K. Rand and S. J. Tester, trans., *Boethius: The Theological Tractates and the Consolations of Philosophy,* Cambridge, MA, Harvard/Heinemann, (Loeb Classical Library no. 74), 1928, 85, 85-92.

Elsewhere I have gone into the nature of sensation, perception, the formation of abstract concepts, and the relation between these operations, judgment and inference as the subject-matter of material logic.[117] To go into this further on this occasion would not only be unduly repetitive, but carry us far beyond the task of this present appendix. Let this suffice for this occasion; we will return to it anon. In the meantime, let us consider some further issues that arise with regard to dualism.

---

[117] See my *The Nature of Inquiry*, op. cit., especially Volume IIA.

Appendix II: Could Sensation be a Bodily Act?

Back in the 1960's, the scientists at the MIT Artificial Intelligence lab created a simple robot designed to mimic the behavior of a living organism. Although inorganic, it was equipped with sensors and programed so that it would be able to detect the presence of solid objects and learn to avoid them. It was thus capable of learning the layout of the furniture in the office in which it was kept and using this acquired pattern to navigate its environment. If the furniture was moved or replaced, the robot's programing allowed it to acquire the pattern of the new layout and quickly master the available movement pathways through its environment. Additionally, it was given an internal sensor that indicated when its battery was running low, at which point the robot was programed to plug itself into the wall and recharge its battery until the power sensor switched off. After this, it would unplug itself and go its merry, if aimless, way.

Much more sophisticated robots are possible today, ones that can simulate many more of the functions of living organisms. Even this simple robot, however, can be credited with a fairly close analogue of the animal visual system. Because it has external, light-sensitive sensors it is capable of being affected by various wavelengths of light and interpreting patterns of such wavelengths as either open space or as potential obstructions, and adjusting its behavioral output in light of the input provided by those sensors. Those sensors themselves, in turn, are directly affected by external. Light-wave based stimuli, and undergo an internal change of state as a consequence, which in turn provides information about the robot's environment that is processed in its CPU and used to generate an appropriate output as defined by its programming: to move around obstructions and into open space in order that its otherwise purposeless ramble through its environment is not impeded.

It would be quite natural to use visual language and intentional attribution to describe its activity: the robot wants to keep moving, it desires to avoid obstructions, it sees potential obstructions and therefore changes course in order to avoid them, and so on. We might even give the robot a name and use that name when ascribing a putative mental state to the robot: "Fred sees the desk...Fred desires to avoid a collision with the desk...Fred therefore changes course in order to get around the desk."

Even today, however, most of us would be disinclined to attach any literal meaning to any of this talk. Fred the robot simulates an organism with a visual system, receiving inputs in the form of light-waves by means of its visual sensors (its "eyes" if you will), causing a change of state in those senses which the robot then interprets and uses to adjust its behavior in accordance with its programming. Its visual system recapitulates, in an artifact, a simplified version of the bodily-based visual system that we find in animals, including human beings. Yet despite this, few of us are likely to say that the robot actually *sees*.

This, of course, is not to deny that the robot is affected by light-waves in such a manner that it subsequently acquires information about the external world that it uses to navigate its environment in accordance with its internal programming. It most certainly is just as modern science tells us we are as well when we engage in what we typically call seeing. It's just that there something more to what we call seeing in the literal sense, something that we think is lacking in the case of the robot, namely, visual mental content accompanied by occurrent awareness of that content capable of being cognitively articulated and linguistically expressed. The same, it seems to me, holds for chess-playing computers and mechanical brains as envisaged by the current US "brain-mapping" and EU Human Brain projects, even if these should prove to be successful.[118]

What is this difference? Most of us, I think, would unhesitatingly respond that seeing, in the literal sense, involves *conscious awareness*, in this

---

[118] For a brief description of these projects – with a total of over 4 billion dollars earmarked over the next ten years for their completion – see Andrea Lavazza and Howard Robinson, eds., *Contemporary Dualism: A Defense*, London, Routledge, 2013, 1-3.

case, awareness of visual content, something of which the robot is incapable. While we would all agree that what the robot does is functionally equivalent to what we do when we see, few if any of us not already in the grips of a theory are likely to ascribe sensory awareness or the power of visual perception to the robot. It is simply an automaton, a clever imitation or simulacrum of a being that can see, merely the sizzle without the steak. Conscious awareness is the steak and something that each human being knows with extrinsic certainty that he or she possesses and enjoys in his or her own case from the first person perspective. This evident fact about what goes on when we see persuades us that this is something that, no matter how completely or closely some artificial, mechanical device imitates the bodily processes that occur in living perceivers, does not constitute literal seeing unless it is accompanied by a particular kind of occurrent, contentful conscious awareness of the world. Of course, if we want to define seeing functionally as simply whatever mediates external stimulation by light-waves (input) and subsequent observable behavior (output) in a being capable of processing, interpreting, and reacting to that sort of stimulation no one can stop us. In that case, Fred the robot does, in fact, see just as we do. Yet those of us not in the grips of some prior theory are likely to protest that seeing, as we engage in it in the course of lived experience, is more than just this and that this functional definition of seeing, while perhaps useful for some purposes, simply leaves out of account what is most important and distinctive about seeing, both as experience and as experienced by us.

In the recent past, materialism has dominated the philosophy of mind. However, after a long and difficult campaign, many prominent philosophers have at last conceded the irreducibility of *qualia,* previously known as sense-data, traditionally constituted by sensory contents such as shapes, colors, sounds, tastes, smells, textures, and bodily sensations such as pain. Even hard-core reductive materialists like Jaegwon Kim have reluctantly concluded that *qualia* are not reducible to properties of brain states or any other physical thing - a conclusion already reached by Wilfred Sellars in 1960, who predicted at that time that sense-data would never be reduced to brain states or their purely physical attributes.[119] The long list of

---

[119] See Jaegwon Kim, *Physicalism, or Something Near Enough*, Princeton, NJ, Princeton University Press, 2005, 168-170. For Sellars, see his *Science, Perception, and Reality*, New York, Humanities Press, 1960, 98-105.

contemporary philosophers of mind who have conceded this includes John Searle, Thomas Nagel, and David Chalmers. All of these figures continue to endorse naturalism and fight shy of substance dualism. Indeed, it seems that any sort of alternative is worth exploring rather than admit that Descartes was right all along: property dualism, panpsychism, emergentism, constitutionalism, neutral monism, etc., etc., have all found proponents in recent years, while substance dualism remains the *bête noir* of all but a small minority of recent philosophers.

Among those who stand with the majority against the few lonely proponents of dualism are philosophers of the roughly Aristotelian and Thomist stripe, who despite their adherence to, or at least tolerance of, traditional religious belief (at least insofar as the fact that a view is compatible with the truth of theism does not in and of itself provide a conclusive ground for rejecting it) insist that they are implacably opposed to dualism.[120] Indeed, they not only oppose Substance Dualism, but also blame it for every evil of modern thought, such as solipsism, skepticism, the decline of religion and traditional sexual morality, along with the attendant evils this has spawned.[121] In opposition to Cartesian substance dualism, Aristotelians and Thomists have opposed their own view, traditionally called *Hylomorphism*. According to this view, to the extent that I understand it, soul and body are not two substances, but rather a single substance constituted by both soul and body standing to each other as (Aristotelian) form and matter. This substance, the human organism, is essentially a body, but a body that possesses a particular kind of soul as its substantial form, one that endows that body with a rational nature. Further, while some of those powers are immaterial insofar as they do not depend on any bodily organ in order to exist or occur, the soul itself is dependent on the body

[120] Actually, some Dualists claim to be Thomists as well; see Moreland and Ray, *Body and Soul*, Downers Grove, IL, IVP, 2000, 199-228, 231-232. On their view, the soul is a substance but the body is not. I find this view attractive and worthy of consideration but have chosen here to hew to the Cartesian rather than what these figures call the Thomist view, one significantly different from both the standard neo-Thomist view and the semi-materialism of Robert Pasnau – see below.

[121] See Robert P. George and Patrick Lee, *Body-Self Dualism in Contemporary Ethics and Politics*, New York, Cambridge University Press, 2008. Indeed, there is a long tradition within Thomism of blaming Descartes for all the errors of modern philosophy; we cannot bother to attempt to answer these claims here. While I will only lightly touch on these claims, a full defense of a traditional account of the intrinsic value and dignity of the human person within a dualist context, see Moreland and Rae, *Body and Soul*, op. cit., 231-342.

both for its existence and its operation[122]. Although Aristotle entertains that notion that one part of the soul (the agent intellect) could survive the death of the body, both Aristotle and Thomas insist that the survival of the soul is not the survival of the person, so that when the body dies so does the person. For this reason Aquinas insists, in his commentary to *I Corinthians*, that the hope for eternal life requires the bodily resurrection of the dead and, indeed, that one receive numerically the same body at the resurrection as one had at the point of death[123] This is because matter is the principle of individuation for finite substances, so that my being the same person after the resurrection as I was when I died absolutely requires the material continuity of my body – a belief enforced as a matter of discipline among Catholics prior to Vatican II, who were forbidden to cremate the dead in order to facilitate the bodily resurrection at the Last Trumpet.

There are many points of contact and convergence between certain versions of Hylomorphism, such as that defended by, e.g. James D. Madden and the form of substance dualism I have embraced and defended in Descartes' name. In some cases, for example, the difference between my version of dualism and Madden's seems to be a verbal one. Madden insists, for example, that the soul is not a substance because it cannot exercise its characteristic activity independently of the body; he thus calls it a "subsistent entity" rather than a substance. However, *every* finite substance (as opposed to God, the Infinite Substance) is extrinsically dependent on conditions and circumstances external to itself in order to exercise its characteristic activities. Existence and essence, matter and form, are always separable in finite things at least in principle. The same holds for the soul and body of the human being as well. As such, if the soul's dependence on the body is sufficient to deny the title substance to it, the same will hold for the human body (whether understood as a material thing or as an organism) and indeed for all finite substances. In that case, either there are no finite substances at all, merely "subsistent entities," or it is not required in order

---

[122] This seems to be the view of George and Lee, see op. cit. 74-81. However, other Hylomorphists, such as James D. Madden, take the soul to be naturally immortal though incapable of conscious awareness apart from the body, a view to which I subscribe; see his *Mind, Matter, and Nature*, Washington, DC, Catholic University of America Press, 2013, 270-272.

[123]See Thomas Aquinas, *Commentary to 1 Corinthians*, 15, Lecture 2, para 924 at the following online link: http://dhspriory.org/thomas/SS1Cor.htm#151

to be a finite substance that one be capable (as God is) of exercising its characteristic activity independently of any extrinsic conditions. I prefer to say that the soul and the body are finite substances, independent in existence but dependent on each other in operation, and that these two finite substances jointly constitute a single, compound substance – a human organism – standing to one another in that unity as substantial form to matter without in any way compromising their status as finite substances possessing contrary natures and separate acts of existence. This, in turn, makes it possible for the substantial soul to survive the death of the body and to serve as the principle of personal identity for resurrected human beings, even if the resurrected body is not materially identical to the body one had at the point of death.

However, there is no space here to consider all of these points of contact, divergence, and contrast. In this essay, I wish to consider just one difference between Hylomorphism and substance dualism, one that I consider both substantive and crucially importance in deciding the case between these two views. This is the Aristotelian-Thomist thesis that, abstract thought aside, all of the functions we assign to the human mind – sensation, perception, memory, imagination, and so on – are bodily acts or activities, such that (apparently) the conscious contents of those acts of sensations, perceptions, episodes of personal memory, imaginative flights of fancy involving mental images, and so on - are the contents of bodily states rather than mental ones. Hylomorphism, as these writers and others describe it, deny that what we ordinarily call mental contents occur or exist in an immaterial conscious subject constituted independently of the body as a result of some causal process occurring in the body and terminating in the affection of the immaterial mind. Instead, they deny that these contents are mental at all, insisting that they are states, features, or properties of the body or of bodily structures, such as our sense-organs. This view deserves consideration; in what follows, for ease of exposition I shall concentrate mostly on cases of visual sensation, although what I say about those sensations should be easily applicable to the other cases under consideration as well.

The Hylomorphic view instantly evokes an obvious question: What does it mean to say that sensations (etc.) are bodily states, i.e. in what manner do bodily states constitute or contain sensations as elements? Surely there is more to this than merely that the sense-organs of the body are affected by and changed as result of the causal influence of external bodies. The same, after all, holds of Fred the Robot, and most of us will deny that these changes in Fred's "visual system" constitute sensation in the same sense that it applies to us. Nor will it do, I think, to evade this problem simply by asserting that Fred is an artifact, or made of metal, or not alive, or has no soul, and thus fails to be analogous to the human case. We need an account of why these differences are relevant differences, if they are, and what makes sensation in our case relevantly different from what happens in Fred's case. This is not obvious, and so needs to be explained. Hylomorphists, however, seem reluctant to answer this question or to provide any account of what it means to say that sensation is a bodily act.

Further, it seems that any such account must accommodate the phenomenological facts about sensation that are evident to us from ordinary, everyday lived experience. Our experience of sensation involves an occurrent awareness of colors, shapes, smells, tastes, textures, sounds, heat and cold, pleasure and pain, tickles and itches, etc. as contents of acts of sensation. If acts of sensation are bodily acts, then the sensory contents or *qualia* we experience in everyday sense experience have to be the contents of those bodily acts, i.e. what we are immediately and occurrently aware of when we sense. It is not immediately clear how this can be the case, as some brief historical remarks easily illustrate.

According to the literalist interpretation of Aristotle's view of color perception, for example, seeing takes place in the eye and thus that visual sensation is a state of the bodily organ itself. According to Aristotle, the eye contains a transparent fluid capable of taking on the visual forms of external bodies. When I am externally affected by a red object, then the fluid in the eyeball becomes red, and this is the redness that we see.[124] Of course, we now know as a matter of fact that nothing like this happens in the eye when we sense the color red. This is just as well, since no theory of this sort has the ghost of a chance of providing a satisfactory account of the broad range of phenomena of which we are aware in visual experience,

Similar remarks apply to the suggestion that, in visual perception,

---

[124] This is the view of Richard Sorabji in "Body and Soul in Aristotle," *Philosophy* (49), 1974, 63-89.

what we are aware of are retinal images produced by light rays on the back of the eye. Such images do apparently exist, and if one were looking for some feature of the eye as it operates in the production of visual experience, this seems a natural candidate. However, there seems good reason to doubt that this is sufficient for seeing. For example, if the impulses traveling from the eye up the optic nerve to the brain are blocked or impeded, then no sensation takes place, despite the presence of a retinal image in the eye. The eye does not see by itself, and the impulses travel toward the brain, rather than from the brain to the eye, suggesting that stimulation of the eye is only the first stage of the visual process and not the location of the act of seeing itself. At any rate, the presence of stimulation and the formation of a retinal image in the eye are hardly sufficient for visual sensation. Neither does it seem to be necessary. It is well known that visual experiences (as well as memories, etc.) can be produced by direct stimulation of the brain, entirely bypassing the standard visual system and the eye altogether. In principle, this suggests that a technology may someday be possible that will allow at least some blind people to have visual experience - to literally *see* - despite not having functioning eyes. In that case, it would hardly be credible to suggest that visual sensation for such persons is a bodily state of the eye.

The immediately foregoing suggests that visual sensation is a bodily act of the brain rather than the eye. In that case, sensory contents as we experience them would have to be contents of brain states and in some manner contained in such states. The difficulty, however, is that there is nothing in the brain that is even remotely like sensory contents as we experience them. While Malebranche may have entertained the idea that my visual sensation of a square involves some process by means of which the outline of a square becomes etched on the surface of my brain, we know better now. We will look in vain for any colors, shapes, or other visual contents as we experience them existing in the brain tissue, no matter how much we dissect or examine that brain tissue. Indeed, brain states are remarkable insofar as they appear altogether to lack qualitative contents of any kind. My sensory acts, however, clearly do have such contents, so it seems difficult to understand how any brain state could be a sensory bodily state.

At one point, Lee and George seem to suggest that brain states could be the bodily states with which sensation is associated and that the difference between our awareness of these states from a first person point of view is simply a different way of being aware of the bodily brain state than that available from the third person point of view.[125]   What the scientist sees is thus identical with what I experience visually. However, an obvious difficulty with such a suggestion is that what I experience as visual content is nothing at all like a brain state as observed from outside by a scientist. Given that what the scientist sees, measures, and examines is the "real" brain state whereas my visual contents are merely subjective qualitative events in conscious awareness, it is difficult to see how those contents constitute an awareness of the brain state *as such*. After all, I am immediately aware of my visual contents, but not, it seems, of any of my brain states. If I were, then I would not need the third person point of view in order to do neurology; I could simply read off the nature of the brain from my own subjective states. To the contrary, however, no matter how hard I concentrate on my visual contents, they never efface themselves in favor of something that looks like a brain state as externally perceived and understood from the third person point of view. At best, it seems that I am *indirectly* aware of the brain state, and in a manner that is compatible with my having no idea that I even have a brain or brain-states. Indeed, given these facts there seems little reason to suppose that I am in *any* way aware of my brain states by means of my visual contents and much more likely that those contents are ontologically distinct from such states, even though perhaps causally dependent on them for their occurrence. Add to this the fact that the scientist's own observation of "brain states" as structural features of the brain are either themselves "theory laden" or at any rate mediated by subjective sensory experiences apprehended from the first person point of view, the question of apprehending brain-states just as such, even in this case there is nothing to be made of the suggestion that we an apprehend brain-states just as such.

In this context, it is common to appeal to cases of referential opacity in order to explain how this underlying identity is possible. For example, it might be suggested that when Medea first sees Orestes she sees a man but does not know that this man is her brother. (Indeed, we may suppose that she does not even know that she has a brother.) However, since the man she sees is Orestes, and Orestes is her brother, in seeing

---

[125] Lee and George, op. cit., 20-21.

Orestes she also sees her brother, since these two are identically the same man. On this scenario, it is thought that my visual contents and some bodily state, such as a brain state, could be identical even if I could not know that this was the case. The analogy here is disputable, however, since we can easily classify Orestes and "Medea's brother" under a common neutral category by means of which we can make the relevant identity claim: both are the same *man*. In the case of my visual contents and one of my brain states, however, there is no neutral category by means of which I can categorize these two things without begging the question. If I say that they are the same state, for example, the next question becomes "What state?" The only answer seems to be "the same brain state." This answer soon leads to the collapse of Hylomorphism into one or another view to which it was supposed to provide an alternative.

Since my sensory contents are not the contents of my brain state (which so far as science from the third person perspective is concerned has no experiential contents at all) we are forced to conceive of the relation between those contents and my brain state along the lines of theories that Hylomorphists insist are different from and inferior to their own. For example, if we try to say that my sensory contents and the external scientific view are simply two global perspectives on the same thing which is neither a subjective mental content nor a brain state, we are back to Spinoza's double aspect theory or Russell's neutral monism. If we attempt to say that the sensory contents we experience are one set of properties of the brain state whereas the properties available to the scientist from the third person perspective are another set of properties of the same thing, then we appear to be back to property dualism: there is one thing to which (as Sir Peter Strawson put it years ago) to which both mental and physical predicates apply, but about which nothing further can be said about that thing's nature that explains how these two sets of properties can inhere in the same thing. If we identify that same thing with the brain state and regard its physical properties as inherent and its sensory qualities as emergent from and strongly supervenient on the brain state *as such* we are back to emergentism. If we treat emergence as the expression of some capacity universally present in matter than only occurs under certain conditions, we are back to panpsychism. If we deny any relevant causal powers to those mental contents, then our view collapses into epiphenomenalism. And so on. These moves have already been tried and successfully critiqued by

Hylomorphists like Madden.[126] From here, there seem only two possible ways left to go - reductive materialism of some kind or Cartesian dualism.

II

Despite their protestations to the contrary, Madden, Lee, George, and Hylomorphists generally are closer in spirit, though not perhaps in what they actually hold, to reductive materialists than they are to substance dualists. In the first place, Hylomorphists are ready to concede to reductive materialists that the entirety of our mental lives other than abstract, conceptual thought are somehow exhausted by bodily states and impossible without them. In the second place, they have a natural antipathy to regarding consciousness (= awareness-as-such) and its features as centrally important to philosophy of mind and psychology. Indeed, another thing that they blame Descartes for is bringing consciousness to the fore in philosophy, something that they claim leads to methodological solipsism, skepticism, and idealism.[127] These charges carry much less weight now than they did a century ago, so perhaps it is time for us to reconsider the case for the immateriality of the mental - all the mental, not just (what reductive materialists will not concede) abstract thought. In articulating that case, I will once again focus on sensory contents (sense-data or *qualia*) as my primary example.

The first thing to note is that sensations are *things we experience* and which are known to us exclusively as such. While neurophysiologists can correlate sensations (or rather, *reports* of sensation uttered by supposedly conscious subjects) with events or states occurring in the brain, even

---

[126] See Madden, *Mind, Matter, and Nature*, op. cit.,. 88-221.

[127] This attitude is evident in the dogmatic, dismissive approach to the problems of knowledge taken by neo-Thomists who, like the Eliminative Realists, find themselves having to deny obvious facts in order not to consider questions that discomfit them. See, for example, Etienne Gilson, *Thomist Realism & the Critique of Knowledge,* trans. Mark A. Wauck, San Francisco, CA, Ignatius Press, 1986, Jacques Maritain, *The Degrees of Knowledge*, New York, Charles Scribner's Sons, 1959 and, for a particularly crude presentation of this point of view, Frederick D. Wilhelmsen, *Man's Knowledge of Reality*, Englewood Cliffs, New Jersey, Prentice-Hall, 1956. Similar sentiments can be found in the writings of Ric Machuga – see his *Life, the Universe, and Everything*, Eugene, OR, Wipf and Stock, 2011, 152. That is not to say that there is not much that is true and valuable in the works of these writers, but only to note that the simple refusal to acknowledge philosophical problems such as that of the nature of knowledge or conscious awareness will not make them go away.

exhaustive examination of these states down to the micro-level reveals nothing special about these states, and no reason at all why these states or events should be accompanied by sensation or any conscious experience, let alone be such that my awareness of these sensations should be direct, immediate, and when clear and distinct, incorrigible for me as descriptions of my current experiential state. In this regard, brain states and events are no different than any other physical event, state, or process such as thermonuclear reaction occurring in a star, a chemical reaction involving *aqua regia*, or the melting of ice by sunlight.

Indeed, without the (in the nature of the case unverifiable) reports of conscious subjects, brain scientists would search in vain for any traces of mentality in the brain. A Martian scientist with complete knowledge of the brain *qua* material thing or *qua* physical object but no direct contact with human beings would never even so much as suspect that there was such a thing as conscious experience going on in human beings. Like Descartes, who believed that animals were mere automata without conscious awareness of any kind, he would explain all of our behavior (including our verbal behavior) using mechanistic physics and see no reason to think that there was anything left out by such an account. Our protests to the contrary would impress him no more than would those of a computer programmed to assert that it was a conscious subject whenever the question was put to it. He or she will, just like we do in the case of the computer, suppose that we need to go with what can be justified from the neutral, third person point of view of external observation, and do this rather than postulate superfluous additional entities that play no ineliminable role in explaining anything simply in order to provide some in-principle unobservable referent for our talk about our putative "inner states."

Yet – and yet – we each of us *know* with extrinsic certainty that we are conscious subjects from the first-person point of view that we cannot but occupy in every waking moment. Further, the third person point of view is not an alternative to this, since we can occupy that point of view only by voluntarily constituting and taking it up within the perspective of lived experience, which is both irreducibly "first-personal" in character and inescapable so long as we continue to be self-conscious rational subjects at all. More than this, the third-person perspective is one that *we* each of us artificially constitute within the first-person perspective that we never cease to occupy and can never transcend. The third person perspective is a stance, whereas the first person perspective is not a stance and is presupposed by the very idea of "taking a stance." In this context, then, there is no fictional or merely dispensable "intentional stance." Quite the contrary, it is the objective, third-person point of view that *is* a stance, one moreover that we voluntarily adopt and cultivate even as it is ineluctably mediated by the first-person perspective rather than being available to us as an alternative to that point-of-view. While there may be powerful incentives for us ignore or "bracket" consciousness in the realm of theoretical inquiry as somehow irrelevant or merely distracting, we cannot succeed in doing so while at the same time remaining conscious of what we are doing. Whatever progress we think that we may be making in solving the problems of mind and cognition will only be an illusion rooted in an act of Sartrean bad faith and self-deception.

If we do take conscious awareness seriously, however, we will have to leave natural science behind as our guide. As I have already noted, from the third-person point of view of neutral external observation, there is absolutely no evidence for even so much as the existence of conscious awareness. From that point of view, the only access to conscious awareness is constituted by reflection on the fact that the scientist him- or herself is necessarily a conscious subject if he or she occupies *any* point of view at all on anything, even the brain.[128] While a curious forgetfulness can lull the scientist or philosopher into forgetting this, and thus making absurd claims about the relation of brain and mind, this is to an extent both predictable and forgivable, inasmuch as adverting to and dwelling upon that fact would make it all too obvious that the self, understood as a self-conscious rational subject, will always slip the surly bonds of any naturalistic entanglement.[129]

But if the third person perspective is little help to us in understanding sensation as we experience it, where ought we to turn to find such a perspective? It seems that we can do no better than to turn inward,

---

[128] See my paper, "How is Neuroscience Possible?" – Chapter 2 above.

[129] As is argued by Raymond Tallis in his book *The Explicit Animal* (New York, St. Martin's Press, 1991) where he notes that the theoretical inquiry engaged in by scientists and other researchers, understood as some sort of rational activity that yields truth and knowledge about reality, is in itself a *reductio* of the naturalistic program that most of them subscribe to as that very truth to which our science leads. Tallis is a geriatric physician, not a philosopher, so his perspective is unique and interesting, as is his argument.

with Plato, Augustine, and Descartes, and allow ourselves to be led by introspection, first to a phenomenological examination of conscious experience and, on the basis of that data, to a metaphysics of mind arrived at using something like Kant' transcendental method, which in this case is very closely analogous to the sort of explanatory inference employed by scientists when they postulate theoretical entities. When we do this, I suggest, we are very quickly confronted with the theoretical need to posit the substantial self or soul as a simple, immaterial substance that is not only the substantial form of the human organism, but also conscious mind, the principle of selfhood, and the foundation for personhood. However, there is no room to go into all of this here. Let me simply illustrate how this works in the case of sensation.

Although there are many external and bodily conditions for the occurrence of sensation, we have no inkling of it in or as part of any bodily state, including states of the brain. We encounter sensation as experienced first in, and only in, conscious awareness as the qualitative content of a mental state. It is natural to suppose that, since these *qualia* or sense-data — the colors, shapes, tastes, smells, and textures of things, the sounds we hear, the heat and cold, pleasure and pain, itches and tickles we feel, and so on — are irreducibly non-physical as we experience them, that the experiencing subject is likewise an immaterial substance whose states and acts contain those *qualia* as contents. This, of course, is the dualist view. According to dualism, the substantial soul that has become conscious is a mind, the subject of contentful lived experience. This subject possesses capacities and powers of its own the activation and exercise of which give rise to mental states and acts. These states and acts being themselves states and acts of an immaterial substance, seem a natural home for non-physical contents such as sensory *qualia*.

To suppose that some bodily state, act, or process contains these *qualia* as conscious contents is difficult to countenance. First of all, if the body is substance that consciously senses, then the body must be a conscious subject in its own right. Yet the body is a material thing and our current best scientific understanding of what that means is that the body is a physical object. That means that all the states, acts, and processes occurring in the body are material, and very likely fundamentally grounded in the physical level of analysis for material things. This means, in turn, that some physically-grounded state, act, or process in the body contains non-physical *qualia* as its contents. As I have noted, there seems to no evidence for this claim to be derived from the third-person point of view of external observation; if we were limited to that perspective alone, we would have no inkling that there was any such thing as sensation at all. Neither do we have any evidence to support such a claim from the first-person perspective provided by conscious awareness. Conscious awareness appears to be non-physical throughout, an intentional field of awareness with 3D-space and A-series time as forms of intuition in which structured, unified sets of sensory *qualia* become constituted as phenomenal objects, putative representations of external objects. Despite the best efforts of philosophers and scientists to show otherwise, we still lack any significant reason to doubt any of this.

Not only is there no evidence for the Hylomorphist view of sensation, it is difficult even to conceive of its being true. In order for the body to be a conscious subject, it would have to be the case that matter is capable of being conscious and entertaining sensory *qualia* just as we are aware of them in lived experience. In turn, these *qualia* would have to be somehow contained in bodily states, acts, or processes, all of which are material and perhaps ultimately physical in nature. I submit that there is no natural way to understand how this could be the case and, to date, Hylomorphists have done little to enlighten us on this topic. Indeed, the problem of how matter could think and be aware of non-physical mental contents is, for the Hylomorphist, the interaction problem as it afflicts that particular theory. Every theory of mind, no matter what its content, breaks down at precisely the point where it tries to provide a precise model of the relation between conscious experience and the bodily processes with which they are associated.

As such, we have to balk when Hylomorphists like Madden claim that there is no interaction problem for their view, since they claim that the human organism is just one substance, not two.[130] That is because it appears that Madden holds the view (and so, perhaps to other contemporary Hylomorphists - proponents of "animalism") that *neither* the soul nor the body is a substance.[131] In that case, we need to draw a distinction between

---

[130] See Madden, *Mind, Matter, and Nature,* op. cit., 275.

[131] Madden, *op. cit.* Actually, as I have already suggested, I think that there is merely a verbal

the body (*qua* material thing/physical object), which is not a substance, and the body *qua* organism (living thing or living body) which is a substance. Materialists, of course, deny this - for materialists, the living body is nothing over and above the body *qua* material thing/physical object, so that Hylomorphists are distinguished from this position so far forth.[132] Even so, the same problem arises as to how it is that these two non-substantial parts are related to one another in the production both of the vital operations of the organism and in the production of conscious awareness and selfhood. This sounds like the interaction problem to me, or at any rate the cognate problem for the Hylomorphist. Nothing that I have read in the writings of contemporary Hylomorphists even seems to recognize this problem, let alone attempt to provide an answer to it. The mystery of mind remains, and another question arises in its place: where Hylomorphism is concerned, is there in fact any view here at all? It is to that question I now turn.

III

Gertrude Stein once described her hometown (Oakland, California) by saying, "There is no there there." For many years now I have had the same opinion about Hylomorphism. Descartes was my introduction to philosophy as a teenager. Although I have always been a theist, this alone

---

difference between what Madden describes as Hylomorphism and my version of Cartesian dualism, which at one time I toyed with calling "Semi-Dualism" in a manner parallel to the "Semi-Materialism" that Robert Pasnau attributes to Aquinas - See Pasnau, *Aquinas on Human Nature*, London, Cambridge University Press, 2002, 57-65. It is to be noted that, while Pasnau articulates Aristotelian Hylomorphism as maintaining that the soul is not a separate substance and that sensation is a wholly bodily act, as he interprets the authentic Thomist view, i.e., the view of Thomas himself in his published writing, it is much more liberal with regard to abortion than is the official teaching of the Catholic Church today - see *op.cit.*, 100-120. More than this, Pasnau recommends the views of Aquinas as a useful correction to the Church's "noxious social agenda" concerning abortion and sexual morality generally - see page 105. This will hardly be welcome news to (e.g.) Lee and George, who base their defense of the Church's teachings on abortion and pro-life on the Hylomorphist conception of the person as essentially a body and only incidentally a conscious mind or self. They have criticized Pasnau's view of Aquinas in print and Pasnau has responded. In this respect, obviously, dualism is a far better position upon which to base a defense of these traditional Catholic teachings, which no doubt contributes to its unacceptability to many moderns who embrace contemporary attitudes toward sex and procreation.

[132] See Hud Hudson, "I am not an Animal!" in Peter Van Inwagen and Dean Zimmerman, eds., *Persons: Human and Divine*, New York, Oxford University Press, 2007, 216-234; see especially 216-217 for a forthright statement of the materialist rejection of Hylomorphism (which Hudson here calls "Animalism").

does not explain my commitment to substance dualism. There are more than a few respectable, and respected, theistic philosophers who are materialists about mind. I have always had too strong a sense of myself as a self-conscious rational subject to find materialism plausible enough to take seriously and have always suspected (though I cannot prove) that those who do are motivated by other commitments (such as ideological atheism or the desire to accommodate theism to the modern mind by conceding some elements of the atheistic worldview) that have nothing directly to do with the philosophy of mind. At the same time, being convinced in my youth by Reid and others that Cartesianism leads to skepticism, I tried to find my way out of the Cartesian problematic. I availed myself of Berkeleyan idealism, then Ordinary Language philosophy, then became a proponent of Direct Realism, all to no avail. Arthur Lovejoy (in his writings) and Laurence Bonjour (as one of my teachers) persuaded me that some sort of Representationalism had to be true, and this led me ineluctably back to the Cartesian problematic and ultimately to the conviction that the Cartesian solution to the challenge of skepticism was first, defensible and second, the only truly satisfying response to that challenge.[133]

During this period I longed for an alternative to dualist interactionism and strongly considered Hylomorphism as an alternative account of the relation of mind and body. Finding myself incapable of giving up either the existence or immateriality of conscious awareness, I found this extremely difficult to do. However, I tried Hylomorphism for a while – after all, I am an old fashioned sort of Catholic and therefore supposed to take the views of Aquinas seriously – and it left an indelible mark on my mind. In the end, however, I could not find any rest in Hylomorphism. No matter how I tried to understand it, it could not hold its ground as a distinct position. When pressed at any point, the view naturally collapses into some other view, and which view it collapses into seems to depend on the point at which it is being pushed. I suspect that this is because the formula *cum* mantra "The soul is the form of the body" admits of just about any interpretation – it all depends on what you suppose

---

[133]See Arthur Lovejoy, *The Revolt against Dualism*, Chicago, IL, Open Court, 1930. Bonjour taught at the University of Washington where I was his occasional student. The solution I speak of is offered in my book, *The Proof of the External World*, Eugene, OR, Wipf and Stock, 2007. Of course, neither Lovejoy nor Bonjour would have agreed with my substantive views on this topic and should not be blamed for the fact that I hold them.

mean by "soul," "body," and so on.

The view that appears to be a new, insightful way of formulating the mind/body relation in a way that avoids the mind/body problem either collapses into some other view or becomes hopelessly obscure. There is no there there. Nevertheless, I see great value in what Hylomorphists are trying to do and have attempted to accommodate substance dualism to many of their insights.[134] In some cases, I think that the difference between Hylomorphism and Dualism are merely verbal, and since Hylomorphism cannot hold its ground anyway, if we want to engineer its collapse we ought to collapse it into dualism, which after is (or ought to be recognized) as the default position in the discussion of the mind/body problem.[135]

Even so, I find myself in fundamental disagreement with Hylomorphists about the immateriality of all conscious states, including sensation. Pasnau says that according to Aquinas, "…sensation is a wholly bodily process," a view that he thinks a modern materialist "could readily welcome." He goes on to explain this as follows:

> That is, Aquinas thinks of sensation as an operation consisting entirely of various bodily parts undergoing change in various ways. There is no further, nonbodily or spiritual operation involved. Aquinas is what I call a semi-materialist, in that he believes some intentional states, and some forms of conscious experience, can have explanations that are, in our modern sense, wholly physical.[136]

Again, this is all very confusing. Sensation, as a form of conscious experience, is occurrent awareness of sensory *qualia* or sense-data, which do not seem to be physical in any useful sense of the term, either modern or ancient. Such awareness is not plausibly thought of as direct or immediate awareness of any bodily state, let alone of the movements of bodily parts in

---

[134] See my Chapter Seven above.

[135] See Tomas Bogardus, "Undefeated Dualism*,*" *Philosophical Studies*, 165, No. 2, 445-466. I have argued the same point in my *Perspective and Personhood*, Amazon CreateSpace, 2022, Chapter II.

[136] See Pasnau, op. cit., 59. Solving this problem, of course, is hardly the be-all and end-all of the philosophy of mind and there is much of value and interest in medieval philosophy mind detailed in Pasnau's valuable book. It is well worth reading even if the philosophers of interest to him fall short on this particular point. I do note in passing that this view appears to be incompatible with Madden's view of Aquinas, though perhaps not unwelcome in this respect to Lee and George.

our sense organs as such. Neither, then, can my sensation of redness be somehow identical with (i.e. *nothing but*) a series of physical changes in the eye. We have already rejected the literalist interpretation of Aristotle's account of color perception as empirically false, and noted that there is nothing for us to put in its place.

So far as I can see, then, there is simply nothing at all to be made out of the Hylomorphist view on this point. At most, we could sensibly mean only that sensory awareness is dependent for its existence and quality on such changes, but this, of course, is just the old mind-body problem again: what exactly *is* the relation between conscious experience and the bodily changes with which it is associated? To date, neither Aquinas nor any other Hylomorphist has given any better answer than that given by Descartes. This does not mean that such an answer is not possible, or that Hylomorphism is ineluctably false. That is just how it seems to me at the current time after many years of study and reflection. Nevertheless, I await correction on any points in which I may have been in error.

Appendix III: Dogmatic Common-Sensism (Or, Does G.E. Moore *know* that he has Two Hands?)

Philosophers in the common sense tradition in epistemology contend that traditional epistemology rests on a mistake, or rather a couple of mistakes about the nature of knowledge. In the first place, traditional epistemologists see knowledge claims as inherently or intrinsically problematic in such a way that they ought never to be accepted at face value, no matter how straightforward, obvious, or unproblematic they may be. The second mistake is to suppose that such claims ought to be accepted only if they can be justified by appeal to some sort of general philosophical account, criterion, or principle that specifies what is and is not knowledge. Perhaps yet a third mistake lies in supposing that to appeal to concrete instances of knowledge as evidence for the reliability of our cognitive faculties is somehow inappropriate or question-begging because it necessarily presupposes the reliability of those faculties in the very act of making these claims.

According to common sense philosophers, traditional epistemologists are committed to the meta-epistemological position known as "Methodism."[137] According to this view, discussion of the nature and scope of human knowledge has to begin with an investigation of the concept of knowledge leading to some sort of definition, general account, or general criterion, usually of *a priori* derivation, for substantive knowledge claims against which such claims must be measured in order to count as

---

[137] See Noah Lemos, *Common Sense: A Contemporary Defense*, Cambridge, Cambridge University Press, 2004, 106-131. The term "Methodism" was coined by Roderick Chisholm.

particular examples of things we know. Common sense philosophers, following in the tradition of Reid, Moore, and the ordinary language philosophers, think that it is proper to begin from clear, particular knowledge claims and use these to evaluate epistemological theories – a view Noah Lemos calls *particularism* in epistemology.[138] According to this meta-epistemological position, we begin from paradigm cases of knowledge, claims to which we can expect universal, spontaneous assent on the part of every sane person, and use such cases to evaluate theoretical accounts of knowledge much as we use particular moral intuitions as the basis for our evaluation of general moral theories. Just as we would reject any general moral theory that claimed that the killing of innocent human beings was a matter of moral indifference or that the highest ethical imperative was to promote the interests of garden slugs on the grounds that such claims are contrary to our deeply held moral intuitions, so too should we reject any account of the nature of knowledge that implies that we do not or cannot know those things that we ordinarily claim to know – such as that we have bodies, that there is an external world, or that other human beings have minds.

G. E. Moore's favorite, and most famous, example of an everyday, common sense knowledge claim was "I have two hands."[139] According to common sense epistemologists, I have far greater certainty of and conviction concerning this obvious, ordinary fact than I could possibly have concerning any general philosophical theory or more general set of principles from which I could justify that claim, or any the premises of any skeptical argument proposing to show that my claim to know this is false. Since it seems clear and evident to me that I do have two hands, nothing prevents me from performing the Moorean *modus tollens* and simply concluding that any argument that implies that I do not know this obvious fact must be unsound and very likely fallacious. For the same reason, to suppose that the propriety of my knowledge claims somehow depends on some sophisticated, philosophical theory about the nature and criteria of knowledge strains credulity. Any such theory would surely be less certain and more debatable than Moore's simple claim to know that I have hands, so I could never reside nearly as much certainty in that theory as I do in in

---

[138] Lemos, loc. cit.
[139] G. E. Moore, "Proof of an External World," in Philosophical Papers, New York, Collier Books, 1959, 126-148; see especially 144-145.

the many particular, garden-variety knowledge claims that theory is intended to justify. To suppose that my everyday knowledge claims are beholden to such a theory, far from making those claims more secure, inevitably seems to weaken my confidence in them – a fact not lost on Hume.[140]

More than this, the very idea of a theory of this kind being necessary for me to possess knowledge or properly claim to know that, e.g. I have two hands is eminently questionable. Here an analogy to moral theory may make things clearer. We take it that we know, in the main, which kinds of acts are morally right and which are wrong: murder, lying, stealing, and so on, are clearly and obviously wrong actions, whereas kind, compassionate, and fair treatment of others count as examples of right or good actions. So much do we take this to be so that a moral theory that claims that we are wrong in making these garden-variety moral judgments is not likely to earn a hearing from us. We take it as the touchstone of a moral theory that it should vindicate judgments of this sort and not their contraries. Particularists propose the same thing where epistemology is concerned.

In that case, epistemology will have the same status as moral theory is understood to have in figures as diverse as Aristotle, Kant, and J. S. Mill. All of these figures stress that they take it for granted that we already know and largely agree about what specific actions are right and wrong, good and bad, obligatory and permissible, constitute our duties and so on. The purpose of moral theory is not to discover or even justify our ordinary moral beliefs, but instead to systematically organize the moral knowledge we already possess and bring to the surface and make occurrent the fundamental theoretical principles upon which that knowledge rests. Ideally, such a theory "leaves everything as it is." In practice, the moral revisions that moral theory introduces are generated by philosophical reflection on the *aporias*, apparent contradictions, paradoxes, and exceptions that prove the rule arising in the attempt to systematize our moral intuitions, resulting not so much in their rejection but in their clarification within the overall project of achieving the maximum of clarity and coherence in our shared moral knowledge. Sometimes, this means that a moral theory, or at least some version of it, must be put aside as untrue; in other cases, it is the

---

[140] David Hume, *A Treatise of Human Nature,* ed. L. A. Selby-Bigge, Oxford at the Clarendon Press, 1888, 180-183.

intuitions themselves that are put aside as groundless or mere expressions of prejudice. Particularists propose the same thing where epistemology is concerned. The suggestion here is that we cannot begin, as philosophers typically do, from some general account or analysis of knowledge or of our epistemic situation and thus arrive at the truth about either the nature or the scope of human knowledge. We have to begin from what we take ourselves to know, accept it as such, and proceed from there.

Initially at least, particularism appears to have a lot going for it. For example, we all implicitly assume that our cognitive faculties are reliable, i.e. truth-directed and self-correcting – except when we are doing epistemology. Yet, in a way, this is perfectly odd. Unless we are willing to assume that our cognitive faculties are reliable, how is any form of theoretical inquiry even possible for us? We cannot call everything into question without calling into question our ability to call everything into question, in which case we will be disallowed from doing so to any purpose. In that case, however, from what point of view are we to even mount a skeptical critique of the reliability of our cognitive faculties? Since any proposal to do so requires that we take some one or another of our cognitive faculties to be capable of reliably establishing the thesis that our cognitive faculties are unreliable in order to make the case, any such proposal must be either self-refuting or impossible to prove.[141] For this reason, global skepticism cannot even get off the ground. On the other hand, given that I have no alternative but to assume the reliability of my cognitive faculties and nothing to fear from an incoherent global skepticism, what is wrong with me arguing for the reliability of those faculties on the basis of the performance of those very faculties themselves? Can't we treat that assumption as an hypothesis and take it to be confirmed by an inference to the best explanation on the grounds that everything is as we would expect it to be if that assumption were true?[142] Epistemologists will argue that this procedure is circular, but is circularity in this case really invidious? Even if this procedure is circular under some interpretation, this means at most that we lack knowledge in some esoteric, philosophical sense that only a few philosophers regard as important. The rest of us will be satisfied with a lower standard, one adequate to the needs of our Humian common life and in accordance with

---

[141] See my paper, "Why Skepticism Fails," also on this website.
[142] Suggested by Ernest Sosa – see Lemos, op. cit., 45-47 and references.

which we can confidently claim to know and even to be certain that we, like Moore, have two hands, and all the rest, without the need for proof or evidence of the sort that a traditional epistemologist might demand.

There is much in the foregoing with which I am strongly sympathetic. At the same time, I find it hard to believe that the problem of knowledge can be solved as easily as this. That, of course, is not an argument; what follows is. I shall attempt to motivate the general problem of knowledge from within the Moorean standpoint. I shall assume that we are within our rights to assume that we have reliable cognitive faculties, that our ordinary knowledge claims do not rest on any implicit theoretical epistemology, and will suppose it is possible in principle that at least some of our substantive knowledge claims are direct or immediate in such a way that makes it superfluous to ask for or supply any further epistemic justification of those substantive knowledge claims. However, even after making these generous (and questionable) concessions, I contend that the traditional problems of epistemic justification can still be motivated within a Particularist account of knowledge with the result that, in a straightforward and intuitively compelling sense of the term "know," G. E. Moore does not just know without further ado that he has two hands. As such, the need to consider the problem of epistemic justification for our common sense beliefs still remains a live – and serious – philosophical issue.

I

Consider Fred, a travelling salesman going door-to-door selling vacuum cleaners. He is currently on a street that is unfamiliar to him, and as he approaches the solid oak door of a house on the block he has never visited before, he suddenly finds himself flooded with the conviction that there is a naked woman behind that door who is strongly desirous of making the acquaintance of the next stranger who knocks on her door. This spontaneously arising judgment, possessing the force and vivacity almost the equal of a Humean impression and the clarity and distinctness of a revelation, irresistibly wins his assent. He approaches the door, knocks, and is in fact greeted by a naked woman who responds to him in the eager, open, and friendly manner he had anticipated. For our purposes here the rest of this story does not matter. My only point I wish to make with this example is to note that very few if any of us would say that Fred *knew* that there was a naked woman behind that door, however strongly he believed this to be the case.

However, it is difficult to see on what ground we could criticize this claim from the point of view of Particularist epistemology. Fred claims that he *just knew* that there was a naked woman behind that door, which according to common sense epistemology is something that we can legitimately claim in many cases. If we ask Fred how he knew that the woman was behind the door, he may shrug and say "I don't know how I knew it. I just did." Given that this is a sincere report of Fred's mental state at the time, it would be churlish for us to doubt or deny his claim out of hand. Further, in rejecting Fred's knowledge claim we cannot accuse him of faulty inference or believing without proper evidence. Fred's belief arises spontaneously and is not the result of conscious inference, nor is it based on evidence. So, since we are taking it to be the case that we have reliable cognitive faculties and thus that most of our spontaneously arising judgments are true, we ought to assume the same in this case as well. Further, since subsequent experience verifies his claim, we cannot challenge it on empirical grounds. So, if Fred sticks by his guns, the common sense epistemologist seems powerless to shift him from his position.

Perhaps common sense epistemologists want to claim that while our spontaneous beliefs are usually trustworthy, in this particular case we should doubt that this is so. For example, they might point out that this belief, not being the product of one our standard cognitive faculties, lacks the credentials necessary to count as an instance of knowledge. However, we cannot simply assume that this because this belief was not caused by one of our "accepted" cognitive faculties that there must be something substandard or suspicious about Fred's belief on this ground alone. Common sense epistemologists countenance basic claims to know without the need for external justification. Further, given that Fred's belief turned out to be true, we have all the same sort of evidence for the reliability of whatever mechanism produced that belief (a new cognitive faculty, perhaps) as we have for sense-perception, memory, and so on. Of course, common sense epistemologists may be inclined to suggest that the source of this spontaneous judgment may be some well-known mechanism that typically produces faulty beliefs and that Fred just got lucky in this case. However, barring some independent reason to doubt that Fred's knowledge claim is true, this just sounds like special pleading. Given the limited critical resources available to proponents of common sense epistemology, it therefore becomes very difficult to find any credible ground for excluding Fred's knowledge-claim from serious consideration. Common sense epistemologists, then, seem to be at loss when it comes to articulating our intuition to the effect that Fred did not, in fact and on that occasion, know that there was a naked woman behind that door.

Using a little common sense on our own parts, we may propose the seemingly obvious reason for doubting that Fred knew that there was a naked woman behind the door, i.e. that Fred's belief lacks any credible grounds within the epistemic situation in which that belief was formed. Common sense epistemologists will likely balk at this, since it threatens to reintroduce the idea that knowledge-claims need to be justified or warranted by evidence, but of course that is precisely what I am trying to show. I am thus suggesting that, since nothing in Fred's cognitive environment provides Fred with any reason for supposing that his judgment to the effect that there is a naked woman behind that door is in fact true in this instance – he has only a powerful subjective conviction concerning the matter – his belief lacks the credentials necessary for knowledge. This lack of epistemically relevant grounds for the truth of his beliefs seems the obvious threat to Fred's knowledge-claim in this case and a reasonable ground, in turn, for supposing that the factual truth of his belief was simply the result of a highly improbable coincidence. (They do happen!) Fred's belief then, being groundless even from his own perspective, cannot count as knowledge for him or for us.

Further, not just any ground that motivates us to believe something will do when epistemic claims are in question. Suppose Fred were to respond that he does in fact have a ground for his belief consisting in the horoscope he read this morning intimating that he would soon meet a new friend. Since Fred takes his horoscope seriously, reading this put him in a heightened state of anticipation, making him more sensitive to the possibilities and more likely to take chances in order to discover what fate has in store for him in this regard. "As soon as I saw that door," Fred might say, "I knew that this was what my horoscope was talking about." However, I suppose that common sense epistemologists will join the rest of us in rejecting Fred's appeal to his horoscope as an epistemically relevant ground for his belief, due to the fact that (for various reasons) horoscopes are not generally accepted by epistemologists as grounds, evidence or justification for substantive knowledge claims. The importance of this, however, is that it suggests that not just any ground for belief, understood as something that motivates us or puts us in a receptive state to believe some substantive claim, is sufficient to make it credible for us. Instead, an epistemically relevant ground for belief has to be something more than this: it must provide proof, evidence, or justification for the truth of that belief, i.e., some sort of reason for affirming that substantive belief *as true*. Epistemically relevant grounds for belief, then, are *truth-connected grounds*, grounds that present reasons for affirming the judgment *precisely as true*. Such grounds do provide motivation to affirm our spontaneously-arising judgments, thereby converting them into beliefs. However, from the epistemic point of view, their providing that motivation has nothing to do with subjective conviction (even if it is accompanied by such conviction) and everything to do with the objective value of the proof, evidence, or justification those grounds provide for that belief. Further, to count as a (subjectively) rational belief, the degree to which one is committed to that belief has to be proportional to the evidential value of the grounds that epistemically motivate it.

Now, to return to Moore, he is undoubtedly going to claim that his belief that he has hands has epistemically relevant, truth-connected grounds: he sees and feels his hands and these facts provide conclusive proof, evidence, or justification for his knowledge claim to the effect that he has two hands. For this reason, he would say, there is no comparison between his knowledge-claim and Fred's. In the end, I want to agree with Moore about this. However, he and I are still a long way from achieving *rapprochement* on this matter. Indeed, at this point I think that the problems for Moore's position are far from being resolved; in fact, they are only beginning.

II

Let us first consider Moore's claim to know that he has two hands within his current epistemic situation. We are granting the assumption that Moore's cognitive faculties are reliable, and that his visual and tactile data constitute epistemically relevant, truth-connected grounds for his belief that he has two hands. Nevertheless, the question can still arise as to whether the epistemically relevant, truth-connected grounds for Moore's belief that he has two hands provide sufficient evidence for his knowledge claim to that effect. Some fairly straightforward considerations quickly provide plausible grounds for doubt that this is the case.

Let us begin by noting a standard distinction familiar from the epistemological literature of fifty years ago between two senses of perceptual verbs like "see" and "feel." On one interpretation, called the phenomenal use or sense, words like "see" and "feel" refer to the qualitative contents of perceptual acts, as what we are immediately and incorrigibly aware of when we are (as it was once popular to say) "appeared to treely." When clearly and distinctly perceived, these contents can simply be "read off" our current state of occurrent awareness as a description of that state's contents. According to the second use or sense, words like "see" and "feel" are "verbs of achievement," indicating that one has succeeded in the completion of a particular task, i.e. seeing or feeling (an actual) tree.

Although there is a natural tendency to suppose that these two notions map the same phenomenon or complement each other (as they certainly seem to do in everyday life) they are quite distinct notions that can be prised apart, both conceptually and in everyday life as well. Not every instance of phenomenal seeing, i.e. my "being appeared to treely," involves the actual perception of a tree. Perhaps the tree that I (putatively) see is actually part of a movie set, a holographic projection, or simply a life-like painting of a tree. Perhaps I am misperceiving my environment somehow or hallucinating. More exotically, I may be a brain in a vat or caught in the machinations of Descartes' Evil Genius…and so on. As such, to see something in the phenomenal sense does not always provide epistemically conclusive grounds for affirming the substantive perceptual judgment that those phenomenal contents incline me to make (e.g., "There is a tree before me.") At the same time, the second, strong "verb of achievement" sense of "sees" or "feels" is generally interpreted as being inconsistent with the possibility of substantive error as to what one sees or feels, so that should one be persuaded that one's judgment about what one is seeing is incorrect, one would also have to admit that neither had one seen or felt the thing that one had supposed (and accordingly judged oneself) to have seen or felt. These latter notions of "see" and "feel" (hereafter *see* and *feel*) cannot function where I have not, in fact, achieved veridical sensory contact with the object about which that spontaneous judgment arises.

We may summarize the relevant difference here as follows. When we see or hear in the phenomenal sense, we have incorrigible certainty about what we perceptually apprehend when that apprehension is clear and distinct, but not incorrigible judgment about the intentional object of that perceptual act. When we *see* or *hear* in the strong "verb of achievement" sense, the truth of the claim that I *see* a tree entails the truth of the judgment that "There is a tree before me." I cannot *see* a tree in this sense unless there is an actual tree to be *seen* and unless I am actually *seeing* it. Thus, if I truly *see* a tree, I cannot be wrong in judging that I do so, or in affirming the judgment that there is a tree before me is true.

Now let's apply this distinction to Moore's claim about his two hands. On the one hand, Moore can be certain that he sees and feels his hands, since in order for him to know this all that is required is that he clearly and distinctly apprehend the contents of his present perceptual act. However, Moore's seeing or feeling his hands in the phenomenal sense is consistent with the falsity of the claim that he actually has hands, since he may be mistaken, hallucinating, or systematically deceived by some outside force. In that case, for him to claim that he has hands on the basis of what he currently sees in the phenomenal sense exceeds what the cognitive grounds available to Moore in his current epistemic situation will support. On the other hand, if Moore claims that he *sees* and *feels* his hands and on that basis knows that he has hands, then since the first claim entails the second on the strong construal of the "verb of achievement" sense of "see" and "feel," if he in fact *seeing* and *feeling* his hands, then he straightforwardly knows that he has hands as well.

However, the difficulty here is that, given that there is no phenomenological difference between seeing and feeling in the phenomenal sense and *seeing* and *feeling* in the strong "verb of achievement" sense, Moore is in no position to determine whether the cognitive grounds for in his current epistemic situation entail the claim that he has hands. He may mistakenly believe that he *sees* and *feels* his hands when in fact he merely sees and feels them. Since there is no intraexperiential way to distinguish cases of *seeing* and *feeling* in the strong "verb of achievement" sense from merely seeing and feeling in the phenomenal sense, the perceptual contents of my acts of seeing and feeling as I apprehend them in consciousness remain ambiguous between these two possible states-of-affairs. So, on either construal, it appears that G. E. Moore does not know that he has hands.

In this context, the *modus tollens* strategy employed by some common sense philosophers is clearly inadequate. Consider the following Moorean response to the foregoing argument:

1. I know that I have hands.
2. If I know that I have hands, then when I am "appeared to handedly" I *see* and *feel* my hands.
3. I am "appeared to handedly."
4. Therefore, I *see* and *feel* my hands.

We cannot suppose (as premise one suggests) that Moore just *knows* that he has hands prior to and independently of all grounds whatever; in that case, we could not distinguish him from Fred in our earlier example. Nor can we argue for this claim solely from some general claim about the reliability of our cognitive faculties without abandoning the epistemic particularism endorsed by Common Sense epistemologists. If Moore is to make this claim about his hands on this occasion, he must do so on the basis of the grounds available to him in his current epistemic situation. This means, then, that his belief that he has hands depends on the epistemic status of those grounds, in this case the perceptual contents of his current mental state, i.e. what he sees and feels in the neutral, purely phenomenological sense.

It is not true, on every occasion, that when I am "appeared to handedly" that I *see* and *feel* my hands; sometimes I am mistaken or deceived in such a manner that I merely see and feel my hands in the phenomenal sense. Since there is no purely intraexperiential way to distinguish mere seeing and feeling in the phenomenal sense from *seeing* and *feeling* in the strong "verb of achievement" sense, the truth of this claim is not guaranteed on *any* occasion that I am "appeared to handedly," since it is always possible that I am merely seeing and feeling my hands in the phenomenal sense and not *seeing* and *feeling* them in the strong "verb of achievement" sense. As such, the fact that I see and feel my hands is not one that can simply be read off my current state of occurrent experience.

For this reasons, then, there is no guarantee that I ever *see* and *feel* my hands on *any* occasion that I am "appeared to handedly," even if I do have hands and even if I do in fact *see* and *feel* my hands on many, even most, occasions, *including that in which Moore claims that he has hands*. This is because the fact that Moore *sees* and *feels* his hands (as opposed to merely sees and feels them) is not accessible to Moore on the basis of the epistemic grounds available to him in that particular epistemic situation, or in any particular epistemic situation in which he could conceivably find himself. Therefore, Moore is in no position to know that he *sees* or *feels* his own hands on this occasion; nothing in his current epistemic situation rules out the possibility he could be mistaken or deceived. This will hold even if, on this occasion, Moore has hands and does in fact *see* and *feel* his hands. As such, the epistemic grounds available to Moore in his current epistemic situation, even if epistemically relevant and truth-connected, are nevertheless insufficient to the task of grounding Moore's claim that he has two hands, because he has no access to the facts concerning their truth-connectedness. As such, his claim to know that he any, let alone two hands exceeds what those grounds, even if truth-connected, will bear.

To put the point another way, consider the following argument:

1. M claims to know that P (e.g. "I have two hands.")

2. In claiming to know P, M affirms the truth of P

3.   However understood, M's grounds for P in his current epistemic situation are compatible with the falsity of P.

4. As such, those grounds do not exclude the possibility that P is false in this case.

5.   Thus, in affirming the truth of P, M exceeds what those grounds will support and his belief to that effect is to that extent gratuitous for him.

6. Thus, M's claim to know that P is likewise to that same extent gratuitous for him.

7. Therefore, M does not know P.

This argument does not rely on any esoteric, merely theoretical account of knowledge, only on the obviously commonsensical notion that since I cannot know what is false, I cannot claim to know that P without precisely claiming to know that P is true.[143] In such case, it is perfectly in order to ask whether the person claiming to know that P has adequate grounds for believing that P is true. If we judge that the truth-connected, epistemically relevant grounds for available to M in his current epistemic situation are inadequate to the truth of P because compatible with the falsity of P, we rightly judge that M does not know P. Returning to Moore, then, we should conclude that since the grounds for Moore's claim that he has two hands are (for all he knows in his current epistemic context) compatible with the falsity of that claim that Moore does not, on those grounds, know that he has hands. In that case, his strong claim to this effect ought to be rejected by everyone, including Moore himself.

III

And yet...and yet...this hardly seems to be the last word to be said on this subject. Even if Moore's claim to know that he has two hands fails to pass epistemological muster, even on its own terms, and even if the account of knowledge it fails to meet is not a dispensable, esoteric account of knowledge of interest only to philosophers, it remains that Moore's position still retains a good deal of intuitive plausibility. Surely, Moore's claim that he has two hands is hardly as gratuitous as Fred's claim that there is a naked woman behind that door. Further, regardless of our epistemological misgivings, outside of the philosopher's closet we are no less persuaded in our own case that we have two hands than was Moore. Only a philosopher or a lunatic would entertain any serious doubt about this, and for philosophers this is mostly posturing in any case.[144] It is a continuing scandal, and one that prevents many from taking philosophy seriously, that reason fails to provide any foundation for the everyday,

---

[143] Even Moore admits this; see Lemos 152. Indeed, the connection here is arguably analytic. It would be incoherent and senseless (and probably pointless, too) for someone to say, "Of course, when I say that I know that I have hands, I don't thereby commit myself to the claim that "I have hands" is true." If I am not committed to the truth of P when I say that I know P, what am I committing myself to? There is no obvious answer to this question; if anyone has one that is also relevant to epistemological questions, I'd like to hear about it.

[144] On the idea of epistemic sanity, see Stephen R. L. Clark, *From Athens to Jerusalem*, Oxford, Clarendon, 1984, 2-6.

common sense claims that we all accept and live by. Can nothing be done to mitigate this problem?

I want to suggest that something can done. Let us suppose that I am right and that ordinary perceptual judgments like Moore's "I have two hands" are not, in fact, epistemically justified or warranted on the basis of the grounds upon which we ordinarily receive them. It needn't follow from this that we must regard such judgments as beneath rational credence or look (as Hume does) to the force of instinct, habit, and custom in order to account for the naturalness of these judgments and the, the study of the canons of judgment. This discipline seeks to discern the criteria for evaluating our spontaneous judgments, proposed to us as candidates for substantive belief and stubbornness with which we hold to them. Indeed, none of these sources is even remotely plausible as the source of the universal, spontaneous judgments that occur to and guide each of us regardless of our theoretical commitments. If epistemology fails us with regard to our common sense beliefs, then perhaps we should seek their vindication in another branch of the theory of knowledge – *criteriology*, the study of the canons of judgment. This discipline seeks to discern the criteria for evaluating our spontaneous judgments, proposed to us as candidates for substantive belief and converted into such by our occurrent, rational assent, and is sometimes pursued in inductive logic or critical thinking courses. Criteriology, which stands to epistemology in the same way that applied ethics stands to metaethics, provides us with normative rules or principles for deciding which spontaneous judgments to affirm or decline in particular cases given particular circumstances, without supposing that the results possess epistemic certainty or are wholly immune from the possibility of revision. Of course, some of these spontaneous judgments, such as those proposed by rational intuition and introspection, do qualify as straightforwardly certain for us, at least on the assumption that we have reliable cognitive faculties. As we have seen, however, others (such as perceptual judgments based on sense-experience) lack this sort of certainty even on the assumption that our cognitive faculties are reliable. In these cases, we are forced to form our beliefs in or under conditions of incomplete information or uncertainty. Despite this, there may well be cases in which we are *subjectively entitled* to our beliefs on the grounds that we have formed them in accordance with the relevant criteria and thus done everything in our power, under the circumstances, to arrive at the objective facts and thus the truth about the matter. In some cases, of course, the best one can do is suspend judgment concerning a particular issue due to the paucity of the available grounds. To some extent, this will be a matter of judgment about which inquirers may reasonably disagree. On other occasions, however, one's subjective entitlement can reach the level of *moral* or *subjective certainty*, a state of mind that excludes all non- hyperbolic doubt of the truth of what one believes even in abeyance of objectively certain grounds, assuming of course (as we must in any case) that we have reliable cognitive faculties. Although there is not space to go into all of this here, let me just illustrate how this might apply to the case of Moore and his two hands.

Consider the following argument, which proposes that our assent to spontaneously arising common sense judgments and in particular, perceptual judgments such as those offered by Moore, could be vindicated for us:

1. I am "appeared to handly," i.e., I clearly and distinctly see and feel my two hands in the phenomenal sense.
2. The *prima facie* best explanation for the fact that I see and feel my hands in the phenomenal sense is that I *see* and *feel* my hands in the strong "verb of achievement" sense. (EP)
3. I have no reason to doubt that I *see* and *feel* my hands and, on the assumption that I have reliable cognitive faculties, am in a position to be aware of those reasons were they to exist.
4. If I *see* and *feel* my two hands, then I have two hands.
5. Therefore, I have two hands.

Now suppose, like Moore, I assert on the basis of the foregoing argument that I know that I have two hands. Since, as we have seen, the epistemic grounds for my belief that I have two hands falls short of establishing that fact, to claim that I know this does not amount to knowledge in the epistemic sense that entails that the conclusion of the foregoing argument is true. Even so, the nature of my epistemically relevant, plausibly truth-connected grounds seem sufficient for me to claim to know this fact in a *weaker* "verb of achievement" sense, according to which I have done everything ordinarily required in responsibly forming my belief that I have two hands and, having arrived at that belief in an epistemically responsible way, am subjectively entitled to that belief and am subjectively certain of its truth *so far forth*. In this way, my belief that I have two hands may possess the highest degree of rationally justified belief compatible with the recognition that this belief might still be false.

This does seem to correspond to one common use of "know," which incidentally is a use that we often see employed in common life as the mark of common sense judgment. When the lawyer in court asks an eyewitness whether he is certain concerning some aspect of his testimony and receives the answer, "I am sure. I know what I saw," neither the lawyer nor the witness intends "certain," "sure," or "know" in the epistemic sense that excludes the possibility of factual error in what was reported. Instead, the witness is only being asked to testify to his or her degree of subjective certainty concerning his or her testimony. For this reason, even if the factual claims to which that person testified are shown to be false, we do not find such witnesses in contempt of court or accuse them of perjury unless we are convinced that they lied under oath, claiming that they were free of doubt when in fact they had, or should have recognized, substantial grounds for doubt concerning the facts to which they testified. Moore's insistence that he knows, is certain, etc. that he has two hands can be understood in the same way. He clearly and distinctly perceives his two hands in circumstances in which, assuming he has reliable cognitive faculties, he ought to be able to discern such facts, and has no reason to suspect that those circumstances do not obtain in exactly the fashion that they appear to do. He thus has epistemically relevant, truth-connected grounds for his belief and no non-hypothetical, non-hyperbolic grounds for doubting the truth of that judgment. He is thus subjectively entitled to believe that he has two hands, affirms that judgment thereby converting it into one of his beliefs, and finds himself in a state of subjective certainty, blissful lack of doubt, in regard to it. None but the epistemically most scrupulous can find any ground for denying that Moore's belief, being the product of a rational procedure, is reasonable so far forth. Moore has done nothing wrong in either forming or affirming that belief given his epistemic circumstances, even though the abstract possibility that his belief is in fact false has not been altogether excluded. This is because given those circumstances he could not have done better and judges the grounds for his belief, while less than conclusive, are sufficient to make his belief reasonable for him. It does not follow, of course, that we will all of us agree with Moore from the third person point of view. However, there is no reason why that should have any influence on Moore's conviction, taken from his first-person perspective. Maybe you just had to be there…

III

The natural home of common sense is the realm of our Humean common life, where we do not have the luxury of suspending judgment. It is not to be extended to the realm of theoretical inquiry, i.e. philosophy and natural science, where the goal is the attainment of truth for its own sake. In that realm, we do have the luxury of changing our minds without any deleterious effects on our daily lives and of seriously entertaining seemingly hyperbolic and even fantastical notions, such as quantum mechanics and the modern Cantorian account of infinity. In this realm, we need to be held to higher standards of proof and evidence than will pass muster in everyday affairs.

Even so, there are many contexts in theoretical inquiry, especially in philosophy but also in natural science, where it is far from clear which of the theories or views on offer is the correct one. In such cases, we find ourselves in circumstances in which substantive beliefs can only be formed in conditions of uncertainty. Nevertheless, and just because the consequences of belief are not particularly life-threatening, one can responsibly commit oneself, tentatively, to substantive theoretical beliefs with the full admission that one's beliefs may be controverted in the course of time as theoretical inquiry continues, even if those beliefs are not shared by all inquirers. In such case, if one has done one's homework, thoroughly examined the case for the other side, and done one's best to make an objective judgment on the basis of the available evidence one may still be subjectively entitled to one's belief even though that belief does not rise to the level of subjective certainty, even for those who accept those controvertible beliefs. In that case, inquirers will be in a position to agree to disagree while respecting each other as entitled to their variant beliefs.

Of course, no one should be satisfied with this state of affairs. Inquiry ought to and undoubtedly will continue so long as there are substantive problems and issues to be examined and resolved. As such, intellectual humility warrants that we treat a good many of our substantive commitments, both in philosophy and natural science, as carefully hedged bets against the results of future research and while a healthy intellectual conservativism bids us not change our beliefs too easily sometimes the weight of the evidence is such that we reasonably judge that a change of belief is necessary. Still, we might conclude by considering briefly what it would take to eliminate epistemic uncertainty and make knowledge possible in the most robust sense of that term. As I have argued elsewhere, two things would secure this, one epistemological and the other gnoseological. First, we need epistemic assurance that our cognitive faculties are *in fact* reliable, which I have argued can be supplied by the strategy employed by Descartes in the *Meditations* to exclude the possibility of any systematic defect in their design or systematic deception in their employment due to the influence of an extramundane power like the Evil Genius.[145] Second, as I have also argued at great length elsewhere, we need to reject Galilean physicalism in all its forms (materialism, mechanism, and determinism) in favor of a Hylomorphic conception of noumenal objects – an ontology of material things composed of matter and form. On such a view, and perhaps only on such a view, can we explain how it is that external, material things can become present in and to consciousness in such a way that they can be apprehended and thus known by us in a manner adequate both to the claims of common sense and the requirements of a realistic (albeit schematic/analogical) interpretation of natural science. This will effect a convergence of research in the three branches of the theory of knowledge – epistemology, gnoseology, and criteriology – with the result that Descartes' fondest dream will be realized in an account of knowledge that transfers the certainty of its first principles to the remotest consequences which find in those principles their ultimate grounds. At present, however, we can but descry the faintest outline of such an account in the crepuscular light of a new dawn. "More light! More light!"[146] We look to the horizon in hopeful expectation while rosy-fingered Aurora slowly, deliberately, and by degrees illuminates the world so that it becomes clear to us at last.

---

[145] As for mundane scenarios of this sort – brains-in-a vat, the Matrix scenario, the experience machine, etc., perhaps Hilary Putnam makes a good start toward a solution in his "Brains in a Vat," in *Reason, Truth, and History*, New York, Cambridge University Press, 1981, 1-21. For several reasons, however, Putnam's argument is not wholly satisfactory as it stands and needs development. This is a topic for another time.

[146] *Mehr licht!* – reported to be Goethe's last words.

Appendix IV: What Do we Really See?

In her 2010 book *The Contents of Visual Experience* Susanna Siegel defends
what she calls the *content view*, i.e. the thesis that all visual perceptual
experiences have contents. "Contents," it appears, is a technical term and
refers not to phenomenological content (i.e. those contents of which we are
immediately aware in visual experience) and instead refers to *representational*
contents of intentional objects existing independently of the perceptual act.[147]
Understood in this way, these contents are analogous to the contents of
other cognitive states, such as beliefs.[148] The contents of visual experiences
are not merely phenomenal contents ("sense data"). They also evoke
spontaneous judgments about what is being visually perceived, which
judgments are either true or false. Considered in relation to the visual
contents that evoke those judgments, the truth or falsity of those judgments
is a matter of how accurately these contents describe those objects to us
and thereby correspond to them. The information contained in a visual
experience, then, is true or genuine to the extent that the spontaneous
judgments that information evokes about the intentional objects of that
experience corresponds to the facts about those objects considered as
things-in-themselves. In this way, the phenomenological contents of visual
experiences are informative about the world in a manner analogous to a

---

[147] This is an interpretation, rather than an attempt to summarize, Siegel's position. I find
much of her technical idiom unfamiliar and a bit confusing, owing no doubt to the fact that I
am insufficiently acquainted with contemporary philosophy of language and "cognitive
science." This is undoubtedly to my cost, but I hope the use of my more old-fashioned
terminology does not completely misrepresent her point of view.

[148] Susanna Siegel, *The Contents of Visual Experience*, New York, Oxford University Press, 2010
(hereafter Siegel), 4.

newspaper story or a map and subject to similar conditions of accuracy.[149]

Her primary argument for this claim is what she calls the accuracy argument but later modifies and replaces with what she calls the argument from appearance.[150] We routinely draw a distinction between veridical and non-veridical perceptual experiences, experiences that accurately depict the world and the objects in it and those that do not. Indeed, for every perceptual event the question of accuracy can be raised. However, for this demand to make any sense, there has to be some possibility of inaccuracy or "mis-presentation" in the perceptual presentation of an object and this in turn can only be possible if we can distinguish between the thing presented and the presentation of it in perceptual experience. However, if the objects of visual perceptual experiences were either nothing but collections of sense data or the objects themselves present to the perceiver just as they exist outside of the mind (on some versions, the naive realist view) we would be unable to sustain such a distinction or explain the apparent need to make it.

Later in Chapter 2, Siegel makes the argument from the weaker premise that every case of visual perceptual experience presents a set of properties as instantiated. Since *in principle* the question can always intelligibly be raised as to whether things really are as they are presented in experience - and we have good empirical evidence from everyday experience that sometimes the answer to that question is "No" – we have good reason to suppose that all visual perceptual experiences have accuracy conditions. As such, we should conclude that that which is presented in visual perceptual experience is something other than the thing itself as it exists independently of our awareness of it or, in other words, that all visual perceptual experiences have (representational) contents and intentional objects.

Siegel then goes on to defend what she calls the *Rich Content View.*[151]

---

[149] Siegel, 30. Actually, Siegel says that visual perceptual contents *are* accuracy conditions. Perhaps she means that they are conditions of accuracy in relation to the spontaneous judgments that are evoked by those contents and this is okay so far as it goes. However, this just seems wrong to me so far as contents, *qua* contents, are concerned so I will use an alternate mode of expression here that distinguishes the conditions for the accuracy of contents from the contents themselves, since this seems to be a separate question.
[150] Siegel, 34 and 45; the entirety of chapter 2 (27-76) is devoted to the articulation, analysis, and defense of the argument from appearing.
[151] Siegel, 7.

According to the Rich Content View, properties and relations other than sensible properties (sense data) and their external relations to one another can be part of the content of visual perceptual experience. On Siegel's view, this includes *K properties* (such as being a duck or being John Malkovich) and causal relations (such as X's pressing down on Y or P's supporting Q.)[152] In the last portion of her book she considers the relation between the contents that represent objects to us and the objects represented by them, asking four provocative questions:

1. Are perceptual contents individuated by their objects?

2. Are visual experiences individuated by their objects?

3. Perception vs Sensation: How Different?

4. Perception vs Hallucination: How Distinguished?[153]

Siegel provides her own answers to these questions and even develops a method - the method of *phenomenal contrast* - as a means of evaluating various hypothetical answers to these questions.[154] However, although I find myself committed to the rich content view, my own answers to these important questions differ from hers and involve the application of a different theory of perception that I have presented elsewhere.[155]

Nevertheless, the Representationalism I endorse naturally finds itself in opposition to two other mainstream accounts of the nature of phenomenological contents. First, there is the view of Berkeley, Hume, and some notable twentieth century philosophers according to which the immediate contents of consciousness are sense-data (shapes, colors, sounds, textures, etc.) and the external relations between them, such as resemblance, contiguity, and temporal succession. The second, which has become increasingly popular in recent decades, is naive or *direct* realism, the view that in perceptual experience generally we are aware of external objects and that the same holds for visual experience as well, so that the contents of perceptual experiences are not *re*presentations, but instead *pre*sentations, of

---

[152] Siegel, Chapters 4 and 5 *passim.*
[153] Neither the order nor the formulation of these questions corresponds to Siegel's presentation of them; see op. cit. 141-143.
[154] For an account of this method, see Siegel, 87-96.
[155] See footnote 144, below.

external things. The version of Representationalism that I will explore and that I have elsewhere called *scholastic critical realism* – or SCR for short – shows how, on a certain account of the nature of material things, it is possible for mental contents to be subjective and mind-dependent, as the Modern tradition holds, and yet for independently existent material things to be present in and to consciousness by means of such contents.

Just as for these other views, accommodation within SCR must be found for four basic kinds of visual phenomena discussed by Siegel. First, there are non-intentional visual contents such as afterimages, phosphenes, "seeing stars," episodes of double-vision, the yellow "tinge" traditionally associated with jaundice, and so on. Second, there are sense-data ("sensible qualities") considered as visual contents. Thirdly, there are the contents of ordinary perceptual experience that appear to be of extramental, independently existing and constituted material things, some of which are veridical and some of which are, as we say, illusory. Fourthly and finally, there are hallucinations, which putatively present/represent material things but which in fact correspond to no such objects at all, even derivatively. I shall now present an outline of the theory and the answers it gives to Siegel's four questions - and I will leave it at that.

Scholastic Critical Realism

I have adumbrated the Scholastic Critical Realist account of perception (excoriated by "the Moderns" as the doctrine of the Schools) in other places, so here I will be brief. First, SCR rejects the Galilean physicalism of the New Science in favor of an Aristotelian ontology of material things. Material things are substances, compounds of form and matter. A thing's substantial form exists in it as an instantiated essence or *nature* and is the principle of all of that thing's qualitative and dispositional attributes, including its causal powers and liabilities. Second, it accounts for the possibility of knowledge of these extramental, material things through a process by means of which the substantial form that exists in a thing as its nature becomes an intentional species and is transferred from the thing, by degrees *via* various media, to the mind of the knower that takes on that substantial form without its becoming the nature of the knower. Due to the fact that numerically one and the same substantial form exists, at the same time though in different manners, both in the thing and in the mind of the knower which, as Aristotle says is the potentiality for all forms, the knower becomes the thing it knows, not materially, but instead formally and intentionally.[156]

The substantial form first enters the mind as the principle of structural unity of the *phantasm*, or mental image, composed of externally-related sense data that form a discrete pattern in experience that varies with changes in the perceiver.[157] From this, the agent intellect abstracts the substantial form (which is not itself a sense-datum) in the form of a *concept*, which exists as the abstract essence or *universal* only in the mind. It then imposes this concept on the phantasm and thereby categorizes *what is seen* as a *thing*, and as a thing of a particular kind. And so it is, and was.

As the principle of structural unity of the phantasm, the substantial form of the extramental thing is already present in and to consciousness, though not in such a way as to be intelligible to us. It is merely inchoately or implicitly present in and to conscious awareness in a manner not yet apprehensible by us. The transcendental (= non-introspectable) mechanism called *abstraction* liberates that substantial form from its matter and converts it into an intelligible species occurrently present in and accessible to conscious awareness in the form of an abstract concept. This abstract concept is not an image of any kind nor is it introspectable. Instead, it exists in the understanding as something apprehended by it in such a way as to be expressible linguistically in the terms for which it supplies the substantive meaning.[158] It is thus by means of that concept we are able to explicitly categorize and recognize that of which we are aware in visual perception as

---

[156] I have reconstructed this process at great length elsewhere in my *The Nature of Inquiry IIA: Apprehension*, Amazon CreateSpace, 2020, 104-190.

[157] Actually, this is only one possible account of the phantasm - scholastic usage here is both technical and vague - there is no one account of what "species," "phantasm," "intellect" and so on mean - these belong to the theoretical realm rather than to visual phenomenology *per se.*

[158] Because the formation and application of concepts is an automatic, pre-conscious and non-introspectable activity, we can and do use words to name, denote, or refer to things before we are able to articulate the substantive meaning of those terms. However, our ability to use words in this way and make ourselves understood in a pre-theoretical fashion demonstrates that we understand these terms implicitly or inchoately prior to being able to do so explicitly. To move from merely inchoate to explicit/occurrent understanding of the substantive meaning of terms requires conceptual analysis in the case of ordinary language and formal definition in the case of theoretical terms. Terms of both kinds can be used to describe extramental reality and, on an ontology of material things, neither is dispensable.

a particular thing, as well as a thing of a particular natural kind.

At this point, the phantasm becomes a *representation* of that particular thing and thus intentional in relation to it. In the representation, then, the thing comes to exist explicitly *in* conscious awareness formally and *for* conscious awareness intentionally as the object it apprehends and thus knows by acquaintance. In this way that thing is thus explicitly and occurrently recognized as present *to* conscious awareness and thus reflectively apprehended by it as well. From here, it may proceed by means of natural science to acquire analogical knowledge by description of that thing *qua* material, i.e., as a *physical object*.

This, of course, is a theory about perception, and thus about visual perception, not itself an instance of it, and one that will strike most contemporary philosophers as outlandish and unmotivated. However, this view shows its value in relation to the well-known difficulties that afflict the other theories of perception that have been proposed by philosophers, including those discussed by Siegel.

Other forms of representationalism associated with Galilean physicalism, such as those espoused by Early Modern philosophers such as Descartes and Locke, lead to skepticism about the external world which in turn undermines both causal and scientific realism and thus ultimately the New Science itself. That is because the New Science guarantees that the external world in no way resembles our perceptual experience and is at best contingently causally related to such a world even if it exists, thus resting belief in that world and the things composing it on a difficult to characterize inference that may in the end prove incapable of justifying those beliefs. Without the divine guarantee offered by Cartesian Theism, secular epistemology in this tradition apparently finds itself unable to escape a Humean result. By contrast SCR explains how, even if our perception is mediated by Cartesian "ideas," it can still be the case that material things can be present in and to conscious awareness in virtue of the mind taking on their substantial forms and thus no difficulty in explaining how it is that mental images can represent extramental material things.

Another major alternative in the theory of perception is the phenomenalist or subjective idealist view propounded by Berkeley and Hume and endorsed by a number of influential twentieth century philosophers, such as Carnap and Quine. According to this view, what we *really* see are sense-data and the external relations between such sense-data. For Berkeley and Hume, the visual perceptual field is a "parti-colored plane," i.e. a two-dimensional array of shapes and colors related merely by qualitative resemblance, contiguity in perceptual space and by relations of succession in time. Everything else is merely interpretation, conjecture, or the product of a combination of instinct, habit, and custom. Hume's constant cry is "Consult your own experience!" Yet the obvious response to this sort of phenomenalism is that, if we consult our own experience, we do not normally see "sense-data" at all, but extramental material things. To see the visual perceptual field as a "parti-colored plane" requires prescinding from the contents of our ordinary visual experience and "flattening" the visual field into a two-dimensional array of meaningless shapes and colors. In the same way, one might argue that, when we look at a landscape painting, all we *really* see are dried, cracking blobs and swirls of dried paint and that the landscape that we think we see is really just an instinctual or habitual interpretation of those blobs and swirls.[159] The natural rejoinder to this is to say that we hardly ever see a landscape in this way and that to so constitute a painting in this way takes a special effort on the part of the perceiver. To the contrary, if we were not aware of more in visual experience than what the phenomenalist claims that we *really* are, there would be no need for this deliberate, artificial "flattening" of the visual field in order to get at its true nature. As such, this account of what we *really* see is tendentious and merely persuasive, a rhetorical strategy intended to get us to buy into a certain picture of things and forget about what visual perception *as experienced by us* is actually like. By contrast, SCR explains how it is possible for us to be aware of things by means of representations partially consisting of the sense-data serving as the matter of visual experience, understanding this in the Aristotelian sense *as that which receives form*, something sense-data do without being either physical or material in the scientific sense.

SCR also explains how what Siegel calls K- (for "kind") properties

---

[159] Of course, at least one phenomenalist has claimed this: see Nelson Goodman, *Languages of Art*, Second Edition, Indianapolis, IN, Hackett Publishing, 1976, Chapter I, 3-43. In one of his works, David Armstrong suggests that representational aesthetic experience is merely illusory. The work of V. C. Aldrich is a good corrective to this extreme view - see the essays collected in Aldrich, *The Body of a Person*, Lanham, MD., University Press of America, 1988, *passim*.

can be actually perceived by us. In the perceptual act, the agent intellect abstracts the substantial form of the thing (as intelligible species) from the phantasm and converts it into what nowadays would be called a concept. Concepts, of course, are *categories* and the words that express those categories names of kinds. The imposition of a substantial-form-*qua*-concept on a phantasm has the effect, then, of classifying it and thus identifying it as an individual of a specific kind. Since substantial forms are the principle of all of the qualitative and dispositional attributes of things for which they constitute their natures, they are also the principles of all other concepts as well by means of which we classify things according to their qualitative and quantitative attributes using words that name those attributes ("blue") and refer to the things that instantiate them as members of the appropriate attribute-kind (e.g., "blue things.")

In the same way, the causal powers and liabilities of things, which are dispositional attributes of things, are also perceivable on SCR, just as we arguably do visually perceive them when we experience instances of pulling, pushing, cutting, burning, heating up, and so on. In such cases, what we see is the application of the causal power of the agent (who is thus designated the *cause*) to a patient capable of being affected by that power in such a way as to give rise to a change in that patient, called the *effect*. In all such cases, the kind of causality exercised is *per se* causation, in which the application of the agent's causal power is simultaneous with the production of the effect in the patient and coterminous with it, so that they are together a single, temporally extended event.

In such cases, the causal relation between agent and patient is also represented in experience. Rational, intentional agents are paradigmatic causes. However, non-rational, unintelligent beings can also be called causal agents by an analogical extension of that term and instances of change produced through the automatic exercise of causal powers in relation to similarly unintelligent patients, as when a brick breaks a window or a rolling boulder flattens a tree, also count as instances of *per se* causation. They are thus also cases in which we see causal relations between things.[160] These

---

[160] Events are not things, and thus neither interact nor are related causally; hence no such relations are visible in their case. *Causal regularities* are constituted as such by embedding them in states of affairs in which the observed events are the product of causal interaction between things or of the operation of causal mechanisms involving a number of distinct things, most of which are hidden and arrived at using the scientific method in the context of

results coincide with the claims made by Siegel for the Rich Context View.

Moving on to the direct realist view, which by implication Siegel rejects, we can note that there is a general agreement between direct realism and SCR on the question of our awareness of external objects.[161] Both views defend the thesis that material things are the contents of visual experience. However, direct realism tries to explicate this thesis by committing itself to the claim that external material things are somehow the phenomenological contents of acts of vision, at best mediated by Reidian sensations ("raw feels".) However, we manifestly do not see external material things if we suppose them to be the physical objects described by the New Science, since such objects considered as things-in-themselves possess only primary qualities and not the secondary qualities that constitute sense data as experienced. Further, there is no way to explain how the phenomenological contents of acts of seeing can literally be the surfaces of external material things: the extromission theory is dead and we know far too much about the physics and physiology of perception to plausibly revive it. The scientific picture of things inevitably commits us to some form of representationalism, regardless of what we take material things to be. SCR supposes instead that we apprehend external material things in acts of vision not by literally seeing their surfaces but instead as a consequence of those external material things being present formally and intentionally in and to consciousness in the way described above, one consistent with the notion that our apprehension of them is mediated by subjective mental contents.

SCR and Siegel's Four Questions

Now let us consider SCR in relation to Siegel's four questions. The first two concern the individuation of visual contents and visual experiences. The position of SCR is that visual experiences are individuated by their contents and that those contents are individuated by their objects,

---

already well-confirmed scientific theories. This is thus the work of discursive reason and theoretical inquiry, not perception *per se*.

[161] On page 76, Siegel says that Naive realism is false unless visual experiences are individuated by their objects and then goes on subsequently to defend the thesis that they are not using her "method of phenomenal contrast" - see page 175. However, I find this method, its application, and Siegel's examples and arguments somewhat obscure, so I may have missed something here.

so that the answer to both questions is "yes." What makes a visual experience an experience of, e.g., some particular person Fred is that, in virtue of its content, Fred is both formally and intentionally present in and to occurrent conscious awareness by means of his substantial form and perceptually individuated by the perceivable qualitative attributes in virtue of which Fred is thus visually apprehended as Fred by the perceiver. This will be the case in every instance in which I visually perceive Fred, regardless of variation in time, place, perspective, or even changes in Fred's appearance, and constitutes a constant, objective, and invariant, element in every such visual experience. In such case, it is to be noted that this fact cannot simply be read off the visual experience like we can simply read off sensible qualities such as shape or color. That which individuates an experience need not be immediately accessible to us.

Consider a Gettier-style case like one discussed by Siegel. Suppose that Fred and Ed are identical twins separated at birth, a fact now known to no one, not even Fred and Ed themselves. Fred, as it happens, is an acquaintance of mine but I am unaware that Ed even exists. One day, I see Ed sitting under a tree, head bowed, body slumped, and evidently depressed. On this evidence, I form the belief that Fred is sad. Suppose further that Fred, who is miles away in his apartment, is in fact sad at the same time that I form that judgment based on my apprehension of Ed. My intuitions, which I suppose that many others will share, is that my belief that Fred is sad, even if accidentally true, is not justified for me because it is not rightly related to its intentional object. My belief that the person that I see is sad is true based on my visual experience, but my belief that Fred is sad is not true based on that evidence, despite the fact that there is no difference between the contents that I see in this case and what I would have seen if it had seen Fred and not Ed in the park. The plain fact of the matter is that I see Ed, not Fred, and my belief that Fred is sad is based on the mistaken assumption that I currently see Fred.

The fact that I do not know this and cannot know this simply on the basis of an introspective awareness or examination of my visual contents, makes no odds. If I was later apprised of Ed's existence and was convinced that it was Ed, not Fred, that I saw on that occasion, I would admit that my belief that Fred was sad was not justified for me on that occasion, even if it happened to be true. Thus, I conclude that my visual experience can be an experience of Fred only if Fred is its intentional object, i.e. the thing represented by the visual contents of my experience, which will be the case only if I am actually perceptually aware of Fred, and not Ed, and my awareness of Fred is the truth-connected ground for my judgments about Fred..[162] In that case, both visual contents and visual experiences are individuated by their objects. I see what I see, i.e. what is actually there, not what I think or believe or infer that I see – and that is not a tautology! Such a result is perfectly compatible with the view that, for the most part, I can simply read off the truth about the world from my visual experiences.

The third question, about the difference between sensory contents (roughly, sense data and their external relations to one another) and perceptual experience, finds a ready answer in the doctrine of substantial form articulated earlier. Substantial form plays two roles in visual experience. First, in relation to the phantasm, it functions as the principle of organizational unity of the sense-data, acting as form in relation to those sense-data considered as matter in the Aristotelian sense, i.e., that which receives form. It thus constitutes the phantasm as a mental image rather than as a mere collection of accidentally and externally related sense data *a la* Hume. Second, in relation to that mental image functioning as a representation of an extramental material thing, which is *in fact* what we actually see in fully occurrent visual experience, that substantial or accidental form as an universal, abstract concept is first abstracted from the phantasm by the intellect and then used by the intellect to classify the mental image according to its type. By imposing this abstract, classificatory concept on the mental image, it thus constitutes it as an image *of* a particular thing *of* a specific kind, either a natural kind like a giraffe or as something belonging to the class of things that exemplify a qualitative or quantitative attribute, such as the class of blue things.

It does not always follow, of course, that we will be able to recognize, distinguish, or classify things on the basis of visual experiences alone. Siegel, for example, notes that the way that things look to the trained

---

[162] Fred's substantial form is an instantiation of the form "human being," not Fred's *haecceity* "Fredness". I have to admit that I have no settled view on the existence of haecceities, but the case of Fred and Ed suggests that there are none, since I cannot detect the difference between Ed and Fred by reference to their distinct individual essences.

eye is phenomenologically different from the way it looks to the untrained eye. The latter looks at the forest and just sees a bunch of trees, whereas the former, and arborist, recognizes and sorts the various species of trees that compose that forest and thus sees more due to his knowledge of forestry. In the same way, the surface of a rock contains a wealth of mineralogical information for a mineralogist that is simply lost on someone who can only see colors and textures.[163] In the same way, the use of abstract universal terms applies with increasing specificity the more contentful the concept happens to be. I can characterize something that I see as a thing, a living thing, a mammal, a human, or as that guy over there, as the Mayor of the City, and so on. Using proper names, like Fred and Ed, I can identify individuals as such and refer to them without explicitly making reference to any of the kinds to which they belong or qualitative attributes they possess.

Question 4 seems the most challenging for a proponent of SCR. Hallucinations are arguably visual experiences (I shall certainly assume that they are) and yet (almost by definition) have no objects. Illusions, mirages, the *fata morgana* and so on can all be explained as the misperception of real external things due to unusual circumstances or defects in the perceptual mechanism itself. In the case of hallucination, however, no extramental object corresponds to the contents of that visual experience *at all*. When Macbeth sees the dagger, he does not misperceive some external object and mistake that thing for a dagger. Instead, Macbeth sees a dagger where there is no dagger, or anything else by way of an extramental material thing, to be seen. Nevertheless, he is prepared, at least temporarily, to entertain the notion that there is a dagger before him, until he is persuaded otherwise by a series of empirical tests.

This suggests a difficulty for SCR. If visual experiences are individuated by their contents, and visual contents are individuated by their objects, how can hallucinations, which after all are visual experiences and have no objects, be individuated? The answer, once again, must be given in

---

[163] Language is another medium through which concepts, hence inFORMation, can be communicated and acquired; indeed, in many cases, we already possess the concept inchoately but are unable to articulate and express it due to the poverty of one's language, which can be relieved in some cases through the acquisition of the appropriate words needed to express one's understanding. In other cases, the concept itself can be conveyed to me verbally, so that I occurrently acquire it prior to my visual perceptual experience of that thing. ("It is just as you described it!")

terms of the doctrine of substantial form.

To begin with, hallucinations operate in some ways, as Siegel notes, like visual sensations - phosphenes, afterimages, "seeing stars," instances of double vision, conditions like jaundice, and so on. Such visual sensations lack any kind of intentional content and are instantly recognized as products of the malfunctioning of the perceptual process itself – no one mistakes the stars they see when "seeing stars" with actual stars. Hallucinations share a lot of the same distinguishing features with visual sensations. Unlike our perception of extramental objects, many hallucinations follow the movements of our heads and stay in the same position in our visual field regardless of our attempts to approach them or look away, continue to be seen even when we close our eyes, and prove to lack solidity ("come, let me grasp thee...I cannot...") and other features that we routinely experience extramental material things to have. However, hallucinations differ from these in possessing *objective* content, i.e. having putative objects and eliciting spontaneous judgments with regard to them. While visual sensations are never or at least rarely taken to be presentations of things, hallucinations do present themselves as such, though the imposture is usually easily detected by a person of sound mind.

SCR suggests the following concerning hallucination. In the case of hallucination, for reasons unknown but about which neurophysiology may be able to enlighten us, the imagination produces a phantasm or mental image out of its own resources that the agent intellect then constitutes as the representation of an extramental material thing. This can only happen because the imagination is able to access the memory, abstract the substantial form from some previously acquired phantasm stored there and clothe it in new sense data also taken from the great storehouse of memory, thereby producing a new phantasm that somehow appears in the intentional field of awareness and which the agent intellect constitutes as a representation by means of the process described above. Hallucinations can be either *global,* in which case the entire intentional field of consciousness is occupied by hallucinatory contents (Siegel's *Airport* and *Amazing Coincidence* examples, with or without the coincidence, would be such cases) or *local,* as in the case of Macbeth's dagger or on one natural reading of Siegel's *Doll* example.[164] In this latter case, one's intentional field of consciousness, or more particularly one's visual field, contains both normal perceptual content and hallucinatory content: one is both seeing extramental material things and hallucinating something that is not an extramental material thing but appears to be so at the same time in the same intentional field.

So, what do we Really See?

According to SCR, what we really, or paradigmatically see, are extramental material things formally and intentionally existing in and thereby present to occurrent conscious awareness by means of subjective mental contents (mental images) that represent them to us. In turn, such contents represent these things in virtue of, first, the presence of the substantial form of the extramental thing existing in that mental image as the principle of organizational unity for its sense-data and subsequently as an abstract concept that the agent intellect extracts from that image and imposes on it to make it a representation of the thing. In this way, the mind apprehends that object by becoming that thing formally and intentionally. Our everyday perceptual experience consists almost exclusively of this kind of content, and the same hold for visual perceptual experience as well. Optical illusions, mirages, and so on are simply the misperceptions of extramental material things that evoke false spontaneous judgments about them.

By contrast, we are hardly ever aware of sense-data, the Aristotelian matter of mental images, as such. To become aware of them in this way, as merely externally related shapes and colors requires a special, occurrent and voluntary mental act called *precisive abstraction*, in which we imaginatively "think away" the formalities of sense perception and introspectively focus just on the matter of sense experience. When we do this, we either constitute the visual field as a two-dimensional, "parti-colored plane" consisting of shapes, and colors or we pick just one such element of that field – such as the shape or the color, and dismiss the other mental contents from one's mind. This is a wholly artificial way of viewing sense perception and sense experience, and it is no wonder that those who have tried to understand perception from this perspective have been unable to avoid skepticism and perplexity.

---

[164] Siegel, 36 and 184-185.

Visual sensations (such as afterimages, phosphenes, etc.) are also visual contents but are not objective contents and so altogether lack intentionality. By contrast, hallucinations have objective content, derived from memory, and thus represent *putative* objects about which they evoke false spontaneous judgments, thus coming to possess intentionality in a different fashion than mental images ordinarily do. However, since these objects fail to exist as extramental material things, all of these judgments are false when construed as claims about their putative objects.

And that, dear reader, is what we really see.

ABOUT THE AUTHOR

Steven M. Duncan (born January 12, 1954) earned his Ph.D. at the University of Washington in 1987 and taught Philosophy at various colleges and universities, retiring from Bellevue College at the end of 2015. He is the author of more than a dozen books, including *The Proof of the External World* and *How Free Will Works*, both available from Wipf and Stock. Steve and his wife Corazon live in Bellevue, WA.